Comprehensive
Business Studies

D0245045

J0

ul

1 2002

09. JAN 03

Comprehensive Business Studies

FOURTH EDITION

Alan Whitcomb
BA, MEd, PhD

PITMAN PUBLISHING

PITMAN PUBLISHING
128 Long Acre, London WC2E 9AN

A Division of Longman Group Limited

First published in 1986
Fourth edition 1994

© Alan Whitcomb 1986, 1989, 1992, 1994

A CIP catalogue record for this book can be obtained from the British Library.

ISBN 0 273 60477 5

Typeset by ⋌ Tek-Art, Croydon, Surrey
Printed and bound in Great Britain by Clays Ltd, St Ives plc

10 9 8 7 6 5 4 3 2

The Publishers' policy is to use paper manufactured from sustainable forests.

Contents

Contents

Preface to Fourth Edition

This book is intended for use as a basic text by students preparing for GCSE Business Studies and other related examinations. The aim has been to present a wide-ranging and comprehensive textbook, produced in a readable and interesting style and which can be used in mixed ability situations. Each chapter is backed by a variety of activities that will help the student to form structured revision notes, to practise test questions at varying degrees of difficulty, and to carry out independent study.

The activities at the end of each chapter give a variety of opportunities for 'differentiation'. The *Make a note of it* exercises could be tackled by all pupils, perhaps with the teacher deleting questions related to topics which particular students find too difficult. Differentiation here is achieved largely by outcome. There is also a collection of *Structured questions* at the end of each chapter. These are 'stepped', that is each sub-part becomes progressively more difficult, thus allowing all students to achieve introductory questions whilst stretching the more able person in the later sections. The weighting of these questions is indicated by the mark allocation suggested. Many of these questions are related to data which adds interest and aids learning. The final activities consist of a variety of *Extended answer assignments*. These are intended to be tackled by the more able student as investigative learning, often giving the opportunity for research and providing evidence of independent thought.

A Message to Students

In writing this book I have deliberately tried to keep the text as easy to read as possible whilst at the same time adequately covering the many topics you are required to learn. Each chapter can be broadly divided into two areas. The first is the reading related to the themes of the chapter. I cannot recommend too strongly the need to read around the topic currently being studied. I attribute the majority of my personal academic development to reading of appropriate material. The second important area of each chapter is the activities section. This consists of three subsections:

- *Make a note of it*
  This section consists of a series of questions based on the themes of the chapter. The questions follow the same order as the text. Consequently, by writing the question followed by the answer you will formulate revision notes, as well as learning through the process.

- *Structured questions*
  These are a series of questions related to a particular area of learning that have been linked together in a structured way to help in examination preparation. These questions are 'stepped' with subsections becoming progressively more difficult.

- *Extended answer assignments*
  A selection of assignments are given here requiring extended answers and personal research. These give you experience in the sort of activities necessary when carrying out course work for some syllabuses as well as helping you to prepare for a higher level of study.

Now for some tips about how you should interpret some of the terminology used in examination questions and what they require:

- *Compare*. Look for similarities and differences and perhaps reach a conclusion about which is preferable.

- *Criticise*. Give your opinion about the merit of one or another of the possible alternatives. Back your judgement with reasoning to support your choice.

- *Describe*. Give a detailed or graphic account of.

- *Discuss*. Investigate or examine. Give reasons for and against, advantages and disadvantages and examine implications.

- *Explain*. Make clear, give reasons for, account for.

- *Illustrate*. Explain the meaning of or make clear, and explain using relevant examples. (It does *not* mean produce diagrams.)

- *Outline*. Give the main features, or the general principles of a topic, omitting minor details.

- *State*. Present in a brief but clear form.

- *Summarise*. Omit details and examples, but concentrate on giving a concise account of the chief points related to a particular topic.

Always read the essay title or examination question very carefully, making particular note of these key terms. Only then will you be sure what the question demands of you. You might find it useful to make a brief plan which organises the essay around the terms used in the question.

Finally, an old maxim: Answer the question, the whole question, and nothing but the question.

Best of luck for your examinations.

Alan Whitcomb

Acknowledgements

The author and publisher would like to thank the following for permission to reproduce copyright material.

The Advertising Standards Authority Ltd
Aiwa (UK) Ltd
Association Container Transportation
  Services Ltd
Barclays Bank plc
BBC
Boots The Chemists Ltd
British Telecom
British Trades Alphabet
Burger King (UK) Ltd
Cadbury Ltd
Canada Maritime Ltd
The Commission of the European
  Communities
Dominique de Buys
Employment News
Executive Post
Financial Times
Ron Freeman (photographer)
The Hammerson Group Developments
Hoover Ltd
Interflora (FTDA) British Unit Ltd*
JVC Manufacturing UK Limited

Kenwood Ltd
D H Letchford
Lloyds Bank plc
Londis (Holdings) Ltd
McDonald's Restaurants Ltd
Midland Bank plc
Mitchell Cotts Freight
Morphy Richards Ltd
National Girobank
National Westminster Bank plc
Office of the Data Protection Registrar
Pandair International Airfreight
Peterborough Development Corporation
Philips Electronics Ltd
The Post Office
Nik Rudge
Safeway Stores plc
J Sainsbury plc
The Stock Exchange
Tesco plc
Wimpey Homes Holdings Ltd
Wimpy International Ltd
Woolworths plc

*In the UK Interflora is a Registered Trademark of Interflora Incorporated. The Mercury Man device is the Registered Trademark of Florists Transworld Delivery Association.

◆1 The Business Environment

Direct production

All people have three basic *needs* – food, clothing and shelter. And much of the activity we engage in is aimed at satisfying those needs. Activities which result in the satisfaction of our needs are often referred to as 'economic activity', therefore Man is sometimes called an 'economic animal'.

Early Man led a simple way of life. He would provide all of his needs himself without the aid of others. This is called *direct production*. He would hunt animals and gather plants and berries. Man was living in a *subsistence economy* – providing just sufficient to survive, but not improve his way of life.

Later Man began to farm in a very basic way, penning animals and planting seeds. This enabled him to settle in one place, build a permanent home and improve his way of life. One of the improvements was that he found he was producing more goods than he needed (*surplus*). He began to exchange his surplus goods with the surplus of others.

Barter

The exchange of one thing for another without the use of money is called *barter*, and this was the way that the earliest form of trade took place. But there are drawbacks to the barter system, as follows:

1 A *double coincidence of wants* has to occur for barter to take place. The person who has a surplus to exchange not only has to find someone who wants his or her surplus, but the person found must also have what is wanted.

2 An *exchange rate* has to be agreed even if a double coincidence of wants has occurred. Imagine the difficulty in trying to agree how many chickens a pig is worth.

3 *Divisibility of goods* is not always convenient. Some rates of exchange will not allow exchange to take place because some goods cannot be split into smaller parts. For example, if one spear is worth half a chicken it is not possible to trade with only one spear because you cannot have half a chicken and also have it alive.

4 *Storage of wealth* is difficult with the barter system. At times there is a need to store a surplus for use at a future time when a scarcity exists. But many items used in barter (e.g. food) cannot be stored for long periods of time.

Money

The use of money solves all of the above problems of barter, but early money was not in the form of coins and notes with which we are familiar today. The difficulties of barter led early Man to the use of generally accepted items which everyone was willing to take in exchange for their goods. These items included such things as shells, dogs' teeth, beads, grain, spearheads, hides, arrowheads, fishhooks and animals, and they became substitute money.

Even today many things are used instead of money in some parts of the world, and when a country's economy collapses the people may revert to using goods instead of money. For example, in Germany during the latter part of the Second World War cigarettes, coffee and stockings were used as money.

Qualities of money

For something to be considered as money, or in the place of money, it must be:

- *durable* (hard wearing)
- *divisible* (easily divided into smaller units)
- *portable* (convenient to carry)
- *acceptable* (people must agree to its use).

The use of money allowed early Man to sell his surplus of goods in exchange for money and use the money to buy his needs from the surplus of others. Money was now acting as a *medium of exchange*, and the process of trading was much simpler.

In time metal became a popular substance used as money in any part of the world where it was common, and the use of metal eventually led to the development of the coins with which we are so familiar today. Look back at the list of the qualities of money. Can you see how metal money so conveniently meets all those qualities?

Functions of money

Money has three basic functions. It is a medium of exchange, a measure of value and a store of value.

1 *Medium of exchange* – money makes trading relatively simple and makes barter unnecessary. It enables workers to specialise in labour and accept money for

wages rather than goods. Workers will accept money because they know it is acceptable to others in exchange for goods.

2 *Measure of value* – money can be used to measure or price the value of goods and services. This is especially important when the items cannot easily be compared. For example, how many hours of work by a farmer is a tractor worth?

Production of cars

Specialisation by process – the car factory:
(a) underframes are automatically welded
(b) bodies are welded by robot
(c) bodies are fixed to underframe
(d) windscreens are fitted by robot
(e) accessories are fitted
(f) finished cars are delivered to garages for customers' viewing.

3 *Store of values* – money can be stored for use at some later time, whereas to store goods such as food for a long time is inconvenient. This makes it possible to 'save for a rainy day', to have some wealth to draw on when a scarcity occurs. In other words, money can be earned at one time and spent at another.

Indirect production

In modern industrial society few people satisfy their needs directly. Instead they co-operate with others to indirectly produce the needs of everyone. This is often referred to as *division of labour* or *specialisation*. Work is divided among several people, allowing them each to specialise in doing what they do best, which is to the benefit of everyone. There are two main ways of looking at specialisation.

Specialisation by product

Instead of everyone trying to produce all they personally need, they each concentrate on contributing to one commodity or service, using the money that they earn to purchase the goods or services of others. In this way the total needs of an individual are met by the contributions of many others.

Specialisation by process

By organising production into several stages or processes workers become more specialised and expert in their work. For example, in a car factory each worker might specialise in a part of the assembly of many vehicles in one day as they pass along the production line. By organising production in this way, workers become

High-speed machine wrapping.
(Courtesy Cadbury Ltd).

more specialised and expert in their work. This enables them to produce more with the same resources.

Advantages and disadvantages of specialisation

Advantages:

- Workers become skilled at doing a particular job.
- Jobs become simpler and easier to learn.
- Time-saving machinery and semi-skilled labour can be used.
- Costs per unit produced are less because of the simple processes and better use of labour and tools.
- Labour is potentially more mobile.

Disadvantages:

- Repeating a single task can become boring.
- Individual crafts and skills are lost by use of machines.
- Greater use of machinery can lead to unemployment of workers.
- All production may be halted by strikes, machinery breakdown or shortage of materials.
- Slow workers may be unable to keep pace with others.

1.2 Scarcity and choice in a modern society

In a world where specialisation has become highly developed with not only individuals but whole communities specialising, it is vital for exchange to take place if everyone's wants are to be satisfied. The bus driver works for wages but needs food, so the wages are exchanged to obtain his needs. This involves making choices.

We have to balance our unlimited wants against our limited resources.

Everytime we go shopping we are involved in a basic economic activity, that of making a *choice* because of *scarce* resources. We have only limited money available, but invariably we would like to buy more than we can afford. Consequently, we have not only to make a choice, but also to form a *scale of preference*. In other words, we put what we want into an order of priority.

Scarcity and choice are not problems that are restricted to individuals alone. Businesses and countries face these problems of choice also. Businesses must decide how to profitably use the capital that shareholders have provided. A country has limited resources and the people or their representatives will try to use or allocate them to the best benefit of the community.

The success with which choices are made has a considerable influence on the well-being of individuals, the prosperity of a business and the quality of life of a country's residents. This is sometimes referred to as the basic *economic problem* – how to use available resources in a community to the best benefit of the needs of society. We are fortunate today in that we have many people, organisations and agencies who are available to advise us and to help us to make wise decisions on the best way to use the scarce resources available. However, it has taken thousands of years of experience to reach this stage of human development.

1.3 Economic systems

The processes of production, exchange, scarcity and choice looked at so far in this chapter take place within a political framework. In other words, the decision of what to produce or what choices to make with the scarce resources available is influenced by the political situation within which the decision is made. No two countries are organised in the same way, but they all have to solve three basic problems:

- *What should be produced?* For example, what quantities of food, machinery or services should be produced?
- *How should production be organised?* What is the best way to combine the factors of production? Should automated or manual methods be used? What technological equipment (e.g. computers) is required? Where should production take place?
- *For whom should production take place?* Should everyone be entitled to an equal share of the production, or should some receive more than others?

Economists distinguish between four different economic systems which answer the foregoing questions. The first of these described here is the subsistence economy.

Subsistence economy

A subsistence economy is one where there is little or no specialisation or trade. In such an economy people tend to live in family groups and grow most of their own food. It is called a 'subsistence economy' because people do little more than subsist – they can provide only the basic necessities to live. This was the form of economy that was a feature of the life of early Man. Today more advanced forms of economy exist.

| What should be produced? | How should production be organised? | For whom should production take place? |

All countries have to solve three basic problems.

Countries differ to the extent to which the government interferes with the economic system. There are three basic approaches adopted by governments in dealing with the economic problem: the free economy, the controlled economy and the mixed economy.

Free economy

A free economy is based on the private ownership of the factors (means) of production and the means of distributing goods and services. Consumers express their wants through their demand for goods and services, and the private producer seeks to satisfy the demand if the profit motive is sufficient. Therefore, in a free economy the purchaser of goods decides demand and not the state. Sometimes such economies are referred to as market economies, unplanned economies, free enterprise, laissez-faire system, or capitalist system. The USA and Japan are typical examples of a free economy.

Advantages of free economy

- All members of the community are free to participate in business enterprise for the purpose of making a profit.
- Those engaged in business enterprise have to compete with many others for custom. This has the effect of maintaining efficiency, keeping prices down and improving the standard of goods and services.
- The consumers play a major part in deciding what will be produced because it is the consumer who creates the demand and the producers who try to satisfy this demand.

Disadvantages of free economy

- Advertising is a major feature of free enterprise and this can be used to create an artificially high demand for some products. In other words, demand may be created by the producer rather than the consumer.

- In a free enterprise society successful businesses may buy out smaller firms in order to obtain control of a larger share of the market. This reduces competition and increases the danger of monopolies arising.
- In response to the profit motive, companies may restrict supplies of some goods or services in order to keep prices and profits artificially high.

Controlled economy

In a controlled economy the state controls the factors of production and the means of exchange and distribution. The state estimates what quantity of goods and services the community will need over a given period, and then directs the factors of production to produce these goods and services. In other words, unlike the free economy, it is the state that decides what the community needs and consequently demand does not originate from the consumers. This type of economy is sometimes called a centralised economy, planned economy, collective economy, or a socialist system. China and Cuba are examples of controlled economies.

Advantages of controlled economy

- The state can assess the needs of the whole community and try to provide benefit for all the population. The means of production can then be directed towards this end and wasteful competition can be eliminated.
- It is not possible for a private monopoly to emerge under this system.

Disadvantages of controlled economy

- The state has control over the factors of production and this discourages enterprise and inventiveness.
- A considerable number of non-productive government officials are required to plan and operate the economy. These officials may not necessarily have the skills needed to decide what the community needs, and decisions may be subject to many rules and regulations. This may result in delays in reaching decisions.
- Centralised production may not respond as quickly to changing conditions and trends as private enterprise.
- The absence of competition and profit motive can hinder both creativeness and efficiency.

Mixed economy

As the term implies, a mixed economy is a combination of elements taken from a free economy and some from a controlled economy. Britain is an example of this type of economic system. Some sections of British industry are owned and operated by the state but large portions of the business world remain in private hands. The contents of this book are largely set in the context of a mixed economy.

1.4 Types of production

Earlier in this chapter we examined direct and indirect production. With direct production, which is a characteristic of countries that are economically backward, individuals or small groups satisfy their wants entirely by their own efforts and unaided by others. Indirect production, which is a feature of all developed societies, involves specialisation, working for wages and using the money earned to buy the goods and services produced by other people. Indirect production can be divided into three categories, primary production, secondary production and tertiary production.

Primary production

Primary production is concerned with the extraction of basic materials provided by nature, which are either above or below the earth's surface. The extractive industries are farming, fishing and mining. Without these much subsequent production would not take place.

Farming involves production of foods in the form of fowls, animals and plants and also other produce of the land such as trees and flowers.

Fishing has always played a major part in the provision of food for Britain which is not surprising as we are a country surrounded by the sea. Deep-sea fishing is carried out in the open sea and is subject to international rules which try to ensure that each country has its own fair share of the catch. Protected fisheries are a growth industry that exists to farm fish in inland lakes and reservoirs, producing high yields from a small area.

Mining extracts raw materials such as coal, ore, oil, gas, etc. from below the earth's surface.

Secondary production

Secondary production consists of the manufacturing and construction industries. They take the raw materials produced by the extractive industries and change their form into some end product.

Manufacturers may be involved in the production of a complete item, or they may make parts which will be assembled into a finished article.

Construction industries take raw materials and partly finished products and change them into buildings, roads and bridges, etc.

Tertiary production

When goods leave the producers they do not usually pass immediately to the consumer. They have to be stored, transported, insured, advertised and sold by traders. These and the many other commercial activities that make up tertiary production further the change of ownership of goods from the producer to the consumers. Tertiary production is sometimes called the service industry, but more often it is referred to as *commerce* and *direct services*.

Commerce

Commerce can be divided into two clear areas, *trade* and *services to trade*.

- *Trade* is the process of changing ownership. Traders are the businesses directly involved in the buying and selling of goods and services. Trade can either take place within a country (home trade) or between countries (foreign trade). Home trade involves the activities of wholesalers and retailers. Foreign trade involves importers (who buy goods from other countries) and exporters (who sell goods to other countries).
- *Services to trade* are the commercial activities that assist trade in its job of selling goods and services.

The activities that provide these services are:

1 *Banking* – providing short-term finance and providing facilities for easy payment transfer.

(a) Which form of production is illustrated here? Why does this form of production also depend on the others shown opposite?
(Copyright: *Farmers Weekly;* photo by Peter Adams)

(b) Fishing

(c) Mining
(Courtesy British Coal))

2 *Finance* – various institutions (e.g. the Stock Exchange) providing long-term finance for industry, commerce and consumer credit.

3 *Insurance* – spreads the risks faced by industrial and commercial businesses.

4 *Transport* – engaged in the movement of commodities from one place to another.

5 *Communications:*

(a) Postal – transfer of written communications through mail services.

(b) Telecommunications – immediate distance transfer of written, verbal or data communications by electronic devices.

(c) Advertising – provides potential customers with information about goods and services available.

All of the elements of both trade and services to trade are the subject of individual chapters in different parts of this book.

Direct services

In addition to commercial services there are groups of people who provide direct services, which are not related to trade but which people use because they provide

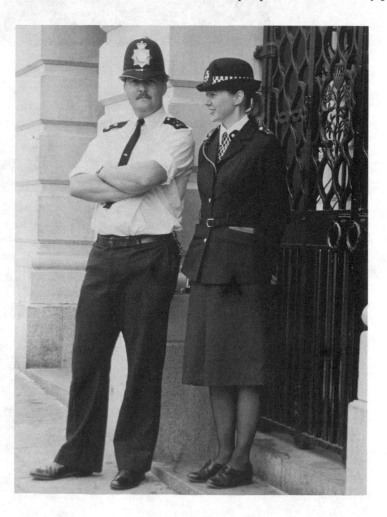

services which are essential to the well-being of the community. Direct service occupations include the services of doctors, nurses, teachers, actors and actresses, policemen, hairdressers, authors and many others who offer a personal service.

1.5 Interdependence of industry

Let us now summarise what we have learnt from this chapter.

- *Direct production* is a characteristic of underdeveloped and primitive economies.
- *Indirect production* is a feature of all advanced economies, and this form of production is most common today.
- *Specialisation* is an essential part of indirect production and it involves people doing what they do best.
- *Commercial activities* are positioned between the producer and the consumer and these provide the means of buying and selling goods and services. They play a vital part in allowing people to specialise, earn wages and then buy their wants. They also play a major role in co-ordinating and promoting the activities of producers. We will now examine some of the ways in which this is done.

Traders support producers by carrying out the distribution of goods and bridging the time gap between production and consumption. For example, retailers and wholesalers order goods from producers and hold them until they are required. Exporters are involved in the distribution of home produced goods overseas. This not only provides work for producers, but also raises foreign capital which is needed to pay for the imports of raw materials that the producer needs. Importers buy from other countries the raw materials and finished goods that we cannot economically produce at home, thus allowing home producers to specialise in manufacturing products for which they are best suited.

The services to trade also play a major part in combining the activities of producers and promoting their enterprise. Finance provides the money for the capital assets needed by business, and also for consumers and businesses who wish to buy on credit. Banking makes transfer of payments between buyers and sellers of goods possible and also provides a variety of other services that facilitate payment and encourage production and trade to take place. Insurance overcomes some of the risks involved in producing and trading such as the danger of loss or damage to capital assets or goods. Transport makes the physical link between producers, traders and consumers, and gets goods to the right place at the right time and in the right condition. Advertising helps producers and traders to bring their commodities to the attention of potential customers. Postal communications and telecommunications enable businessmen to communicate with each other and their customers at the various stages of production and distribution.

We can see from this section that commercial activities are essential to production, but many of the commercial activities would not be needed if it were not for producers and specialisation making exchange necessary. In other words, primary, secondary and tertiary production are interdependent.

Make a note of it

1 What is direct production and why does it limit the quality of life?

2 Define surplus. Why is the production of a surplus important?

3 What is barter?

4 Briefly describe the difficulties involved in trading by the barter system.

5 List six examples of substitute money.

6 What are the qualities necessary for something to be suitable for use as money?

7 What do we mean when we say that money is a medium of exchange?

8 Describe the functions of money.

9 What is indirect production?

10 Define division of labour.

11 Explain the difference between division of labour by product and division of labour by process.

12 List the advantages and disadvantages of specialisation.

13 Why is exchange so important to the success of specialisation?

14 What is the relationship between choice, scarce resources and scale of preference?

15 Why is making wise choices important to individuals, businesses and the country as a whole?

16 State the four basic problems that economic systems have to attempt to solve.

17 What is a subsistence economy and why is it not a satisfying way of life?

18 'The free economy and the controlled economy are completely contrasting forms of economic systems.' Give a detailed explanation of this statement.

19 Give a brief description of a mixed economy.

20 Why is primary production also referred to as the extractive industries?

21 Name three examples of occupations found in primary production and three from secondary production.

22 Why is tertiary production so important to the other forms of production?

23 Briefly define tertiary production and distinguish between trade and services to trade.

24 List ten commercial occupations and briefly describe the functions of each.

25 What are direct services? Give three examples of occupations that provide a direct service.

26 Why are commercial activities as important as production?

Structured Questions

1 Refer to the diagram on page 9 and answer these related questions.

   (a) Why are the extractive industries also referred to as primary production? (1)

   (b) How does secondary production differ from primary production? (2)

   (c) State two specific differences between home trade and foreign trade. (2)

   (d) Why are advertising, telecommunications and post all recognised as forms of business communication? (3)

   (e) Why is trade particularly important to producers? (4)

   (f) In what ways do the services to trade support trade? (8)

2 Consider the following illustration.

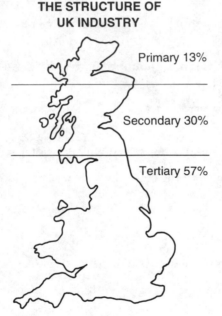

THE STRUCTURE OF UK INDUSTRY

Primary 13%

Secondary 30%

Tertiary 57%

Contribution to UK Gross Domestic Product

Our basic needs vary from one part of the world to another, and so does our ability to satisfy them. There are three stages of production in the development from natural resources to consumption.

Production in the UK can be divided into these three stages or categories: primary, secondary and tertiary. The percentage contribution each makes to UK production is shown in the illustration.

   (a) Why do the basic needs differ from one country to another? (2)

   (b) In what ways does the ability of the UK to satisfy its needs differ from that of a Third World country? (2)

   (c) Explain the difference between primary, secondary and tertiary production. (3)

   (d) Using the data in the illustration, produce a pie chart that shows the percentage each type of production contributes to the UK economy. (3)

   (e) Draw a flow chart showing the development of a product through all three types of production. Include an explanation at each stage. (4)

(f)　The tertiary sector has been the fastest growing element of production in the UK for many years. Give some reasons why this has been so.　(6)

3　Refer to the illustration on page 3 which shows the processes involved in the production of cars.

(a)　In what way is division of labour shown in this illustration?　(1)
(b)　Why is division of labour also referred to as specialisation?　(2)
(c)　Why does division of labour often result in increased production output?　(3)
(d)　The illustration (a) to (f) shows the processes involved in car production in logical order. Form a flow chart that shows the progression in the production of an item of furniture.　(4)
(e)　State three advantages and three disadvantages of division of labour.　(4)
(f)　Explain the difference between specialisation by product and specialisation by process. Give examples to illustrate your answer.　(3)

4　The flow diagram below shows the way that a subsistence economy can develop and eventually result in a better standard of living.

(a)　What is meant by a 'subsistence economy'?　(2)
(b)　Why is a subsistence economy sometimes referred to as a 'trap'?　(2)
(c)　How can division of labour help a community to escape from the subsistence trap?　(3)

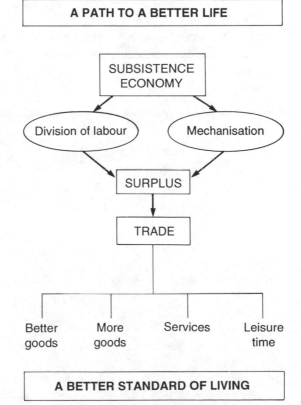

A PATH TO A BETTER LIFE

SUBSISTENCE ECONOMY

Division of labour　　Mechanisation

SURPLUS

TRADE

Better goods　　More goods　　Services　　Leisure time

A BETTER STANDARD OF LIVING

(d) In what ways does division of labour help to make mechanisation
    possible? (3)

(e) How does the combination of division of labour and mechanisation
    usually result in the creation of a surplus and make it important to trade? (4)

(f) Why do the combined processes shown in this flow diagram result in
    'a better standard of living'? (6)

Extended Answer Assignments

1 Make a survey of small production industries in your area (perhaps on an
  industrial estate). Present your survey on a simple colour-coded diagram/map
  to show different categories of production. See if you can identify any
  relationship between the size of premises and the legal identity of the firm.
  Comment on your findings.

2 Using library resources make a comparative study of the USA, China and the
  UK as illustrations of different types of economy. To what extent do you think
  these are changing?

3 Visit a local factory that has a production line and find out the following
  information about the organisation of production:

  (a) What elements of the manufacturing process are done on the production
      line and which are not?
  (b) To what extent does the factory employ 'modern technology'?
  (c) How do wage rates differ between workers within the firm and why does
      this occur?

2 Organisation of production

Aims of production

Production refers to the creation of goods and services, i.e. the creation of utilities. The purpose of production is to provide people with the goods which they need or want to consume. *Needs* are things that are essential to human survival. There are three primary human needs. They are:

- food
- clothing
- shelter.

Production also provides the many things that Man *wants* to consume but are not necessary for survival. These things help to make the quality of life better, for example televisions, cars, books, etc.

In what ways can what you see taking place in this photograph assist in the provision of primary human needs?

19

Levels of production

In Chapter 1 we said that production for the country as a whole can be divided into three main sectors: primary, secondary and tertiary. It can also be classified according to the levels of operation. These levels are dependent upon the resources available, and the extent to which the country has developed to exploit those resources. There are three basic levels of operation: *subsistence, domestic* and *surplus.*

Subsistence level

This level of production meets only the basic needs of the country in which it takes place. In other words, sufficient is produced only to enable the population to survive, but not enough to improve the way of life. This is the kind of problem faced by many of the under-developed communities of the world. Subsistence economy is a term usually applied where agriculture is the main source of production. In other words, people live almost entirely by what can be obtained from natural resources, and this could lead to a poor quality of life. Usually the subsistence level of production is inefficient and very dependent upon the climate and weather. Periods of drought or other bad climatic periods result in severe hardship. Fortunately the subsistence level of production is not as common today as it has been in the past, but it still exists in many under-developed countries.

Domestic level

At the level of domestic production everything is produced locally, that is in the home country. This level involves the minimum of imports from foreign countries. Both human and natural resources are employed and the whole economy is particularly dependent upon what it can produce from these resources.

Some developed countries, such as the USA, try to grow all the food they need because they have the resources to do so. The governments of developing countries encourage domestic production in order to make full use of the resources available in their country, e.g. promotion of self-sufficiency in agricultural produce.

Surplus level

Developed countries, such as the USA, Britain and Germany, have a wide variety of resources and exploit these to the full. They also have advanced technology which enables them to take full advantage of their resources.

Such countries are able to achieve a level of production which not only satisfies domestic consumption, but also produces a surplus that can be exported to other countries. This results in a better quality of life for the population because there is access to a wider variety of products and competitive prices, and an ability to earn more from production.

How a business may organise production

The way we have looked at production so far has been largely from a national point of view, i.e. a whole country. We also need to consider how production can be organised by an individual business. There are three basic methods:

1 *Job production* – where a single product is made from start to finish, to a customer's requirement, and in response to an individual order.
2 *Batch production* – where products are made in lots, with a complete lot being finished before starting the next lot.
3 *Flow production* – where products are produced continuously, e.g. mass production on an assembly line.

Which of these production methods a firm chooses will be influenced by the form of the orders it receives:

- special one-off orders (e.g. a fitted kitchen) – *job production*;
- orders from several customers, likely to be repeated – *batch production*;
- orders for production in continuous demand (e.g. bread) – *flow production*.

The foregoing factors will obviously affect the *scale of production* and will give rise to other decisions a firm must make. For example, flow production in particular will mean that the producer must decide what *levels of stocks* of raw materials will have to be held, and how much stock of finished goods will be permitted. The *number of employees* and the skills and equipment they require will also be influenced by production. And of course all firms involved in production are concerned about the *quality* of their products, and the *efficiency* of their employees and the methods used to produce their goods.

2.2 The factors of production

In Chapter 1 we learnt that there are only scarce resources to meet our unlimited wants. The scarce or limited resources which are used to produce the commodities people want to consume are collectively called the *factors of production*. They are:

- land
- labour
- capital
- entrepreneurship.

Each of the factors receives payment or reward in return for the contribution it makes to production. Land receives rent, labour wages, capital interest, and entrepreneurship (which some people argue is a fourth factor of production) is rewarded with profit, although some factors actually receive more than one return.

The factor of land

Land as a factor of production includes not only the land itself but all natural resources found in the earth and sea. Land in this sense includes:

- geographical surface area
- rivers, lakes and seas
- minerals and chemicals.

Land is fixed in supply; in other words, the supply cannot be increased, although the quality of the soil may be improved by the use of fertilisers, drainage, land reclamation, contouring and reafforestation. The search for minerals below the surface of the land and sea continues.

Production cannot take place without land. Primary, secondary and tertiary production and all economic activity involves the use of land.

The factor of labour

Labour is the factor of production which is Man's physical and mental contribution to the creation of goods and services. It is the factor that converts resources into goods and services that people want. This contribution to production is generally rewarded with wages, although sometimes profit or interest is the return received.

All production requires some labour. Even the automated factory requires workers to supervise machinery, to program computers, to operate equipment and to process paperwork. Therefore, it is important that there is an adequate supply of labour, with the appropriate skills required. In this respect, labour is often divided into three broad groups:

1 *Semi-skilled and unskilled* – jobs which involve little or no special training and usually involve working with the hands – drivers, cleaners, street sellers and some factory production line workers, watchmen, etc.
2 *Skilled* – engineers, mechanics, electricians, plumbers, trained machine operators, computer operators, clerks, junior supervisors, etc.
3 *Managerial and professional* – business executives, teachers, doctors, nurses, solicitors, architects, pharmacists, senior supervisors, etc.

These groups generally reflect differing qualities and levels of training.

Many businesses improve the quality of their labour force through education and training. This results in efficient use of the capital goods the business employs and, therefore, contributes to the growth and development of the firm. But there are many other factors which determine the supply and quality of labour.

Determinants of the labour supply

Labour supply is influenced by:

- *The size and structure of the population.* A large population will give a greater supply of labour. But a high proportion of very young or very old people will tend to reduce the supply of labour. These will be influenced by the school leaving and retirement ages.
- *The number of women at work.* This is influenced by many factors such as economic conditions in the country, wages and attitudes towards working mothers, etc.
- *Hours of work.* If there is a general trend towards a shorter working week (which is the case in developed countries), this has the effect of reducing the supply of labour.
- *Quality of labour force.* It is not enough to have sufficient numbers of people available for work. They must also have the appropriate skills that are needed. If the required skills are not available the effect will be to limit the supply of labour.

Labour quality is influenced by:

- *Quality of education*. Education plays an important part not only in producing a knowledgeable workforce, but also contributes towards making people more mobile and adaptable to change.
- *Training facilities*. A shortage of workers with particular skills can be overcome by training more of these specialists through the education system or through in-service occupational training.
- *Natural talent*. Some skills are important but are natural talents and cannot be taught, although they may be increased by training, for example acting, drawing or playing a musical instrument.
- *Health*. The standard of health of workers obviously affects their efficiency and productivity. Health is affected not only by living conditions, but also working conditions.

The factor of capital

Capital is the money and all other assets (possessions of value) which are employed in the process of production. Capital includes the buildings, machinery, equipment, stocks and many other things (producer goods) used in making the items we consume (consumer goods).

Capital in this sense takes two basic forms, fixed capital and working capital:

- *Fixed capital* – buildings, machinery and other equipment with a long life which are used many times over in the production of goods and the creation of further wealth.
- *Working capital* – stocks of raw materials, cash, bank balances and other items required for the day-to-day operation of the business and which are continually being used up.

The entrepreneur

Some people argue that entrepreneurship can be considered as a fourth factor of production. Entrepreneurs are those who organise and co-ordinate the other factors of production. They are the owners of business enterprises who, by taking risks and making decisions, enable production to be carried out in anticipation of demand. This book is very much concerned with entrepreneurship.

If entrepreneurs successfully predict future demand they are rewarded by a special form of income called *profit*. If, however, their judgement is incorrect they may get no reward or may even make a loss. For example, a shopkeeper may buy stocks of a new brand of confectionery but will have no guarantee of being able to sell them. There would be far fewer businesses in existence if there were not entrepreneurs around willing to take the risks involved.

In order to participate in entrepreneurship the entrepreneur must be willing:

- to raise capital, from savings or by borrowing, necessary for investment in the business;
- to organise the various levels of labour required;

Can you identify the factors of production in this photograph?

- to define and clarify business policy decisions so that all levels of personnel can understand what the firm is trying to achieve.
- to make any changes necessary in the interests of the growth and development of the business.

2.3 Location of business

A major decision that all firms have to take is where to site their premises. A variety of factors will influence this decision, including the size of the organisation and the expected scale of its operations, but most choices of site are a compromise between several advantages and disadvantages. The summary chart on page 25 shows the main influencing factors.

Government influence on business location

Governments can play a particularly important part in influencing where a firm sites its premises and it is worthwhile looking in greater depth at the reasons why, and how, they do so.

The main reasons the government may wish to influence the location of industry is to improve the regional balance of employment, in other words to draw production into regions of high unemployment and areas where industry has declined. Such areas are sometimes referred to as 'depressed' or 'problem regions'. These can be distinguished by the following:

INDUSTRIAL INERTIA Sometimes firms stay at a particular site even though the original reason for siting in that area (e.g. near source of raw materials) no longer applies.

RAW MATERIALS Closeness to raw materials or to the port where they enter the country may influence choice of site.

TRANSPORT ACCESS Siting near to good road, rail, sea or air links can save in distribution costs or in the movement of raw materials.

LAND Availability of sufficient suitable land, at an economically viable price, in a suitable position will attract business.

MARKET PULL Businesses are attracted to sites close to where potential customers can be found; shops near where shoppers will be, hotels near tourist areas.

INFLUENCES ON LOCATION OF BUSINESS

LABOUR Availability of suitable labour with a good no strike record. This will be influenced by availability of social amenities such as housing and medical facilities.

GOVERNMENT INFLUENCE Some governments try to influence the location of businesses, e. g. to improve regional balance, to reduce overcrowding in cities and towns.

ENVIRONMENT Climatic conditions are important to some businesses, particularly those involved in agricultural products.

FUEL OR POWER Closeness to fuel or power are less important today than in the past, but some firms still need to locate near to sources such as water.

LINKAGE INDUSTRIES Firms will locate near other businesses on which they depend, or near to other firms in a similar line of business.

- unemployment rate higher than national average;
- average income of residents is below the national average;
- large numbers of workers are leaving the area;
- workforce generally retains outdated skills;
- there is less industry than in other regions;
- factories, housing, hospitals, roads, etc., are generally outdated.

The ways in which the government can influence the location of industry include offering grants, subsidies, relief from taxes or prohibiting industrial development in other areas.

Regional development grants

Over the years the government has created areas where grants are available as incentives to businesses. Currently these are defined in the following way:

Development areas

These are areas of high unemployment and declining basic industries. Grants are available to firms to contribute to new buildings and the creation of new jobs. The grants are particularly for manufacturing industry, although some service industries also qualify.

Intermediate areas

These are areas where unemployment is high, but not as high as in development areas. Often there are indications that unemployment is increasing. The grant in

REGIONAL AID MAP

Dundee
Glasgow
Newcastle
Sunderland
Middlesborough
Belfast
Leeds
Manchester
Liverpool
Sheffield
Wrexham
Wolverhampton
Birmingham
Newport
Swansea
Cardiff
Bristol
London
Plymouth

**Assisted Areas
from 1.4.88**

Development Areas
Regional Development Grants abolished 31.3.88.
New Regional Selective Assistance.
New Investment Grants for firms employing fewer than 25 people:
15% of capital expenditure (max. grant £15,000).
New Innovation Grants of 50% for firms employing fewer than 25 people (max. grant 25,000).
New Enterprise Initiatives (govt. grant towards 2/3 of cost of business consultancy schemes).

Intermediate Areas
New Regional Selective Assistance.
New Enterprise Initiatives.

Northern Ireland
Separately funded aid.

an intermediate area will vary with the type of project but can include cheap rents on government-built factories and training grants for workers.

Enterprise zones

These are small geographical areas where businesses of all types are encouraged to locate or expand. Enterprise zones are particularly identified in run-down inner city areas where economic decay is particularly problematic. These areas offer incentives such as:

- rate free accommodation (ten years);
- tax advantages to firms locating in zones;
- simplified planning procedures.

In addition to the foregoing government policies, local authorities also spend considerable funds encouraging businesses to locate in their areas, and back this up with local incentive schemes.

2.4 Business size

What is large?

It is generally accepted that a large business has certain advantages over a small one (these are examined later in this chapter), but deciding whether a firm is large or small is not as simple as it appears at first sight. How do we measure the size of a firm?

The physical size of the business, e.g. how much area its premises cover or how many branches it has, can be an indicator. Another measure could be the number of people that are employed. But these tell us little about the profitability of the business, which is an important factor. However, large businesses do not always make big profits – some make very big losses.

The total value of all the assets being used by a business (the capital employed) is a good measure of the size of a business because it is through this that a firm creates its profits. But even this can be deceiving because a factory located in a busy city is generally of higher value than the same size property in a rural area.

It is generally recognised that a combination of factors needs to be taken into account in deciding whether a business is large or small. The turnover of the business is one of the most useful measures of business size because this generally indicates how 'busy' the firm is. When turnover is combined with other factors such as the value of assets owned and the number of people employed we end up with a pretty reliable measure of the size of a business.

Economies of scale

The producer has to decide how to use the factors of production to the best advantage, because the chances of making a good profit depend upon how effectively the factors are employed. The entrepreneur also has to decide on what scale to produce and what size of business to operate, because the size of the business and the scale of production can also influence profitability. These decisions have to be taken by all entrepreneurs. Obviously, the entrepreneur should aim for the scale of production which yields the greatest profit margin.

Large businesses tend to dominate certain industries because their size gives them advantages over smaller organisations. For example, by producing larger quantities they can reduce their production costs. These advantages of size are called *economies of scale*. Sometimes business growth results in disadvantages; when this occurs they are referred to as *diseconomies of scale*. You should realise that there can be advantages to a business remaining small as well as advantages to being large.

In addition to large-scale and small-scale economies of scale, there are external and internal economies of scale. *External economies of scale* refer to the benefits gained by all of a certain industry, or the whole of society. For example, a particular invention may result in benefits to all firms in an industry, or to the whole of society. Internal economies of scale refer to the benefits gained by one particular industry. Internal economies of scale can be grouped into four categories:

1 technical
2 managerial
3 marketing
4 financial.

Technical economies of scale

Greater size allows more opportunities for division of labour, the use of machinery and automation, and other methods of increasing efficiency. It also allows a company to allocate more resources to research and development, which can result in further economies through increased efficiency and effectiveness.

As a firm increases its output and employs more workers there are more opportunities to divide work into stages and, consequently, workers become more efficient in their work. Dividing the work into stages in this way also makes it easier to introduce machinery and other labour-saving equipment.

Managerial economies of scale

Larger firms are able to employ more highly skilled personnel. Such employees will be attracted to the company not only by the higher salaries offered but also by the prestige of a larger organisation and greater scope for advancement.

The employment of skilled specialists in charge of functions such as design and production results in the advantages of division of labour. Small firms often do not have sufficient work to enable them to form separate specialist departments and, therefore, managers have to undertake a variety of tasks which makes them less effective.

Marketing economies of scale

Larger firms can purchase their supplies in bigger quantities than small firms. They can also engage in mass production and they save in advertising and distribution costs. The important result of these advantages are that such firms can market their goods more cheaply than smaller competitors, and obviously consumers will be more likely to give their custom to such firms.

Most firms see public relations as an important part of their marketing strategies, because if potential customers regard the reputation of the company as 'good' they will be more likely to want to give their custom to the firm. Large businesses are in a better position to sponsor sports and public events and offer attractive prize-giving competitions, thus promoting good public relations.

Financial economies of scale

A major advantage of being a large firm is that, because they own more assets, they find it easier to borrow money and they are more able to withstand the financial pressures (e.g. of cash flow) than smaller businesses.

Banks and other lending institutions feel safer in loaning money to large companies because they feel there is less risk involved. Similarly, creditors (e.g. suppliers) feel more confident to give trade credit to larger firms than smaller ones.

Large businesses

It is generally the case that larger firms achieve bigger profits because they enjoy 'economies of scale'. That is, the cost per item falls as output increases. However, *diseconomies* of scale can also occur and these are reflected by unit costs increasing as output increases. Both of these possibilities can be examined by looking at the advantages and disadvantages of large-scale business.

Advantages of large businesses
- They find it easier to raise large amounts of capital.
- More capital is available for:
  - extensive advertising
  - research and development
  - employing specialist personnel
  - labour-saving machinery.
- Mass production allows greater possibilities of specialisation.
- They can obtain special prices and discounts.

The advantages of large businesses summarised in this list refer only to *internal* economies of scale, but there are also *external* economies of scale.

Sometimes many related businesses in a particular industry are located in one area. This will encourage the provision of skilled maintenance and other backup services such as training facilities which benefit all members of the industry. In addition, all firms engaged in a particular industry may combine together for the purposes of advertising, research or technical developments. Groups of industries will also attract good transport facilities, or special treatment from banks and other financial institutions.

Disadvantages of large businesses
- Can become too complex to manage.
- Lines of internal communication and management become unwieldy.
- Customers may find the large organisation too impersonal.
- Mass production can lead to boredom for workers and reduce quality.
- Workers find it easier to organise restrictive working practices.

The law of diminishing returns

A firm cannot continue to grow indefinitely unless some factors change. If you continue to blow up a balloon it will eventually burst because the fixed factor (the balloon) cannot contain the varying factor (the added air). The same principle applies to a growing business. If the fixed factor is factory space and the firm continues to add more workers, initially there will be more production, but eventually additional workers will result in less output per person as too many workers in a restricted space get in each other's way.

As a firm grows, it is subject to the law of diminishing returns. When a firm is growing rapidly it experiences increased returns and rising profits. But there is a point in any productive organisation when diminishing returns will begin to operate. The additional output (marginal output) achieved as a result of the addition of a unit of labour begins to fall, therefore the average output also falls. We can illustrate this by means of a table as shown below.

Units of workers	Total output	Marginal output	Average output
1	5	5	5
2	18	13	9
3	30	12	10
4	36	6	9
5	35	-1	7

Small businesses

In spite of the benefits of large-scale operations small firms continue to exist because they have their own special advantages, and in some cases (e.g. direct services such as hairdressing) do not lend to large-scale operations.

Generally there is only limited management structure in small businesses and often the only management will be the owner(s) of the firm. This has its advantages in that there is less need for consultation when making decisions because the manager or owner performs all the important functions. But this person also requires a wider range of management skills than his counterpart in a large organisation.

Advantages of small businesses

- Closer communication exists between employees.
- Easier to have good working relationships.
- Employees feel a personal involvement in the business.
- There is more personal contact between employees and customers.

Disadvantages of small businesses

- Limitation on capital for expansion.

- Are not in a position to take advantage of the benefits of the economies of scale available to larger organisations.
- Cannot employ specialist workers such as accountants and information technology experts.
- Product development, market research and other important activities cannot be financed.

2.5 Technological change

The previous section of this chapter included an examination of economies of scale. One aspect of this was technical economies. What we said was that the large size of some businesses enables them to use labour-saving machinery and automation. We will now look at this in more detail.

Automation refers to the use of sophisticated machinery which is electronically or computer controlled to carry out some form of production with the minimum of human intervention.

Demand for material goods has increased dramatically throughout the world, and many of these commodities are more sophisticated than ever before. The profit available to those who can produce goods and services most economically has always required businesses to look for the most economic way to meet this demand.

The most dramatic development that has assisted this has been the relatively

Technological change: use of microchip in control panel of washing machine.
(Copyright: Hotpoint)

recent innovation and application of the silicon chip which has put computer technology within the reach of small businesses and even individuals.

Computers

Computers have had an important effect on businesses. A computer is an electronic information processing machine. It can handle databases and spreadsheets as well as operate as a word processor.

A computer can accept data from a user (input), supply information to a user (output), sort, select, store and retrieve information and do calculations (process). The text or data may be in words or numbers. Computers operate on instructions (called a program) input by the operator.

A computer consists of the following main unit parts:

- *Keyboard* – an electronic keyboard used to feed information into the system.
- *Visual display unit (VDU)* – a television-like screen (monitor) used to display text prior to printing.
- *Central processing unit (CPU)* – sometimes called the computer's brain. It is the main part of the computer where the data is processed and the entire system is co-ordinated.
- *Memory system* – all computers have at least some internal memory, but this can be extended for long-term storage by recording data onto magnetic disks.
- *Disk drive* – a device that is used to feed in extended memory from disks.
- *Mouse* – some computers have a device such as this. It is a hand-held device that is used to move an icon (graphic image) across the screen. The mouse usually

A computer system.

has two or three buttons which are used to select objects on the screen. The action is known as 'clicking'.

- *Printer* – used to print out final text (hard copy).

Computers in business

The following are just some of the ways in which computers are increasingly being used in business operations.

- *Company registers*. A company's register of shareholders is constantly changing as its shares are bought and sold, and the current holders of the shares have to be paid their share of the company's profits. The register of shareholders can be kept in the computer system and rapidly updated.
- *Stock records*. Records can be automatically updated as stocks are removed from the warehouse or from the display shelves and recorded out through the tills. The computer can automatically issue a warning when stocks fall too low, and a valuation of stock is also immediately available.
- *Accounts*. Invoices and statements of account may be issued and records of customers' accounts maintained.
- *Payroll*. The maintenance of a company's wages system can be operated by computer, including automatic deduction of income tax etc.
- *Banking*. Banks use computers for automatic cheque clearing, keeping branch records, issuing bank statements and standing order payments, and the operation of cash dispenser systems. They also use computers for immediate updat-

Use of robots in car production.
(Photo courtesy of Ford of Britain)

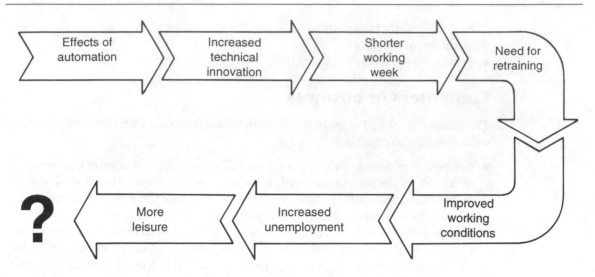

Some effects of automation. What next?

ing of customer accounts when deposits and withdrawals are made.

● *Word processing.* Computers can be used as word processors. Copies of letters, invoices, statements of account and other important paperwork can be keyed into a computer and stored for later retrieval for review on a VDU or by printout.

● *Production line applications.* Many machines in factories are used to perform repetitive tasks and, therefore, there has been an increasing use of computers to perform these tasks, e.g. automated robotic welding.

The effects of the increased use of technology in production can be summed up as follows:

● Increased standardisation of production results in increased output and reduced costs.

● Business risk is increased because sophisticated, expensive machinery must be purchased well in advance of the sale of products.

● Often results in workforce being made unemployed.

● Leisure time can be increased by a reduced working week and a lower retirement age.

● The need for tertiary services is considerably increased.

Make a note of it

1 What is meant by the term production?

2 Name the three primary needs.

3 In your own words explain the difference between 'needs' and 'wants'.

4 What is the aim of production?

5 Briefly describe the three levels of production.

6 Give examples of how the different levels of production can be seen in countries at different stages of development.

7 Describe separate circumstances when job, batch or flow production would be most appropriate.

8 Give a brief description of each of the four factors of production.

9 Describe some of the factors that affect the supply and quality of labour.

10 Define capital.

11 Explain the difference between fixed capital and working capital.

12 To what extent would you agree that the entrepreneur can be considered a factor of production?

13 Give an account of what you consider are the main influences on the location of businesses.

14 What special contribution can the government make to the location of businesses? Why would the government want to contribute?

15 What factors can be reliably used to decide whether a firm is large or small?

16 What do you understand by the term 'economies of scale'? Why do 'diseconomies' also occur?

17 Briefly describe the various forms of economies of scale.

18 What are the advantages enjoyed by large firms? Why do large organisations also have disadvantages?

19 Briefly explain the difference between internal and external economies of scale.

20 In what way does the law of diminishing returns show the limits of large-scale production?

21 Why do small firms continue to exist even though large organisations have many advantages?

22 Why do you think some people are apprehensive about technological change?

23 Word processors are making considerable impact on office work. What is a word processor? Briefly describe the functions of the main parts of a word processor system.

24 In what ways are the functions of a computer wider than those of a word processor?

25 Describe four examples of the use of computers, including at least one application to office work and one related to production.

26 Define automation. What are the possible results of automation?

Structured Questions

1 Look at this photograph taken in a chocolate factory and answer the questions that follow it.

(a) In what way is secondary production illustrated here? (1)

(b) Name two factors of production that can be identified in the photograph. (2)

(c) The system of production illustrated is called 'division of labour by process'.
  - Explain what is meant by 'division of labour by process'. (2)
  - Describe one example of this process that operates within your school or college. (2)

(d) Many firms have introduced new technology into their production process, and increased the productivity of their workforce.
  - Define the terms 'new technology' and 'productivity'. (2)
  - State two costs and two benefits new technology can bring to a workforce. (4)

(e) One of the possible disadvantages of division of labour by process is that it can result in alienation of the workforce. What do we mean by 'alienation' and what methods might a firm use to combat it? (7)

2 The data opposite is used by Peterborough Development Corporation to encourage businesses to locate in its industrial areas. Answer the questions that follow the data.

(a) Give one reason why British Sugar moved from London to Peterborough. (1)

British Sugar – one of Europe's largest sugar companies – moved its national headquarters from London to Peterborough in 1974.

Three hundred staff were employed as the central offices opened alongside the company's existing Peterborough factory.

Since then the number of headquarters staff has almost doubled through the emergence of Silver Spoon as a national brand leader.

A further 235 people are employed in the factory (part of a network of sugar manufacturing plants in East Anglia and the West Midlands) and this rises to about 350 during the annual autumn sugar making season.

British Sugar's Managing Director, Mr Gordon Percival, said: "From Peterborough we control the operations of all our factories and co-ordinate supply and delivery of more than one million tonnes of sugar and more than 600,000 tonnes of animal feed every year.

"We have never looked back from the days when we moved from cramped and expensive headquarters in London.

"In Peterborough the company and its workforce have prospered to the extent that sales have doubled in the last ten years to make our Silver

Spoon brand the retail brand leader and largest of all grocery brands in the UK.

"In 1984, the company relaunched its range of sugars with new pack designs in an extensive advertising and promotion campaign which highlighted speciality sugars. We are continuing to invest heavily in further product development".

Mr Percival said that Peterborough, with its excellent road and rail network, housebuilding programme, leisure facilities, growth prospects and a good available workforce, was an ideal location for the company.

The company describes its locally-recruited employees as 'hard-working and dedicated professionals'.

Location of British Sugar. (Courtesy of Peterborough Development Corporation)

(b) Why has British Sugar been able to double its headquarters staff? (1)

(c) How could the data shown here help Peterborough Development Corporation encourage businesses other than British Sugar to move into the area? (2)

(d) Give two reasons why both British Sugar and its workforce have prospered at Peterborough? (2)

(e) Why would British Sugar be likely to need larger premises than a producer of computer software? (2)

(f) What advantages might there be of siting the central offices alongside the company's factory? (3)

(g) In siting its business in Peterborough British Sugar would consider the provision of local facilities such as housing, schools and transport. Why would it consider these important? (3)

(h) Take the area in which you live and design an advertisement that aims to attract businesses to locate in your area. The advertisement must clearly identify the benefits that would appeal to firms considering relocation or setting up initially in your locality. (6)

37

The bar code reader reads the following code into the computer

5	000171	010070
Country of origin	Manufacturer's number	Product number

For the above label

JOHN WEST

Tuna Steak 200g ← The computer uses the code to link the code with this information

Bar codes and supermarkets.

Bar codes were introduced:
- *to record which goods have been sold*
- *to speed up customers checking out at the tills*
- *to replace price labelling of goods.*

They also provide:
- *the customer with an itemised bill*
- *the supermarket with accounts*
- *the supermarket with data for sales analysis.*

This illustration is referred to in Question 3 on page 40

3 The following questions are all related to the use of bar codes in businesses which are shown on page 38.

(a) What is a bar code? (1)

(b) How does a computer 'read' a bar code? (2)

(c) In what way does a bar code help a supermarket to easily provide a customer with an itemised bill? (2)

(d) How could a supermarket use its bar code system to update its stock records? What would be the main advantage of doing this? (3)

(e) Describe two examples of the ways that a supermarket would use data collected from bar codes for 'sales analysis'. (4)

(f) Libraries combine bar codes on books and on membership cards to control the issue and return of books. Describe in detail how a business offering the hire of video cassettes could usefully operate a similar system and what the benefits would be compared to a manual system. (8)

4 Look at the diagram below of a computer system. It consists of the following parts: mouse, VDU, processor, keyboard.

(a) What do the letters VDU stand for? (1)

(b) List the names of each of the four parts of the system shown and beside each give the identifying letter A, B, C and D shown in the diagram. (2)

(c) Describe the function of any three of the items of equipment contained in your list in Part (b) above. (3)

(d) *Hardware* is the name given to any device which is part of a computer system, e.g. VDU, mouse, processor. *Software* is the term given to the programs that are used on the computer. They are stored on either a floppy disk, hard disk or on a network fileserver.

Complete a table similar to the one below placing the software and hardware terms listed in the correct column:

- laser printer
- personnel records
- keyboard
- customer accounts
- bar code reader
- address file
- graphics scanner
- spreadsheet.

Hardware	Software

(4)

(e) The six main areas of computer software are:

(i)   word processing   (iv) graphics
(ii) control   (v)   desk top publishing
(iii) databases   (vi) spreadsheets.

Choose any five of these aspects of computer applications and for each describe a different specific business application. (10)

Extended Answer Assignments

1 Consider the extent to which the siting of businesses in your area can be seen to be influenced by local or national government.

2 Consider any new business which might wish to locate in your area and examine the different factors which would help them to choose between two contrasting sites.

3 Take any vacant business premises in your locality and put forward rational arguments for starting a new type of business in those premises.

4 Use a relatively local map to illustrate the main area of location of primary, secondary and tertiary production. Make observations on the reasons for site choice in each case.

5 Your school art department has decided to start a mini-enterprise which will produce ornamental pottery for marketing locally. A local bank has offered to finance the rent of a small shop in the town, if it is not too expensive. What are the cheapest but most practicable premises you can identify? Give reasons for your choice.

6 Investigate two contrasting businesses in your locality that are involved in manufacturing. Make a comparison of the extent to which they use information technology in their production processes.

7 Produce personal research evidence that proves at least two businesses you have personally investigated achieve 'technical economies of scale'.

3 ▸ Business organisation

<table><tr><td>3.1</td></tr></table>

The role and functions of a business

The main aim of any business is to make profits in order to give the best possible return to the owners for the money they have invested in the company. Businesses achieve this aim mainly through their major functional areas of production, finance, marketing and personnel.

Production

The broad function of production is to satisfy human wants. In order to do this through the production of goods and services the firm will have to co-ordinate:

- the purchase of stocks and raw materials;
- the design of goods;
- research, development and experimental work;
- the manufacture of the company's products;
- control of the quality of production;
- storage of the raw materials and finished goods.

We can see this reflected in the production of furniture. The firm may design prototype furniture from raw materials it has purchased. It will research the market to investigate the best ways to market such items. This research will also reveal what need there may be to amend the design of the prototypes, and to produce samples to show prospective customers and obtain orders. Only then will full-scale production take place, during which quality control will be maintained to ensure that what is produced is of the required standard, and workers called *progress chasers* will make sure that goods are produced within the timescale required. The finished products will then be stored until they are required for the intended market. Chapters 8 to 11 give further details on marketing.

Finance

Finance is required to form a business and to fund its operations. It is required, for example, to purchase plant and machinery, raw materials, and to pay wages to workers. A business also needs finance to meet day-to-day running expenses and maintenance costs.

There are four main sources of business finance (also called capital): (a) savings of the entrepreneur(s); (b) capital borrowed from a bank or some other financial

LEEDS METROPOLITAN UNIVERSITY LIBRARY

institution; (c) capital raised by the sale of shares in the business; (d) profits of the business reinvested ('ploughed back' or 'retained').

The finance of businesses is examined in more detail in Chapters 15, 16 and 17.

Marketing

The marketing function of a business aims to anticipate consumer demand in order that the right products are manufactured. Once the commodities have been produced it is then the function of marketing to promote sales to the consumer. Marketing is not confined to goods alone; labour, capital, land and buildings must also be marketed as well as the many services that are needed. Chapters 8 to 11 examine marketing in detail.

Personnel

The personnel function of a business is concerned with recruitment, selection, training and welfare of employees. Theoretically, the more businesses that exist, and the more successful they are, the greater is the number of personnel needed. However, in reality the provision of employment is far more complex than this simple view. For example, technological developments which lead to increased efficiency and business growth can also result in a reduction of the number of employees needed in a particular industry.

The integration of the two broad technologies of computers and telecommunications has led to increased efficiency and business growth. The revolution in electronics has transformed many of the traditional areas of employment. For example, many of the functions of office workers have been by-passed by computers and word processors; methods of communication have rapidly changed with telecommunication making an even greater contribution. And the automated factory is now becoming more commonplace.

Part of the personnel function of business is the management of these aspects of the business: to recruit people with appropriate skills, care for their welfare, and ensure that where necessary in-service training is provided to update their skills. The personnel function is examined in Chapters 5, 6 and 7.

3.2

Management

Responsibilities of management

The foregoing functional areas of a business have to be co-ordinated and managed to ensure that the resources of the business are used to the best advantage.

All members of an organisation have some responsibility, even if it is only to have regard for their own safety and that of their work colleagues. But the higher in the hierarchy of the organisation that a person is, the greater will be that person's responsibility. Consequently, the greater degree of responsibility lies with the managers of an organisation, whether they are managing directors, or managers of departments. Managers in this respect are those who have the responsibility to direct, control and co-ordinate others.

PRODUCTION

FINANCE

MARKETING

PERSONNEL

The functional areas of a business.

The management of an organisation are responsible to the firm's:

- *owners* – to achieve the best possible return for the capital they have invested and to re-invest or 'plough back' sufficient capital in order to ensure sound future growth and development of the business;
- *customers* – to provide goods or services of good quality, within the agreed period of time, and at a fair and economic price;
- *employees* – to provide the safest and most comfortable working conditions possible, to pay a fair wage and to secure future employment as far as possible.

The management also have some responsibility to the government, and to society. The responsibility to the government is to ensure that the company abides by the law, and behaves in a manner that is compatible with the country's trading practices both at home and overseas. The responsibility to society is to ensure that the firm's operations do not cause harm to the general public, e.g. through being environmentally aware.

In order to meet these responsibilities the management must organise and co-ordinate the work of others. The manager will, therefore, at times be required to:

- appoint and train new staff;
- communicate company policy;
- give instructions and set tasks;
- assess performance;
- discipline and dismiss staff.

Superiors are expected to be responsible for the actions of their subordinates. Although they can delegate the power or authority to carry out tasks to subordinates, the responsibility for actions cannot be delegated and ultimate responsibility always remains with the manager.

Management functions

The functions of management can be grouped into six areas:

1 *Planning*. This involves methodically looking ahead, making decisions, and formulating policy on the intentions and objectives of the organisation and the methods to be used to achieve these objectives. It assists the efficient utilisation of the firm's resources and it emphasises preventative rather than corrective measures.

2 *Direction*. This involves giving instructions to workers so that they are clear as to how their work should be done to best benefit the organisation.

3 *Delegating*. This involves assigning tasks or goals to subordinates while at the same time granting them the necessary authority to carry out those tasks. The subordinates must recognise their responsibility and accept their accountability for the expected performance.

4 *Controlling*. This involves supervising and checking the activities and performance of subordinates to ensure that instructions are being carried out properly and plans and methods are being followed.

5 *Organising*. This involves ensuring that workers can get on with their jobs by making sure that people, materials and machinery are available in the right place at the right time. Good organisation involves planning of what is to be done, who is to supervise it, time frames and the most efficient method of doing it.

6 *Co-ordinating*. This involves directing and integrating the activities of the team under their direct supervision and contributing to the overall co-ordination of the activities within the organisation in order to form a united strategy of operations to achieve the organisation's objectives.

7 *Motivating*. This involves encouraging other members of the organisation to carry out their tasks properly and effectively. Although extrinsic incentives such as wages help to motivate people, the ability to motivate others is very much

dependent upon leadership qualities which are discussed later. Intrinsic incentives such as job enlargement and job satisfaction also help to motivate people.

Leadership

People who are in a supervisory position in business need to have some understanding of group dynamics, that is the way that people interact in a group situation. The extent to which people work effectively (or not) together affects the overall success potential of the business. In the business sense there are four basic elements of group behaviour: the group, an objective, the individual and the leader.

The group

Groups can be divided into two categories:

1 *Informal groups* have usually come together voluntarily (e.g. a music group) and the purpose of the group is not defined too specifically. There are no set rules (although an informal group may have an objective, e.g. to raise money for charity) and the leader will be chosen by the members of the group. Informal groups just develop because those involved recognise they have some common interest, e.g. interest in a particular sport.
2 *Formal groups* are usually created for a specific purpose, e.g. a department in a firm. This type of group has a formal structure, a specific objective, and an appointed leader. In fact, the leader may be the one who chooses the members of the group, and consequently enjoys the power of authority. People in businesses and factories generally work in formal groups, with expected standards of production and behaviour.

An objective

Because most groups in business are formal ones they required a clear objective, e.g. to formulate a marketing campaign for a new product. Unless the objectives are clearly defined (i.e. by the leader) the group will lose direction; the objective will be liable to be misinterpreted.

The individual

Even though they are part of a group each person still has to work as an individual in order to make their contribution to the group objective. However, this can result in a problem if the views of the individual or their attitude or behaviour are not in harmony with the rest of the group. Under such circumstances the importance of the objective may be sufficient to solve the conflict. Alternatively, it may be the skill of the group leader that will be the deciding factor.

The leader

Whereas the leader of an informal group may be chosen by the group members, with formal groups the leader is often appointed, e.g. managers, chairperson, etc. In this position the leader may have the power to regulate the group behaviour (e.g. in a position to be able to direct someone to do something), but to use their authority in this way may adversely affect the group morale and attitudes. For this reason a good leader will try to identify the parameters within which the group can operate, often delegating some responsibility to members of the group.

The main function of the leader in a business is to ensure that the group works effectively and carries out the tasks assigned to it. It is often the case in formal groups that it is part of the leader's role to supervise the work of individuals and make recommendations to superiors. In informal groups, however, the leader may be the reason why the individual has chosen to join the group. Whilst the latter is an example of group harmony it can also be a source of discontent when some individuals see themselves as alternative leaders.

Earlier in this chapter we saw that it is important that workers feel motivated. Wages are often assumed to be a motivating factor, but an unlimited amount of capital to provide wages cannot be guaranteed, and wages alone are limited in the extent to which they can be relied upon to encourage people to work hard and effectively.

The success of management and the ability to motivate others very much depend upon the ability to lead. But leadership qualities are difficult to identify and to define, firstly because they depend on the manager's own attitude towards the responsibilities delegated to him or her and to his or her subordinates. Secondly, the ability to lead is considerably influenced by the attitude of the manager towards the problems of his or her subordinates. Thirdly, some of the qualities required to lead others differ from one occupation to another.

To be able to motivate others managers must also be inspired. They need to be committed to their organisation and must have interest and pride in the products or services which they produce or sell. Leadership qualities are particularly revealed by the willingness of superiors to listen to, and understand, problems from their subordinates' point of view.

Styles of leadership

There are four basic styles of leadership and a leader may combine any of these:

1 *Authoritarian or autocratic*. Such leaders are the absolute authority on all matters. They decide what to do and, whatever others may think, it is done. It is often the case that this type of leader frequently uses his or her position in authority to exert his or her will over others.

   Such an approach to leadership is often effective, but not necessarily the most efficient. Although work may be completed in the way that the leader has specified, at the same time employee input and innovation is discounted.
2 *Participative or democratic*. The leader will consult with those likely to be affected before making a decision, although the leader will reserve the right not to act on a majority view.

   This style of leadership is popular because it enables workers lower down in the hierarchy to participate in the decision-making process. Consequently, they are more highly motivated and need less supervision.
3 *Laissez-faire or free-rein*. In this style of leadership the leader gives limited directions to workers. They are given general directions on the tasks to be tackled and then left to achieve them in the way they think is best.

There are circumstances where this type of leadership is appropriate (e.g. where the employee acts in a consultancy capacity), but generally, most employees prefer to work under some degree of authority from a superior.

4 *Charismatic*. A charismatic leader is one who influences and motivates others because he or she has an outstanding personality or character. This type of leader is relatively rare but can be very successful in the extent to which they can motivate others to do things to support them.

Management communication

The success of any organisation is greatly influenced by the participation of all its members in its activities. We have seen earlier in this chapter that managers have an important part to play in co-ordinating and motivating all workers to achieve a common goal. But for all the workers to make a contribution they need to know what goals they are expected to achieve. Experience has shown that people are more committed to involvement in an organisation where they are well-informed of policies, and even more so when they have participated in making decisions.

Good communication is important in involving all members of an organisation in its activities. The most effective management communications require a two-way flow of information – downwards from management and upwards from employees.

Downward communication is initiated by management and is used to inform employees of the company's proposals, policies, decisions and progress. There are two main methods of downward communication, oral and written:

- *oral* – direct command, discussions, meetings, loudspeaker, intercom, closed circuit television, telephone;
- *written* – letters, memoranda, notice-boards, reports, company magazine, handbooks.

Upward communication may be initiated by employees but it is often 'collected' by management. For example, management may well require specific information from employees. This feeds back to management the views, suggestions, proposals and problems of employees. Upward communication can be 'collected' by direct and indirect methods:

● *direct* – by managers talking to employees and elected representatives;
● *indirect* – suggestion schemes, attitude surveys.

3.3 Small and large businesses

The internal structure of a firm is influenced by its size. The small business is organised fairly simply, whereas the larger company has a more complex structure and more divisions.

Small businesses

Small businesses cannot easily be divided into departments because they do not have the people or floor space to organise in this way. Consequently, workers in small firms tend to specialise less and they are required to have a wider range of skills and a broader knowledge of the way that the business is organised. This is because the workers are required to be able to carry out a wider variety of tasks, whereas in a large organisation they would have more opportunity to specialise in a particular activity. However, the variety of the work in a small organisation is considered to be an advantage by some workers.

Large businesses

Large businesses are generally private or public companies which are dealt with later in Chapter 4. These types of organisation are owned by shareholders. These shareholders elect a board of directors to decide the general policies that the firm

A large business can be divided into separate departments, each with its own manager and internal structure.

ACCOUNTS

Records all payments in and out of the firm. It is particularly concerned with incoming and outgoing invoices, and maintaining the firm's money flow. Payment of wages is frequently included in the responsibilities of this department. The modern accounts department has an extensive data processing system backed up by computers.

LEGAL

Most legal matters are dealt with by the company secretary, although a very large organisation might have a legal department. The department's activities include legal matters such as contracts, guarantees, insurance, compensation, etc.

SALES

To plan and organise the selling of goods or services offered by the firm. This department is one of the most essential because without it other departments would not be needed. Sales representatives provide an important link between the company and potential customers.

PURCHASING

The purchasing or buying department is responsible for all items bought by the firm. It obtains quotations from suppliers and issues orders, ensuring delivery is made on time. It also checks that prices, quality and quantity delivered correspond with the quotation and order. This department also deals with 'requisitions' which are written requests for supplies from other departments in the firm.

ADVERTISING

May be a separate department or it can be incorporated into the sales department. The aim of this department is to make potential customers aware of the goods or services the company offers and to encourage custom. Smaller firms may employ the services of an advertising agency to carry out this work for them.

TRANSPORT

May operate the company's own fleet of vehicles, or alternatively it organises other forms of transport using agencies outside the firm. The function of this department is to arrange for delivery of goods to customers on time, in good condition, at home or overseas, and by the most economical method and route applicable.

ADMINISTRATION

Many firms have a general office concerned with co-ordinating the activities of the various departments of the firm. The administration department may include back-up facilities such as centralised filing, typing pool, mail room, reprographics and data processing. The administration department is frequently closely related to the managing director.

PRODUCTION

Where the company is involved in production of some commodity, a production department may be used to co-ordinate the work of the factory unit. 'Progress chasers' may be employed to ensure that delivery schedules are adhered to, and 'quality controllers' can be used to maintain production standards and investigate complaints or deal with goods returned as faulty.

PERSONNEL

Concerned with finding the right person for vacant jobs, dismissing unsuitable workers, dealing with resignations and providing references. It is involved directly in any induction training or staff training school the company operates. It maintains personal records of all employees and is involved in the welfare and happiness of all personnel.

The departments of a large firm.

will follow. The board of directors will appoint a managing director to supervise the day-to-day operations of the business, and to ensure that the policies decided by the board of directors are carried out. A company secretary is also appointed to deal with legal matters such as contracts of employment, product guarantees and government legislation.

3.4 Organisational structure

Chain of command

Many companies are organised in the form of a pyramid. The person at the top of the pyramid has the most authority and the steps down the pyramid indicate less authority. Each person in the pyramid is responsible to the person immediately above them (sometimes referred to as their 'line manager'). The sections of the following pyramid show the person in the managing position is at the top of the chain of command. This shows the lines of communication between the person in the supervisory position and his/her subordinates. Each manager delegates work to the people below him/her in the chain.

Pyramid organisation charts.

Span of control

This is sometimes also referred to as 'span of management' because it refers to the number of subordinates a manager supervises, or the effective limit to the number of others that a manager can supervise efficiently. There are a number of factors that influence the span of control and they include the following:

- *The complexity of the work.* Some work is easy to check whilst other work demands closer supervision by the manager.

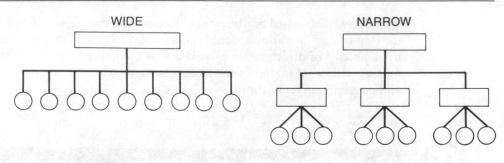

Span of control.

- *Self-discipline of workers*. Where workers are well motivated and have a professional approach a greater number can be supervised.
- *Method of communication*. Some methods of communication (e.g. face-to-face) are more demanding than others (e.g. electronic methods).
- *Frequency of supervision*. The more frequently that a manager needs to see subordinates the more limited will be the span of control.
- *Capability of the manager*. Some managers have more ability to lead and motivate than others and this will extend their span of control.

If workers do not need close supervision then the span of control can be wide and flat. Where there is a need for closer supervision the span of control will be narrow and contain more people in sub-supervisory positions.

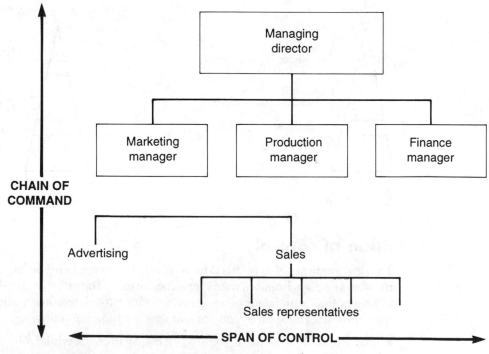

Combined chain of command and span of control.

Organisational structure

To enable a firm to achieve its objectives satisfactorily it relies on two types of relationship between personnel. One type is 'formal' and the other 'informal'. Together these relationships are called the 'organisational structure' of a firm.

Formal organisation

Formal organisation is concerned with the official lines of communication followed by employees to carry out management decisions. It allows those in charge to define objectives for each section/department to enable the organisation to achieve its corporate aims. It helps to define responsibilities and to ensure that tasks are not duplicated but are co-ordinated between functions within an organisation, so that each department blends its activities with those of other departments to form a corporate strategy.

A formal organisation chart shows the structure or relationships through which a firm intends to work. But in addition to this *formal structure* there usually exists *informal links*. These links can be useful to a firm because they can help to support the organisation; for example, if a group of workers organise social events it can have the beneficial effect of motivating workers. However, informal contacts can also be damaging; for example, groups of workers meeting outside the business may discuss aspects of the firm's operations and promote mistrust and ill-feelings based on rumour rather than fact.

The functions found in organisations will vary depending on their type or size, and this will affect the organisational structure used.

There are basically four types of formal organisational structure and a business might incorporate more than one:

1 line organisation
2 staff organisation
3 functional organisation
4 committee organisation.

Line organisation

This is a traditional form of organisation which involves a direct flow of authority, and responsibility is dispersed and delegated from top to bottom. The owner, or chief executive, will instruct those below him, e.g. the departmental managers.

Line organisation in a small firm.

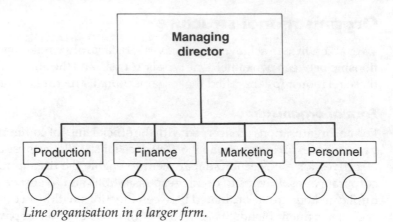

Line organisation in a larger firm.

They, in turn, will instruct the employees who then comply with the instructions. (This is looked on as a narrow span of control.)

Within this hierarchical form of organisation everyone has some responsibility. The higher the position in the hierarchy the greater is the responsibility, and this responsibility cannot be delegated. Tasks or objectives, however, can be delegated, and so can authority or the right to use power. This right is defined by the hierarchy and should correspond with the delegator's position in the hierarchy.

The benefits of this method of organisation are that it is easy to understand and has an uncomplicated chain of command. Decisions can be reached quickly. It is particularly suited to a small business. However, this type of structure ties up the owner/chief executive with administration, leaving little time for policy-making and planning. It also restricts the inclusion of specialist personnel where services

Staff organisation: the service departments supply facilities to the operating departments and also to the other service departments. The dotted lines show how one department of an organisation might provide a service to all or many other sections.

are required by more than one department. A small firm could 'buy in' these services, e.g. legal advice and the information offered by research agencies, but this would be uneconomical for a large firm which would prefer to employ its own specialists. For this reason the line organisation tends to be less suited to a large firm.

Staff organisation

Staff organisation is a development of a line organisation. Some activities of a business cut across the departments of a linear structure because they offer a service facility (e.g. legal or research activities) to several if not all departments. As mentioned earlier when looking at line organisation, a large firm would find it more economical to employ specialist staff to offer these services and advice to other departments. Staff of these 'back-up' services can advise, but generally not direct or control, the other departments.

A major advantage of this system is that it allows employment of specialist workers. The main disadvantage is that the lines of responsibility and authority are less clear and this can result in disputes between specialist personnel and heads of departments.

Functional organisation

This type of organisation is set up in departments to carry out the basic functions of the business, e.g. finance, production, sales, warehouse/delivery, etc.

The head of each specialist department supervises, controls and is responsible for just the one function with which it is involved. However, a subordinate employee, carrying out a task, will be in the unenviable position of receiving orders from, and being accountable to, possibly all the specialist department heads.

This is a wide span of control and this type of organisation requires a lot of co-operation and common sense to avoid confusion and conflict in the workforce.

This method of organisation has its place in a business which has branches located around the country, or in a situation in which there is the need to have specialist functions based at a suitable location, e.g. a shipping office or warehouse positioned near docks. Under these circumstances the specialist departments would probably

Functional organisation: within a functional organisation's structure a member of a department might receive instructions from many or even all of the other departments.

Functional organisation: in a large functional organisation structure the branches might use any of the departments at headquarters, and those departments might also use each other.

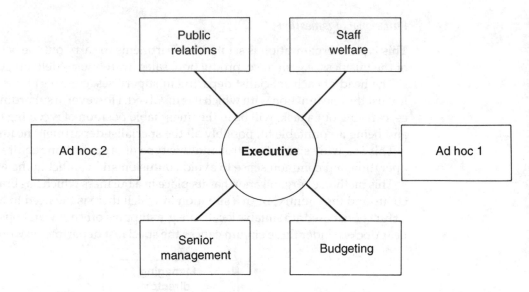

Committee organisation: a group of specialists is brought together to advise top executives and help them develop policy and procedures.

be based at the head office and control of the branches would emanate from there. However, the branch managers would retain a certain amount of autonomy whilst also being able to draw on the functions and expertise at headquarters.

Committee organisation

The committee organisation is based on the management principle of grouping specialists in committees to advise the executives and to assist them in developing policies and procedures. Some committees will have authority to recommend to

A horizontal organisation chart.

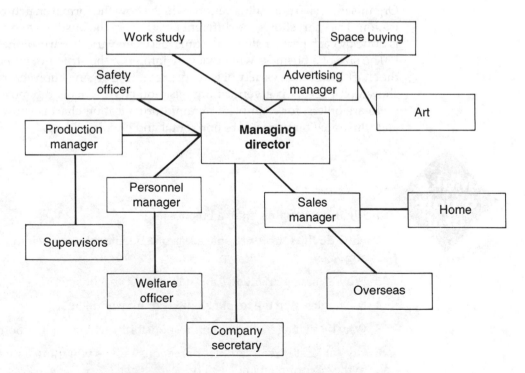

A circular organisation chart.

supervisors (upward communication), others are formed purely to receive information (downward communication), and some will undertake management functions, e.g. policy-making. Some will be permanent working groups whilst others will be 'ad hoc', i.e. set up to examine a particular problem, and then dissolved once they have achieved their goal.

Committees invariably slow up the decision-making process, but they improve morale by allowing employees to participate. The combined judgement of several specialists in similar or diverse areas also promotes sound decision-making.

Informal organisation

Some groups have an influence on an organisation but do not necessarily have the interest of the business directing their actions. Workers tend to form into informal groups based on their interests or skills. For example, a group of workers might get together to organise a social function. The reason for this grouping is not intended to benefit the organisation, although it may well have a good influence on morale which is in the firm's interest. In another example, workers might form a group of people concerned about a new development the firm wants to undertake and in which they want to express an adverse opinion.

It is important for management to recognise the way in which informal groups work if they are to minimise the damage they can cause, or to maximise the benefits to be gained by utilising such groups wherever possible.

Organisation charts

Organisation charts are illustrations which show the formal structure of an organisation. The chart shows the different positions in the business and indicates what is done by each part, or shows the links between various parts of the organisation.

The size of a business will obviously influence the structure and complexity of the chart. There are a variety of ways of presenting organisation charts. The method shown on page 49 is a vertical organisation chart. This is the most popular, but there are others, for example a pyramid organisation chart is shown on page 51, and illustrated on page 57 are horizontal and circular charts.

Make a note of it

1 What is the main aim of a business?

2 How do the four functional areas of a business help it achieve its general aim?

3 Why is management an important aspect of a business?

4 Briefly describe the responsibilities of management.

5 Why do managers have more responsibilities than their subordinates?

6 Give at least three examples of responsibilities you think a manager has to the government and society.

7 In what ways do management meet its responsibilities?

8 Describe the main functions of management.

9 Why is it important for a manager to have an understanding of group dynamics?

10 Explain the difference between informal groups and formal groups.

11 Why is it important that a firm's objectives are clearly understood by its employees?

12 Why is it that wages are limited in the extent to which they can be relied on to encourage people to work hard and effectively?

13 Why is it difficult to define the qualities needed to lead others?

14 List in your own order of priority ten qualities you would look for in a potential manager of a medium-sized manufacturing company.

15 Briefly describe each of the four styles of leadership.

16 Why is communication an important factor of management?

17 'Effective management requires a two-way flow of communication.' Explain this statement.

18 Make an outline comparison between the organisational structure of a small business and that of a large business.

19 How does the function of a managing director differ from that of other directors?

20 Describe the functions of six departments of a large company.

21 Why are there so many variations of span of control?

22 How does chain of command differ from span of control?

23 Describe the four types of formal organisational structure.

24 Produce simple diagrams and concise explanations to illustrate the four types of organisation chart shown in this chapter.

Structured Questions

1 The chart on page 60 shows the percentage of UK managers who, at the time of a survey, felt that the top management of their organisation were doing a 'good' or a 'very good' job of handling several critical aspects of the business.
   On balance, the survey concluded that the majority of UK managers were far from satisfied with the task or business related aspects of their company's management.

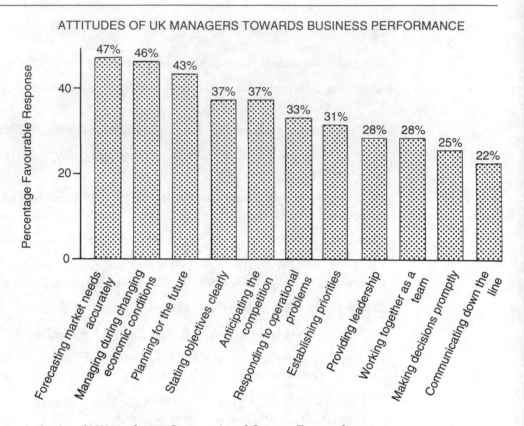

ATTITUDES OF UK MANAGERS TOWARDS BUSINESS PERFORMANCE

Attitudes of UK employees, International Survey Research.
Source: Roger Maitland (1988)

(a) For which aspects of business performance do UK managers have least confidence in the top management of their organisation? (1)

(b) Which aspect of top management activities do other managers feel are carried out most effectively? (1)

(c) How would you define the difference between 'managers' and 'top management'? (2)

(d) There is a clear functional link between some parts of the survey data. For example, what do you see as the links between the aspects 'providing leadership', and 'working together as a team'? (4)

(e) Give three contrasting examples of objectives that top management would need to state, and say why they would be important to lower managers. (6)

(f) Take the three aspects of the survey most highly rated and for each give a separate explanation for why they are important to business organisation. (6)

2 Refer to the diagram on page 50 and answer these questions.

(a) Name the department of a company that would be particularly concerned with the firm's money flow. (1)

   (b) Give two examples of matters that are likely to be dealt with by a
      company's Legal department. (2)
   (c) Why are larger organisations more able to divide into a departmental
      structure than smaller ones? (2)
   (d) Give three examples of work carried out by a Purchasing department
      other than buying items. (3)
   (e) The Sales and Advertising departments have a close association and
      they are sometimes incorporated in a larger department called
      Marketing. What is the important association between these two
      departments? (4)
   (f) The Personnel department is stated to be involved in 'induction
      training or staff training'. What does this involve and why is it
      important to business operations? (8)

3 Look at the diagram on page 49 showing a typical example of the structure of
a public limited company and answer these questions.

   (a) Which of the labels in the diagram refers specifically to the owners of
      the business? (1)
   (b) The chairperson of a board of directors is an 'elected' position whereas
      the managing director is an 'appointed' position. Explain the
      difference between the words in inverted commas in relation to these
      positions in an organisation. (2)
   (c) How does the work of a managing director differ from that of other
      directors? (3)
   (d) Why is the Transport department particularly important to both the
      Sales department and the Factory department of a large organisation? (4)
   (e) Describe the work of two of the following business occupations,
      including mention of who their line managers would be in the
      diagram:
      (i) wages clerk;
      (ii) progress chaser;
      (iii) sales representative. (4)
   (f) Clearly describe the work of three managers in the diagram and in
      each case say to what extent they need leadership qualities. (6)

4 Consider the article that follows on page 62:

   (a) What is a multinational company? (1)
   (b) Why is the question of centralisation and decentralisation particularly
      relevant to large organisations rather than small ones? (2)
   (c) List at least three benefits you feel a firm gains from centralisation. (3)
   (d) List three advantages that can occur as a result of decentralisation. (3)
   (e) How would centralisation of a company's reprographic services save
      in the overall cost of equipment if the firm consists of 15 departments? (4)
   (f) Discuss the view that decentralisation of control of the decision-
      making process can have the effect of motivating those with
      management responsibilities. (7)

Centralisation refers to a situation when a business is organised in such a way that policies and decisions for all branches of the firm are made by a central body. It is also used to describe a situation whereby internal services of a firm, e.g. reprographics or filing, are carried out by one department for the whole of the organisation.

Decentralisation exists when the policies and decisions of a firm are made away from the central control. Each branch of the firm makes its own decisions on how it will operate.

A major problem large organisations face is the degree to which control is centralised or how much decentralisation there should be. Most firms such as multinationals use a mixture of centralisation and decentralisation.

Extended Answer Assignments

1 Make a diagrammatic 'map' of the organisation structure of a small and a medium-sized local firm with which you are familiar. Comment on the differences observed.

2 Make a comparative study of the organisation structure of a local department store and that of a local manufacturing unit.

3 Select two competing businesses situated within your locality and show:
(a) how they compete;
(b) why they are both able to survive in spite of the competition they are part of.

4 Write to two multinational companies with questions that aim to find out which policies are decided centrally. Produce a report that summarises your findings and suggest reasons for the decision process of each firm.

5 If you were the managing director of a bakery firm with a central bakehouse and 20 shops selling your products, what kind of organisation structure would you have? Give your reasons.

6 Produce an organisation chart to represent the structure of your local council. Explain why you think it is divided into departments and describe the function of six of the departments.

7 'All managers are required to lead, but not all managers are leaders.' Discuss this statement using specific examples to illustrate your answer.

8 Investigate a business to which you can gain relatively easy access. Describe the extent to which the firm achieves its aims through the functional areas of production, finance, marketing and personnel.

4 ▸ Types of business

Private and public enterprise

Britain is said to have a 'mixed' economy because it consists of both private enterprise and public enterprise.

Private enterprise refers to businesses that are owned by private individuals (some of the public) engaged in the production of goods or services. There are four main forms of business ownership in the private sector of the economy:

1 sole traders
2 partnership
3 private limited companies
4 public limited companies.

There are also some private organisations which have a special relationship with the owners of the business. Co-operative societies and holding companies are examples of these special forms of private enterprise. These special relationships are examined later in this chapter.

Public enterprise refers to industries and services owned by the state (all of the public) and run by central or local government.

4.2

Limited liability

The business entrepreneur faces many risks when participating in business activity, especially if the firm has unlimited liability. This means that if the business goes bankrupt and cannot pay its creditors, the owner's personal possessions such as car or home and its contents can be taken and used to pay the debts owed.

Although many small firms do have unlimited liability, larger organisations face so much greater risks that only some form of security for personal assets encourages people to invest and accept the greater risks involved.

The status of limited liability allows people to invest in a business without having to face the risks of unlimited liability. Limited liability indicates that the liability of shareholders for the debts of a business is limited to the amount they have invested in the business and not their personal assets.

Limited liability can be applied to the shareholders of a private or public limited company and a limited partnership. The private company and limited partnership must show the letters Ltd at the end of the company title. The public company must indicate limited liability by the letters plc (public limited company) at the end of the company title.

Limited companies are said to have a 'separate corporate identity', in other words, an identity separate from their shareholders. They can sue and be sued in their title name.

4.3 Private ownership

The sole proprietor

This type of firm is owned by one person who provides all of the capital needed to form, operate, or expand the business. The sole proprietor (sole trader) is the simplest and most common type of enterprise. It is the easiest form of business to set up and it is also more likely to fail than any other.

Such businesses as sole proprietors tend to have only a few employees and less machinery or capital than larger businesses. They also have less plant facilities and fewer opportunities to make economies of scale. Their market tends to be less diversified than that of larger businesses because their levels of operations limit their output.

Advantages

- The small size of this type of business requires a relatively small amount of capital for formation.
- The owner does not have to consult with anyone else when making decisions.
- The owner does not have to share profits with anyone else.
- The owner will be familiar with all aspects of the business.

Disadvantages

- The owner's personal assets are at risk because the business has unlimited liability.
- There can be difficulty in continuing business (lack of continuity) if the owner is on holiday, ill, or dies.

- Division of labour may be difficult to organise because of small size of business.
- Shortage of capital can occur because all capital has to be provided by one person.
- This type of business finds it more difficult to borrow money than others.

Partnerships

Some of the problems faced by the sole trader can be overcome by incorporating more owners into the business to form a partnership.

Partnerships are regulated by the Partnership Act. This Act allows partnerships to have from two to twenty members although there are two exceptions to this rule.

1. Banks which operate as a partnership are not allowed to have more than ten partners.
2. Some professional partnerships are allowed to have more than twenty partners (e.g. accountants, solicitors, members of the Stock Exchange).

A deed of partnership sets out the rights of each partner, such as the way in which profits are to be divided. If there is no partnership deed, the provisions of the Partnership Act are assumed to govern the partnership, and that Act provides for equal sharing of profits.

All partners are equally responsible for the debts of the business. A 'sleeping' partner is one who invests in the business but takes no active part in running it, but such a partner is fully liable with other partners for debts incurred by the business.

It is possible to have a limited partnership but at least one partner must accept unlimited liability. Consequently, limited partnerships are relatively rare.

Some professional bodies prohibit their members from forming a limited company and, therefore, the partnership is particularly suitable for them. Solicitors, doctors and accountants are examples of professions that are not allowed to have limited liability status.

Advantages

- Easily formed.
- Greater continuity than sole trader.
- More people are available to contribute capital to the business.
- Expenses and management of the business are shared.

Disadvantages

- Generally unlimited liability.
- Possible conflicts between partners.
- Each partner is fully liable for the debts of the business.
- Membership limit of twenty restricts resources of business.

Private limited companies (Ltd)

Any company which is not registered as a public company is a private limited company. This type of business must include Limited (or Ltd) in its title name.

Both private and public limited companies are sometimes referred to as joint stock companies. This is because the money contributed by many shareholders is combined to form a joint stock of capital assets, which is used in some form of business enterprise to generate further wealth or profit which is divided between the shareholders.

The private company is allowed from two to an unlimited number of members (shareholders). The capital of the firm is divided into shares, but the shares are not sold on the Stock Exchange and they cannot be advertised for sale publicly. Consequently, shares have to be sold privately – hence the name 'private'.

Some firms may wish to keep ownership within a particular group of people, for example, within a family or a religious group. The private company may restrict share transfer if it wishes by writing a rule into its articles of association requiring members to offer shares to existing shareholders before attempting to sell them to non-members.

Advantages

- Has more people contributing capital than a sole trader or partnership.
- Has greater continuity than smaller businesses.
- Has limited liability.

Disadvantages

- Capital raising possibilities are limited because shares cannot be offered for public sale.
- Capital raising may be further limited if the company decides to restrict share transfer.
- Audited accounts have to be available for inspection.

Public limited companies (plc)

The public limited company must indicate its public status by including the letters plc (public limited company) in the title name.

The public company in formation must have at least the minimum amount of share capital laid down in the Companies Act 1985. It is allowed from two to an unlimited number of shareholders, and it can advertise shares and debentures for public sale. Capital raising is also helped by the fact that public company shares are listed on the Stock Exchange. This encourages people to contribute to the original share capital because they know they can easily sell their shares second-hand on the stock market. Consequently, this type of business organisation can raise almost limitless funds.

When an investor buys shares in a limited company they become a part owner. This not only entitles them to a share of the company's profits, but also gives them the right to some say in the way that the company is operated. It is usual for the shareholders of a company to elect a small committee called a board of directors to decide overall company policy on behalf of the shareholders. A chairperson is also elected to regulate board meetings.

Even a board of directors consists of too many people to take an active part in the day-to-day operation of the firm so the board appoint a managing director to carry out this function. Both private and pubic companies elect a board of directors and a chairman and appoint a managing director.

Advantages

- Have limited liability.
- Enjoy maximum continuity.
- Can raise large sums of capital.
- Large size enables them to enjoy 'economies of scale', such as being able to buy supplies in bulk.
- Size allows them to buy special equipment which will save in labour and expense.
- Find it easier to borrow money than smaller businesses because they are less risk than smaller firms.

Disadvantages

- Formation involves considerable documentation and expense.
- Company, employees and shareholders become too detached from one another because of large size.
- Ease of transfer of share ownership can lead to 'takeover' bids for company.
- Tend to develop too many rules ('red tape').
- The annual accounts of the company are open to public inspection which reduces confidentiality of the firm.

Forming a limited company

All types of private businesses, including sole traders, partnerships and private and public companies, must register with the Registrar of Business Names if they wish to operate under a name other than that of the owner.

When a limited company is being formed it must register with the Registrar of Companies. This registration is carried out mainly by presentation of two completed documents, the memorandum of association and the articles of association, by those initially forming the company. Both the private and the public company follow a similar procedure, except that the private company passes through fewer stages than the public company.

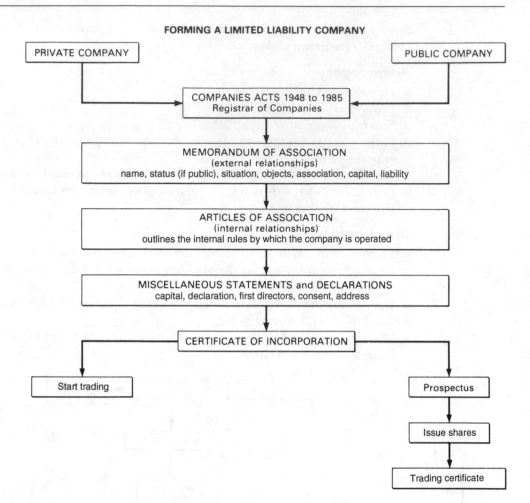

FORMING A LIMITED LIABILITY COMPANY

Memorandum of association

This document states the external relationships of the company, for example the relationship between the company and others. The memorandum of association consists of a number of clauses.

Name clause

This states the trading name of the company. The Registrar of Companies ensures that no two companies are formed bearing the same name. The Registrar of Companies also looks for misleading names, suggestive names (i.e. of a connection with, say, the Royal Family) and similar names.

Status clause

The memorandum of a public company has to state that it is to be a public company. The public company indicates its status by the letters PLC (or plc) at the end of its title name, whereas the private company ends its title with Limited (or Ltd). The Welsh equivalent 'ccc' is also acceptable under relevant circumstances.

Situation clause

This identifies the country where the registered office of the company is situated. The company can move its registered office within the stated country.

Object clause

This clause states the object for which the company is established, for example to manufacture toys, or to publish books.

Liability clause

This states that the liability of shareholders is limited to the amount they have invested in the company.

Capital clause

This is a statement of the amount of capital with which the company is to be registered and the manner in which it is to be divided into shares, for example £500 000 divided into 25p shares or £1 shares. A public company must have a nominal share capital of at least £50 000.

Association clause

This is a declaration implying that those signing the memorandum wish to form the company and that they are prepared to take up and pay for the number of shares shown on the form by their name. The minimum number of signatories is two.

Articles of association

The articles of association outline the internal relationships of the company, that is the broad way in which the internal organisation will operate. This document must be signed by the same people who sign the memorandum of association.

The contents of this document are more flexible than those of the memorandum of association and they can easily be changed by the shareholders. However, any alterations to the articles of association must not conflict with the memorandum of association.

Contents of the articles of association

- The rights of shareholders.
- Methods of election of directors.
- The manner in which meetings are to be conducted.
- Division of profits.

Miscellaneous statements and declarations

In addition to the memorandum of association and the articles of association the promoters of a company must also make the following statements and declarations to the Registrar of Companies.

Statement of nominal capital

This shows the amount of registered capital and the manner of its division into shares (similar to the capital clause in the memorandum of association).

Declaration

A statement made under oath by the company secretary of a director confirming that all the requirements of the Companies Acts have been met.

List of first directors

The names of the first directors of the company are listed.

Statement of consent

Signed by each of the proposed directors confirming that they are willing to act in this capacity.

Address of registered office

This states the precise registered address of the company. Any changes in this address must be notified to the Registrar within twenty-eight days of change.

If the Registrar of Companies is satisfied that all the requirements have been met, a certificate of incorporation is issued. The business now has an identity separate from that of its owners. A private company can now start trading and a public company proceed to raise capital.

Raising capital for a public company

The directors of a public company can now attempt to raise the capital stated in the capital clause of the memorandum of association. This is done by issuing a prospectus, which is a printed circular or an advertisement, giving a frank outline of what the company hopes to do, and detailing the amount of capital required to start trading.

When the Registrar of Companies is satisfied that the company's share capital is not less than £50 000, and that at least a quarter of the nominal value has been paid on each share, a trading certificate is issued allowing the company to begin trading.

4.4 Special business relationships

Franchising

In franchising, a company allows someone to buy the right to use their products or techniques under their trade names. This is one of the fastest growing sectors of the economy and over 20 per cent of retail sales is accounted for by this form of trading, and the trend is growing each year.

Franchising offers a 'ready-made' business opportunity for those who have the capital and are willing to work hard. The potential entrepreneur or franchisee pays to use the name, products, or services of the franchisor who receives a lump sum and a share of the profits of the business.

The franchisee receives the majority of the profits, but must also meet most of any losses. In addition to allowing use of their name, products, techniques, or services, in return for the money they receive franchisors usually provide an extensive marketing back-up.

Fast food giants such as Wimpy, Kentucky Fried Chicken and Burger King are particularly well known in the franchising sector, but the range of franchise activities is much wider than just fast food. The following are a few other examples of this type of business:

- developing and printing films
- home tuning of car engines
- drain clearing
- door to door ice-cream sales
- bakeries

Co-operatives

Co-operation sometimes develops in production when small units of agriculture or manufacturing owned by people with small and limited amounts of capital combine together for the purpose of sharing labour and buying or hiring equipment which individually they would be unable to afford.

By co-operating in this manner the members of the co-operative not only have access to the economic use of equipment purchased or hired through their pooled resources, but they can also enjoy economies of scale such as bulk purchasing of supplies and wider advertising and marketing possibilities.

Productive co-operation is less familiar in Britain than it is in many other European countries, and in this country most examples of co-operatives are found in distribution (*see* Chapter 10) rather than in production.

Holding companies

For a variety of reasons, businesses sometimes form a temporary or permanent combination to achieve a certain aim. For example, the combination of three or four businesses might usefully bring together several separate processes into one production unit.

This kind of partnership of companies is usually incorporated as a holding company. Each member company retains its legal entity, but overall control lies with the holding company.

Building societies

Building societies are a further example of a special business relationship. They operate on a non-profit-making basis. They are concerned with personal rather than business matters and, consequently, they are considered to be on the fringe of commercial activities.

Building societies are intermediaries between 'small' savers who wish to invest funds and people who wish to borrow money to purchase or improve property. Building societies lend by means of a *mortgage* which is a long-term loan, often repayable over a period of twenty years or more. Most of the deposits to building societies are lent out in this manner, but some of their funds must of course be retained to meet demands for cash withdrawals.

It is usual for the deeds of the property purchased by a borrower to be held by the building society until the mortgage has been repaid. If the borrower defaults in repayment of the mortgage, the society can sell the property to recover the debt.

Building societies have always competed with the commercial banks to obtain deposits from savers. Since the Building Societies Act 1987 the societies have been allowed to compete more openly with the banks, offering many of the financial services that have traditionally only been provided by the banks. The range of services the societies offer remain relatively limited, and the Act ensures that they keep primarily to their traditional areas of business. At least 90 per cent of every society's commercial assets has to consist of first mortgages on residential property. Some banks have also begun to provide mortgages and these developments are providing the basis of healthy competition between building societies and banks.

4.5 Business growth

Reasons for growth

Most of the large firms that exist today started as a small business and have grown. Many of today's small firms are tomorrow's big businesses. Businesses grow and expand for a variety of reasons:

- they are successful and expansion is necessary to meet the demand for their product;
- they wish to make a greater level of profit;
- they are trying to gain economies of scale;
- they wish to reduce competition and become market leaders, maybe even gain a monopoly;
- they wish to secure their sources of supply or outlets for their products.

Expansion will only take place if the business can benefit and make extra profits.

Methods of growth

Basically firms can grow in four ways:

- by working existing plant and machinery harder, pushing it towards full capacity;

- by extending existing capacity or moving to a new bigger site;
- by a *merger* with another company – mergers take place when both businesses involved are in agreement about joining together;
- by a *takeover* of another company – a takeover occurs when one company gains control of another against its wishes by buying the existing owners out.

Directions of growth

Businesses need not expand simply by doing more of what they are already doing. Depending on the motives for expansion they can grow or integrate in a number of directions.

Horizontal integration

This is when a business extends its current operations, doing more of what it already does. It expands at the same level in the chain of production (e.g. a car manufacturer expands and builds another plant to produce more cars).

Chain integration

This is expansion to produce the same product, but for a different market (e.g. a car manufacturer producing more cars to sell in a new overseas market).

Lateral integration

This is expansion into a similar area of production, using similar techniques and processes, but making something different (e.g. a car manufacturer expands to produce tractors).

Vertical integration

Vertical integration may be 'backwards' or 'forwards', or in both directions.

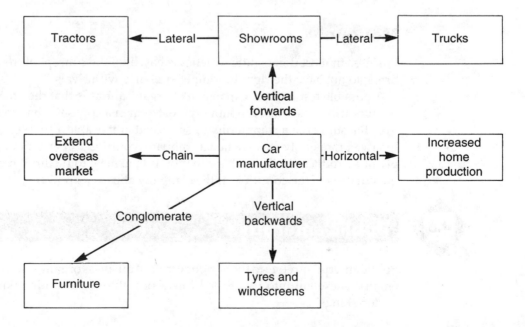

- *Expansion backwards* along the chain of distribution occurs, for example, when a business begins to produce the components and raw materials the business needs (e.g. a car manufacturer begins to produce tyres or windscreens for use in its own cars).
- *Expansion forwards* involves extending along the chain of production, for example taking on the selling of the products (e.g. a car manufacturer opens up its own car showrooms).

Conglomerate integration

This is expansion into an area that has nothing to do with the current operations of the business (e.g. a car manufacturer begins to produce furniture).

Multinationals

It is not unusual for expansion to take place across international borders. In other words, companies sited in different countries may combine to form a multinational company. The multinational is an enterprise that has subsidiaries or branches in more than one country.

The main objectives of a multinational are to expand its operations into other profitable areas. It will do this in order to gain as large a share of the world market as possible, and to use its expertise and skills to the benefit of all the companies in the group.

The decision-making process is controlled by the parent company and implemented through its foreign subsidiaries. These subsidiary companies are firms that have either been set up by the parent company, or they are foreign businesses which have been taken over. The parent company may own the subsidiary completely, may have a controlling interest (own a majority of the shares), or may just own a large and influential number of shares in the subsidiary.

Monopoly

Business in most democratic societies is based on the concept of free competition. firms do not have the right to compete unfairly with rivals.

A possible result of the expansion of organisations is that they may end up in a monopolistic position. A monopoly exists when a company has so much control over the supply of a commodity or service, that it is able also to control the price. In law, a monopoly exists when a company controls 25 per cent of the total supply of a product. Whilst such a situation is beneficial to the firm, it can be against the interests of the consumer if the company abuses its power.

Public enterprise

Public enterprise refers to the various forms of business organisation in public ownership. These fall into two broad categories: municipal undertakings and state undertakings.

Municipal undertakings

Municipal undertakings are businesses or services operated on a commercial basis by local authorities. They are financed by local taxation such as the Council Tax and charges made for the use of the service. Sometimes municipal undertakings are subsidised by grants from central government. Examples are sports centres, theatres, bus services, conference halls, art galleries, museums and street markets.

State undertakings

State undertakings, state ownership, public ownership, public enterprise, public corporation and nationalised industry are all terms that are used to refer to a variety of businesses that are operated by the government on behalf of the public.

Each public corporation is set up by an Act of Parliament to provide commercial or industrial functions, often in a monopolistic position.

Each corporation has a legal identity separate from the government.

In effect, a public corporation is owned by all the public. General overall policy is decided by the government in consultation with the corporation board, which is selected by the government.

Financially speaking, corporations are expected to at least break even. However, sometimes other priorities may be decided as more important than making a profit.

Profits are used in three ways:

1 to pay interest on capital borrowed;

Sports centres are a typical municipal enterprise. What municipal enterprises can you identify in your locality?

British Rail is a state undertaking.

2 set aside for future repayment of loans;

3 reinvested to improve or expand the industry.

Losses must be met by the Treasury, which in effect means the taxpayer.

Nationalisation and privatisation

Some public corporations have been set up by the government in the first place (e.g. the Post Office and the BBC), others have at one time been in private owner-ship (e.g. British Rail) and have been taken into state ownership (nationalised). When nationalisation takes place the original owners are paid compensation.

When a publicly-owned business is sold back to the private sector it is said to have been *privatised*. There are many reasons why the government might return a state-owned business to the private sector. Obviously the sale will raise revenue for the government, but it can also result in increased choice and improved qual-ity for consumers.

In the past Labour governments have favoured nationalisation whereas Conservative governments have preferred private ownership of industry.

Reasons for public ownership

- To take a monopoly out of private ownership.
- To keep a natural monopoly in public ownership.
- Sometimes the initial capital cost of setting up an industry may be too high for private enterprise.
- Some forms of enterprise may be essential to our welfare but uneconomic for private business.
- National security may have to be protected through state ownership (e.g. atom-ic energy).
- To standardise equipment and avoid duplication of services (e.g. British Rail).
- To save an ailing industry and protect jobs.

Advantages of public ownership

- Government has the resources to fund a vast industry, even if it is uneco-nomic.
- Will ensure provision of essential services.
- Reduces possible duplication of equipment.
- Enables large sections of the economy to be planned towards a single strategy.
- Profits benefit the whole nation as opposed to a limited number of private indi-viduals.
- Large size of public corporations allows them to enjoy maximum economies of scale.

- Personnel are appointed and promoted because of proven ability as opposed to personal contact or share of business owned.

Disadvantages of public ownership

- Can be over-cautious due to the fact that they are answerable to the public.
- Bosses are politicians who may not have the necessary business expertise.
- Local issues may be disregarded in favour of policies of national importance.
- State monopoly can lead to inefficiency and insufficient profit motive.
- Losses have to be met by taxpayer.

Make a note of it

1 Why is Britain said to have a 'mixed' economy?

2 How does private enterprise differ from public enterprise?

3 Explain the meaning of limited liability.

4 Why is the sole proprietor the most common type of business? What are the advantages and disadvantages of this type of business?

5 What advantages would a sole proprietor gain by becoming a partnership?

6 Why are limited partnerships relatively rare?

7 Make a detailed comparison between private and public limited companies. Include a list of the advantages and disadvantages of each of these forms of business ownership.

8 Give a description of the process followed in forming a limited company.

9 Give a brief description of the various forms that co-operatives may take.

10 Why can a franchise be said to be a 'ready-made business'?

11 Why are building societies an example of a special business relationship?

12 What is a holding company?

13 What are the reasons for business growth?

14 Explain the difference between a merger and a takeover.

15 Describe the different forms of integration.

16 What is a multinational company?

17 Why are monopolies generally not in the public interest?

18 Explain the difference between municipal undertakings and state undertakings.

19 What is nationalisation? Why might government decide to nationalise an industry?

20 List the advantages and disadvantages of public ownership of business.

Structured Questions

1

Going it Alone

There has never been a better time to start a business of your own, but our Business Correspondent Amira Shah reports, it's a rocky road before you can hit the big time.

Instant success is rare in business and budding entrepreneurs need to be aware of the five stages of growth of a business:

Existence At the existence stage the founder is technically orientated and using all the energy to design and manufacture a product (or provide a service). The business is run by the owner who often performs all the managerial functions.

Survival At the survival stage the business becomes more aggressive in seeking new customers and a small standardised product line appealing to a wider set of customers is developed. The number of employees starts to expand and the owner becomes much more burdened with management responsibilities.

Success At the success stage the business credibility and technical feasibility has been established. Economies of scale are introduced in the production process. The owner has to make a decision, either to concentrate all his or her energies on expanding the company with the consequent risks or to keep the company stable and profitable and provide a basis for alternative interests.

Take off If the owner decides on the expansion route and is successful then he or she should reach the take off stage. At this stage there are multiple product lines and a divisionalised organisation structure to cope with the increasing complexity of the business.

Resource maturity At the resource maturity stage, the business is now very well established. It is successful and the owner and the business have become quite separate financially and operationally. However it can become very bureaucratic and stifle innovation.

One of the major challenges for independent business people is that both the problems faced and the skills necessary to deal with them change as the business grows. You need to anticipate these changing factors based on the stage of development of your business.

Similarly at the success stage, you have to decide whether or not to commit all your time and risk everything you have worked for to date in order to grow further.

(a) Explain the words 'founder' and 'entrepreneur' used in the above newspaper article. (2)

(b) Why does the owner of the business tend to be carrying out all the managerial functions at the 'existence' stage of business development? (2)

(c) Advertising tends to become an important feature of a business at the 'survival' stage. Why is this so? (3)

(d) What does it mean in the article when it says that the business 'credibility and technical feasibility has been established' at the 'success' stage? (3)

(e) What 'economies of scale' are likely to be introduced during the 'success' stage of development? Why are these not likely to be introduced earlier in the development of the business? (4)

(f) Why do the skills required of a business person change as the business grows? (6)

2

> Dai Evans holds a majority shareholding in Easy Electronics plc, a company that owns a large chain of shops that sell a wide range of household electrical goods. Hightec Electrical plc produces a range of electrical items such as kettles, irons, hairdriers, etc. Hightec have been trying to take over Easy Electronics for some time. They have been openly buying ordinary shares on the Stock Exchange over the last year, but they have not managed to obtain sufficient shares in order to make a bid for the company. They have now offered to buy Dai Evans shares at a price above the current market price.

(a) What do the letters plc stand for? (1)

(b) What implications do the letters plc have for companies? (2)

(c) What is meant by the wording 'Dai Evans holds a majority shareholding'? (2)

(d) What do you understand by the term 'takeover' as used here? (2)

(e) State at least three ways that the takeover could affect the workers of Easy Electronics if it were to take place. (3)

(f) What factors might Dai Evans take into account before agreeing to sell his shares? (4)

(g) Suggest reasons why Hightec would want to take over Easy Electronics. (6)

3 Refer to the article about franchising on page 80.

(a) In your own words explain what franchising is. (2)

(b) Explain the terms franchisee and franchisor. (2)

(c) What is meant by 'start-up costs'? (3)

(d) The article says that profit projections generally show that franchisees should get their money back in 3–4 years. What are 'profit projections'? (3)

(e) State four disadvantages of being a franchise holder. (4)

Franchising can offer success in self-employment

FRANCHISING is a method of starting up on your own by buying, not a business as such, but a licence from a franchisor to use his name and his tested operating methods and the exclusive rights to sell his products or service in a privileged territory for a fixed but renewable period of time.

The idea is that if you follow the methods that he lays down and that other franchisees have followed, you will achieve a predictable level of results.

The start-up costs vary from under £10,000 to over £250,000, but the average is around £40,000-£50,000 and profit projections generally show that you should get your money back in 3-4 years. Furthermore you can borrow up to 70% of the cost of an approved scheme from the bank.

There are about 350 franchises on the market and a number of them are household names: Tie Rack, Prontaprint, Pizza Express, Budget Rent a Car and Body Shop, are just a few.

Rapid expansion

In the USA, franchising accounts for 30% of all retail sales, and though it has a long way to go to reach anything like that figure here, it is expanding even more rapidly. Latest figures show that annual UK sales are at £2.2 billion and that they are expected to top £5 billion comfortably by the end of 1990.

Franchising is seen by the banks and, increasingly, the government, as one of the major avenues into self-employment, because using a business format in this way has proved to have a high success rate as compared to starting out entirely on your own.

Source: *Executive Post*, June 1988.

(f) Why is a franchise business seen by banks as more likely to be successful as a form of self-employment than starting out on your own? (6)

4 Answer the following questions which are related to the illustration on page 68 showing the procedure involved in forming a limited liability company.

(a) At which of the stages in the flow diagram shown is a business given an identity separate from its owners? (1)

(b) How can the general public readily tell whether a business is a private or a public company? (2)

(c) If two limited companies were formed with the same name this could cause confusion. How is this avoided? (2)

(d) What are the implications of a business having limited liability? (2)

(e) The diagram shows that a public company raises its capital eventually by issue of shares. How does a private company raise its capital? (3)

(f) Briefly state the differences in function of the memorandum of association and the articles of association, giving a separate example of an item included in each that is not contained in the other. (4)

(g) Explain the differences between a private limited company and a public limited company. (6)

Extended Answer Assignments

1 Make a survey of all (or a section of) the businesses in your high street and discuss the appropriateness of the various forms of legal identity for the nature of the business enterprise.

2 Carry out a survey of municipal undertakings in your locality and assess to what extent it would be more appropriate if they were in private ownership.

3 Make a study of any local issue which has implications for local businesses, e.g. introduction of a one-way system or parking restrictions.

4 Form a diagrammatic 'map' of the organisation structure of a small and a medium-sized local firm with which you are familiar. Comment on the differences observed.

5 Locate a well-established local entrepreneur who started his or her business from 'scratch'. What factors can you identify as making contributions to its apparent success?

6 Complete a survey of all the public sector activities within your locality which are controlled by a public corporation, central government or local government. To what extent do you consider the source of control appropriate to local needs?

7 Choose one of the nationalised (or one that has been privatised) industries and trace its development from the time of nationalisation to its present status.

8 Interview the owners of any relatively recently established business in your locality:

(a) Discover what are the main problems faced by the owners.
(b) How did they overcome the difficulties?
(c) What problems are they still faced with?

9 Imagine that you are a skilled craftsman who has recently been made redundant and you have been awarded £30 000 redundancy pay. What local help is available to assist you to set up your own business?

5 ▶ Recruitment, selection and training

5.1 ▸ Seeking employment

Looking for a job

Those seeking employment will want to investigate all available possibilities. The following are the main sources of information about job vacancies:

- job centres run by the government's Training Agency;
- employment agencies run by private firms;
- local careers officers;
- newspaper advertisements;
- friends and relatives.

Advertisements are the most common way of publicising a job vacancy and inviting applications. These advertisements are important to the firm because they must be carefully formulated so that they attract the right sort of applicant. They must clearly state what is required otherwise valuable time will be wasted investigating the suitability of applicants. They are also important to the job hunter because they help to ensure that they only apply for the kind of job they really want.

OFFICE JUNIOR £4500 pa to check invoices and calculate insurance and freight costs.	Is the pay suitable?
	Will you enjoy the work?
Experience preferred, but school leaver with Business Studies background considered. Neat handwriting, aptitude for figure work and minimum GCSE Grade	Have you the qualities required?
C in English and Mathematics required.	Do you have the right qualifications?
• Luncheon vouchers	
• Flexible hours	Are there any fringe benefits?
• Sports and social club	
• Pleasant offices near railway station	
Applications in writing to: Mr B Mason, The Personnel Officer, Astor Publications PLC,	What form of application is required?
7 Pleasant Street, BIRMINGHAM B10 9UB	Is the job within convenient reach?

Job advertisement.

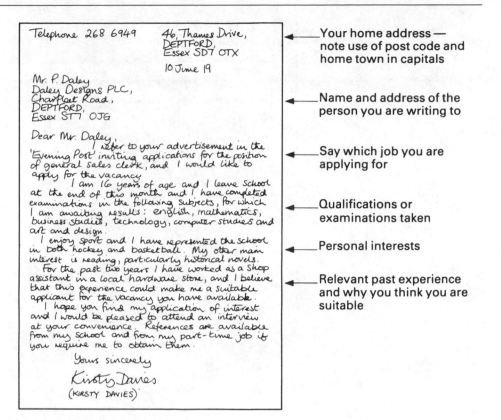

Telephone 268 6949   46, Thames Drive,
DEPTFORD,
Essex SD7 OTX

10 June 19

Mr. P. Daley
Daley Designs PLC,
Charfleet Road,
DEPTFORD,
Essex ST7 OJG

Dear Mr. Daley,
    I refer to your advertisement in the 'Evening Post' inviting applications for the position of general sales clerk, and I would like to apply for the vacancy.
    I am 16 years of age and I leave school at the end of this month and I have completed examinations in the following subjects, for which I am awaiting results: english, mathematics, business studies, technology, computer studies and art and design.
    I enjoy sport and I have represented the school in both hockey and basketball. My other main interest is reading, particularly historical novels.
    For the past two years I have worked as a shop assistant in a local hardware store, and I believe that this experience could make me a suitable applicant for the vacancy you have available.
    I hope you find my application of interest and I would be pleased to attend an interview at your convenience. References are available from my school and from my part-time job if you require me to obtain them.
    Yours sincerely
    Kirsty Davies
    (KIRSTY DAVIES)

Your home address — note use of post code and home town in capitals

Name and address of the person you are writing to

Say which job you are applying for

Qualifications or examinations taken

Personal interests

Relevant past experience and why you think you are suitable

Letters of application

In some cases it may be acceptable to type a letter, in others the advertisement may state that the application should be in 'first hand', in which case the letter should be handwritten, preferably on plain paper. It is sensible to make a rough draft of the proposed letter before writing it out in detail.

Curriculum vitae

Job advertisements today frequently ask for a curriculum vitae (CV) from applicants. A CV is a brief history of the applicant, for example school, qualifications, relevant experience, etc. This should be typed to accompany the letter of application, thus making it possible to make the letter shorter and more concise. Sometimes names, addresses and telephone numbers of the referees are included at the end of the CV.

Application form

These are standard printed forms which are sent out by firms for applicants to fill out providing specific information to support their application. The form may be sent to the applicant for completion prior to interview, or it may have to be completed under supervision at the interview.

```
CURRICULUM VITAE     SUNILA PATEL


ADDRESS              21 Courtfield Road
                     Nottingham

DATE OF BIRTH        12 October 1969

SEX                  Female

PLACE OF BIRTH       Nottingham

NATIONALITY          British

EDUCATION            St Martins School
                     Ladyfield Road
                     Nottingham

                     1981 to 1986

GCSE                 English language
                     Mathematics
                     French
                     Biology
                     History
                     Business studies

INTERESTS            Reading
                     Outdoor sports
                     Music

WORK EXPERIENCE      Saturday job in family general store
```

Example of a curriculum vitae.

There are two main reasons why firms use an application form as part of the recruitment and selection process. First, it acts as a check on personal details, qualifications and experience, and it ensures that key information is included in the minimum space. Second, it allows selection panel members to easily make comparisons between candidates.

References

Most employers will require applicants to provide the names of persons (*referees*) willing to testify as to the character of the candidate, or written declarations (*testimonials*) from reliable persons testifying to the good character of the applicant. Referees should be contacted by the applicant for permission before using their names on the CV.

5.2 The Personnel department

The Personnel department is concerned with finding the right person for vacant jobs, and if necessary giving them induction training. This department also deals with resignations, providing testimonials and dismissing unsuitable workers. It maintains personal records of all employees and is involved in the welfare and happiness of all personnel.

Applications for employment are received and considered by the Personnel department which is headed by the personnel manager.

Short-list of applicants

From the many applications received in response to the advertisement, the Personnel department lists a few of the most promising applicants and invites them to attend an interview. For this reason, the written application is very important if the applicant is to reach the next stage in being successful in applying for the job.

Interviews

Short-listed applicants for employment are invariably interviewed (usually in the Personnel department) before any job offer is made. The aim of the interview is not only to assess the suitability of the candidate for the vacant position, but also to give the applicant the opportunity to seek further information about the job. During the interview the applicant may be required to complete an aptitude test designed to assess their suitability for the job available.

The interview is crucial for the applicant because it is at this time that the interviewer assesses the candidate's appearance, ability to communicate and general manner. Consequently, it is important to be thoroughly prepared for the interview.

Preparation for the interview
- Do a little homework about the job for which you have applied.
- Use your common sense about your appearance.
- Remember the name of the person you have to see.
- Know exactly where the interview will take place.
- Plan the route to get there.
- Arrive promptly for the interview.

During the interview
- Only sit down when invited to.
- Do not smoke.

- Try to be relaxed and confident.
- Concentrate fully on the interviewer.
- Be prepared to answer questions.
- Try to ask some sensible questions when you are invited to do so.

At the interview

- Dress carefully.
- Take the letter inviting you for interview.
- Arrive promptly.
- Appear confident but not flippant.
- Do not be over-familiar.

Questions to be prepared for

- Why do you want the job?
- What qualities do you have to offer?
- What is your future ambition?
- What do you do in your spare time?
- What do you read?

Questions you could ask

- What does the job involve?
- What hours are involved?
- What is the salary?
- What are the opportunities for promotion?
- What are the holiday arrangements?

 ## 5.3 Staff orientation and training

All new members of staff need to be acquainted with other members of the firm, as well as becoming familiar with the organisation of the business. Many firms organise an induction programme to help new employees to become a useful part of the organisation, and to introduce them to their new job and work colleagues. The induction programme will often be managed by the Personnel department.

Staff training does not only apply to new employees. Sometimes existing staff will be transferred to other departments or other jobs which may require training in new skills. A large firm may operate its own internal training school, or alternatively staff may be encouraged to attend college courses to learn new skills.

 ## 5.4 Welfare of employees

Welfare refers to the concern for the physical well-being of people. Social facilities, lighting and heating, hygiene and canteen services are all examples of things that contribute to the welfare of employees. These all come within the functions of the Personnel department in a large firm.

The Personnel department may be responsible for the operation of the company's sports and social club, organising activities and events which encourage employees to mix socially. A member of this department may also have the responsibility of visiting employees who are sick, or those who have retired.

The firm may have its own house newspaper or magazine which is used to keep the workers up-to-date with events in which the company is involved, as well as providing a means of general communication.

Most firms recognise that good working conditions not only keep the employees happy, but also help to make them more productive and efficient. For this reason, firms try to provide good working conditions, but there are five Acts which are particularly concerned with staff welfare. These are dealt with together with other aspects of working conditions in the next chapter.

1 Factories Act 1961
2 Offices, Shops and Railway Premises Act 1963
3 Contract of Employment Act 1972
4 Health and Safety at Work Act 1974
5 Employment Act 1988.

5.5 Staff records

The letter of application for employment, the curriculum vitae or the completed application form, together with the results of any aptitude tests taken when the new employee joins the firm, form the basis of the record of the individual held by the employer.

Over the years of employment the file held is added to by progress reports from other more senior members of the firm. These reports and other records of progress will include reference to the following aspects of the employee:

- punctuality
- health
- academic progress
- promotions and salary increases
- suitability for further promotion
- misdemeanours.

From the foregoing it will be obvious that the contents of personnel records are highly confidential. For this reason, people who work in the Personnel department are expected to be discreet. In addition, security of personnel records is of utmost importance.

5.6 Dismissal and Redundancy

In the following chapter reference is made to the Contract of Employment Act which requires all employees to be given details of the terms of their employment. The Contract of Employment includes the length of *notice* (length of time as notification of ceasing employment) to be given by the employer and the employee. When a worker wishes to take up new employment elsewhere they are required to give a period of 'notice' which allows the employer to look for a new employee. Similarly, if the employer wishes to dismiss the worker a period of notice is generally observed, although there are exceptions to this, such as when the employee has been guilty of a serious misdemeanour. In such circumstances it is usual that certain steps will have been followed:

1 oral warning
2 written warning
3 suspension
4 dismissal.

Obviously the employee may get instant dismissal for breaking substantive rules of the organisation, e.g. stealing, or putting other employees in danger.

Today workers are protected against unfair dismissal by the Employment Protection Act which requires an employer to show that there are good reasons for terminating employment. An employee who feels that they have been unfairly dismissed can complain to an Industrial Tribunal. If the Tribunal finds that the employer has acted unfairly or unreasonably, it can order reinstatement of the employee. If this is not practicable, the Tribunal can award compensation against the employer.

Redundancy

This refers to a situation when an employee loses their job because it no longer exists. This may occur because the business has been forced to cease trading, or when the firm no longer has the capacity to employ the same number of workers.

When an employee loses their job as a result of redundancy they need financial help to enable them to make the transition to new employment.

The Redundancy Payments Act requires employers to make a lump sum payment to employees being made redundant (so long as they have served a minimum period of time). The amount of redundancy compensation depends upon the age, length of service, and pay of the employee

Grievance procedure

An employee has a 'grievance' in the following situations:

● an existing employer/employee agreement has been broken;
● a labour law has been violated by the employer;
● the employer has acted in an unfair manner;
● the health or safety of the employee has been put at risk.

The first point of contact for the employee is their *work supervisor* who may be willing and able to offer a remedy for the circumstances. Certainly this person would be the point of contact between the aggrieved person and the firm's management.

Should representation through the supervisor be inappropriate or unsatisfactory, the worker will contact their *union representative,* often another employee of the company. This person will be familiar with the rights of the worker and will act on their behalf, or direct the grievance to the union for advice and guidance. The union may even decide that the employee does not have a real grievance, and it is part of their function to advise the worker of this.

Make a note of it

1 List five sources of information about job vacancies.

2 Why are job advertisements important to both the firm and the applicant?

3 List four specific pieces of information that the job applicant can obtain from the advertisement.

4 What does it mean when an advertisement states that applications must be in 'first hand'?

5 Make a list of six suggestions you would give someone to help him or her write a letter of application for a job.

6 What is a curriculum vitae? What information does it contain?

7 In what way does an application form differ from a CV?

8 What is the function of 'referees' and 'testimonials' in relation to applications for employment?

9 Give a brief summary of the main functions of the Personnel department of a firm.

10 What is a 'short-list'?

11 What is the main purpose of the interview?

12 Why might a job applicant be required to complete an aptitude test?

13 In what way can someone usefully prepare for a job interview?

14 List six points the candidate should observe during the interview.

15 Give four examples of questions that might be asked of an applicant at the interview.

16 Suggest four questions the job applicant could ask when invited to do so.

17 Why would a firm be interested in the welfare of its employees?

18 In what way might a firm show its care for the welfare of its employees?

19 How would the Personnel department in particular be involved in the welfare of employees?

20 Briefly describe the kind of information likely to be found in personnel records. Why is security and confidentiality important to personnel records?

APPLICATION

Surname ...... Mc Meakin .... (Mr/Mrs/Ms)
Forename(s) Richard David ....
Address 10, Juniper Close, CATERHAM, Surrey CR3 6SZ ......
Nationality British .... Date of birth 24/12/69

EDUCATION

School or college	Dates	Examinations taken
King Edward Caterham Surrey	1982 – 1987	GCSE: English, Maths, Science, Art, Business Studies, Geography

PREVIOUS EMPLOYMENT

Name of employer	Dates	Position held
The Bargain Shop High Road Caterham	1985 to present	Part-time shop assistant, some experience on cash till

Other relevant experience: Two weeks of work experience arranged by my school in a local estate agents. I answered the telephone, did some duplicating, and prepared mail for the post. Sometimes I went out with one of the agents visiting properties.

Hobbies and other interests: I belong to a local drama group presenting small shows for charity

Referees
Name Dr. K. Beasely   Name Mrs. B. Rose
Position Headmaster   Position Manager
Address King Edward School   Address The Bargain Shop
Southwick Road CATERHAM   High Road CATERHAM

Signature R. Mc Meakin .... Date ....

OFFICE USE ONLY

Medical Report		References Received	
Date appointed	Department		Position

21 What regulations exist to protect an employee from unfair dismissal?

22 Explain the purpose of redundancy payments.

Structured Questions

1 The questions below are all related to the application for employment on page 90.

(a) Name the person who is applying for employment. (1)

(b) How important is it to the employer to know about details of the applicant's previous employment when it was only done on a part-time basis? (2)

(c) Why is the employer interested in the applicant's 'hobbies and interests' even though they may have no relevance to the vacant position? (2)

(d) What is the purpose of 'referees' and why are two requested? (4)

(e) Briefly state the purpose of each of the small sections within the part of the form marked 'office use only'. (5)

(f) What is a 'short-list' and what factors might an employer take into account in deciding whether this particular applicant should be short-listed? (6)

2 Refer to the newspaper article on page 92 related to a sales career and answer the questions below.

(a) What work do you think a careers' counsellor does? (1)

(b) Why is it in the interest of both the employer and the employee that the salesperson is successful? (2)

(c) What do you understand by the word 'extrovert' in the context that it is used in this article? (3)

(d) Why does age and previous job experience affect a person's chance of success in a sales career? (6)

(e) The article states that the type of person most suited to sales work is determined by the type of business or product involved. Take two contrasting types of business and explain why they require a different type of salesperson. (8)

3 The questions below are all related to the 'sales career' article on page 92.

(a) Why do salespeople need to be able to 'understand and manipulate numerical data and to be able to read and understand product information'? (2)

(b) The article says that 'sales effectiveness tends to increase up to the age of about forty and to decline in later years'.

(i) Give two reasons that support this statement. (2)

(ii) Give one example of the type of sales where this statement may not apply, giving reasons for your choice. (3)

Discover if you've got what it takes for a sales career

By ROGER LAY

THE EXPERIENCE of careers' counsellors is that very few people have in mind a sales career as their first choice.

But the sales team is an essential element of any commercial enterprise. Quite a lot of people therefore, find themselves in selling roles.

Clearly, if you are faced with the prospect of a sales career, it is in both your interests and that of your future employers that your chances of success be as high as possible. How can you tell if you are likely to make a successful salesperson?

The popular image of the successful salesperson is of someone who is highly extroverted or outgoing, socially confident and who tends to be fairly agressive in their approach to people.

Although there would appear to be an element of truth in this, research into the question reveals a far more complicated picture.

Some of the factors which determine the type of person most suited to sales work are;
- The type of business or product involved.
- The selling techniques used (telephone sales, face-to-face contacts, cold calling, maintenance of major accounts etc.).
- The extent to which technical product knowledge is required.

Age and previous job experience also effect a person's chance of success in a sales career.

Although the factors which determine success in sales are complex, it is clear that personality type is important.

The difficulty in predicting what type of person is likely to be successful, is that even where the type of business and selling techniques are known, there are still quite wide variations in personality type. Nevertheless, there are some common factors:
- Social confidence or social sophistication, and the ability to relate easily to others.
- Organisational effectiveness and independence, and the ability to formulate and carry out a plan of action without close supervision.
- Emotional resilience, and the ability to keep going even when the customer says 'no.'
- Energy, enthusiasm and competitiveness, and the ability to go out looking for a sale rather than waiting for the telephone to ring.
- Persuasiveness, and the ability to change a person's inclinations, opinions or decisions.
- Lack of modesty also appears to be a characteristic of some successful salespeople.

It is perhaps worth noting that there is little support for the idea that successful salespeople need to be outgoing in nature and aggressive in their approach (although some people with these characteristics do in fact succeed in sales work).

Most recruiters who are looking for salespeople refer to the importance of motivation — by this they usually mean the motivation induced by monetary rewards.

However, research evidence suggests that financial motivation is only significant where a commission pay system operates.

As far as abilities are concerned, successful salespeople tend to be above average in intelligence. More specific aptitudes which are relevant include the ability to understand and manipulate numerical data (eg: price lists, numerical tables) and to be able to read and understand product information.

Where the product or service being sold is highly technical in nature, a salesperson is likely to be more effective if they have a good familiarity and understanding of technical aspects.

A number of special psychological tests have recently been developed to assess sales potential. These tests typically concentrate on evaluating personality factors relevant to selling.

Age is another factor related to sales success — sales effectiveness tends to increase up to the age of about forty and to decline in later years.

A final observation — although as observed earlier, quite a wide range of personalities can be successful in selling roles, sales managers (having almost always been successful salespeople themselves) usually believe that only people in their own image will be successful and recruit accordingly.

Source: *Executive Post.*

(c) 'Most recruiters who are looking for salespeople refer to the importance of motivation – by this they usually mean the motivation induced by monetary rewards.' Briefly explain how most firms motivate their salespeople. (3)

(d) Salespeople need to be able to work on their own initiative. What does this mean? Quote from the article to support your answer. (4)

(e) If you refer to the list of common factors identified as likely to influence a person's success as a salesperson, some of these tend to contradict the later statement – 'There is little support for the idea that successful salespeople need to be outgoing in nature and aggressive in their approach.' Discuss this observation. (6)

4 Look at the following 'Situations Vacant' advertisements on page 93 and answer the questions following.

SITUATIONS VACANT

PERSONNEL ASSISTANT
AGE 17+ £7500 pa
Excellent benefits

Additional team member to join this busy personnel environment. Sense of humour, bags of stamina, good typing/administrative skills essential. Good telephone manner. Ref 134

RECEPTIONIST
TO £6000 pa Age 16/18
Young, bubbly, well presented young lady required for superb reception area. Excellent benefits to include gym, subsidised restaurant. Typing an advantage, pleasant personality essential, willingness to learn PABX switchboard as relief operator. Ref 166

TELEPHONIST/TYPIST
We require a Telephonist Typist for our large car showrooms. Will train on switchboard but accurate typing is essential – 40 wpm. Some clerical work involved. Good salary and some perks. Ref 281

SHORTHAND SECRETARY

£9000. Good s/h skills/audio. Working on a one-to-one basis for partner. Lots of variety. 5 weeks' holiday. Early finish Friday (4.30). Ref. 294

SALES OFFICE CLERK
We are an extrovert team working in a busy sales office and we need help? If you enjoy dealing with people, have legible handwriting, numeracy skills and a good telephone manner – contact us now. Salary negotiable. Ref 207

ACCOUNTS CLERK
LV's, pension scheme ideal opportunity for a person with all-round knowledge of accounts and experience of computerised systems. Immediate interviews. Salary £6250. Any age. Ref 222

AUDIO TYPIST
£6000   Age 16+
Busy office needs extra pair of hands typing correspondence, reports, etc. Duties will include client/telephone liaison. Solicitors. Good salary offered. increments for RSA/LCCI qualifications at higher levels. Apply in writing in first instance. Ref 285

WP SECRETARY – LOCAL £8000
Lovely position for a confident secretary with a flair for admin. Meeting and greeting clients, cross-train on our WP system and Telex. Never a dull moment! Qualifications required in word processing. Ref 298

All applications quoting reference number to:
Topline Employment Agency
17 Primrose Park
UXBRIDGE
Middx
UB10 9TZ

(a) Considering that a typed application is easier to read, and a telephone application quicker to deal with, why do many job advertisements ask for applications in writing? (2)

(b) Why do all the jobs here quote reference numbers and no individual addresses? (2)

(c) What is meant by 'a good telephone manner' and why is this important to both a firm and its clients? (3)

(d) One of the advertisements shown states 'good salary and perks'. What are perks? Give some examples. (3)

(e) These jobs are all advertised through an employment agency. What services would such a business provide to help a firm to obtain appropriate new employees? (4)

(f) Applicants for jobs would be 'short-listed' by the firm looking for new staff. What is a 'short-list' and what factors might the employer take into account when deciding who to include in the list? (6)

5 The questions below are also related to the 'Situations Vacant' advertisement on page 93.

    (a) What is meant by the wording apply 'in the first instance'? (2)

    (b) Take any two *contrasting* job advertisements shown here and briefly explain the work involved. (2)

    (c) Choose any one of the jobs advertised and draft a letter of application for yourself. (6)

    (d) All of the following terms have been used in the job advertisements shown here. Briefly explain each one:

£6000 pa	PABX
Salary negotiable	LVs
S/h skills	Increments
WP system	Subsidised
One-to-one	40 wpm

    (10)

Extended Answer Assignments

1 How do local employers attract staff? Provide evidence to support your findings.

2 Select four contrasting advertisements for business jobs and describe how you would ensure that you accept the most appropriate applicant for the vacancies.

3 Make a study of the induction programme of a firm with which you are familiar or can gain access to and suggest ways in which it might be improved.

4 Design an induction programme to introduce pupils new to your school/college, or those joining a business with which you are familiar.

5 Describe the facilities the government provides which help people who want to train for new employment.

6 While out on work experience make a comparative study of your job and another in the same organisation.

7 Make a survey of job vacancies at your local Job Centre and find out from the Centre how many local people are unemployed. Give suggestions why such jobs remain unfilled while there are people unemployed.

6 Motivation of employees

6.1 Job satisfaction

People spend a large percentage of their life at work. Therefore, it is important that they get some satisfaction from their job. Not all jobs can give satisfaction, and people have different ideas of what constitutes a good job. For some people pay is the most important factor, others will have some other priority. Often it is a combination of many factors which makes a job satisfying. The following are just some of these factors. What others would you include? What would be your order of priority?

- Pay and opportunity for wage increases.
- Promotion prospects.
- Working hours and times of attendance.
- Holiday arrangements.
- Job security.
- Friendship and relationship between employees.
- Conditions in which work is carried out.

Most jobs will include a combination of the above factors. Some are within the influence of the employee, but the employer has by far the greater effect on working conditions. There are, however, laws which ensure that working conditions do not fall below an agreed minimum standard. Some of these laws are examined later in this chapter.

There are various specific strategies that are used by employers to positively promote job satisfaction. Two of these are job enlargement and job enrichment:

- *Job enlargement*. This is where additional tasks are built into a job in order to make it more interesting or more satisfying for the worker and perhaps to relieve monotony by making it more demanding.
- *Job enrichment*. This is where the management of a business attempt to make a job satisfying, and more motivating for the worker, by changing the tasks and responsibilities it involves.

Appraisal of employees

Appraisal is a method of assessing how well an employee is carrying out his or her work. Performance is often rated against predetermined or negotiated criteria and usually targets are identified for achievement in the future. If managed effectively, appraisal is an important motivating tool. It recognises the achievement and the effectiveness of the employee, and it also gives them a direction for future development.

6.2 Wages

Wage Differentials

Wages are the reward paid for labour. Not surprisingly wages are considered more important to most people than many other things in life. This is because the level of earnings has such a considerable effect on the quality of life. The amount of income received influences the type of house and furnishings one can have, the quality of car owned and where and for how long holidays are taken. The poorly paid person cannot hope to compete with the highly paid person with regard to standard of living and leisure facilities. But for a variety of reasons some people are better paid than others, and it is important to understand why this is so.

The key to the reason for wage differentials is demand and supply. For the purpose of comparison we can take the wages of doctors and bus drivers as examples of where differences in wage levels exist. Both of these occupations are important to the community, but the doctor's wage is considerably higher than that of the bus driver. In other words, the cost of the doctor's services is far higher than the cost of the bus driver's services. Alternatively, we could say that the supply of doctors is smaller than the supply of bus drivers, forcing up the price of the doctor's services.

The supply of doctors is smaller than that of bus drivers for the following reasons. These same reasons can also be applied to many other examples of occupations where wage differences exist.

- The occupation requires a high degree of skill and academic ability.
- The training period is too long for many people.
- There is a degree of risk involved (e.g. infection).
- The work requires a special aptitude.

What other reasons can you think of for wage differentials?

Rates of pay

There are several ways that wages may be calculated, and sometimes a wage payment may combine more than one of these.

Flat rate

A set rate of pay per week or month based on a standard number of hours. Many workers are paid by this system but it does not always provide incentive to give extra time or effort.

Time rate

The worker is paid a set amount for each hour worked. The worker is paid 'overtime' at a higher rate of pay for additional hours worked.

Piece rate

This is not as common today as it has been in manufacturing in the past. A payment is made for each good quality item produced to encourage the production worker to give maximum effort.

Bonus

Paid to employees as a share of additional profits gained by the employer due to increased effort or efficiency of the work group.

Commission

A payment made additional to a flat or time rate as a percentage of the value of sales or business promoted.

There are various ways that rates of pay are established, two of these are *productivity deals* and *job evaluation*.

Productivity deals

These are negotiated by the employer with employees (or their representatives).

They are agreements where targets are set or changes in working practices are implemented in order to achieve improved productivity. In return for the increased output employers give increases in wages.

Job evaluation

This refers to ranking jobs in order of importance, particularly for the purpose of deciding rates of pay.

Deductions from pay

Gross pay is the total amount earned by the employee before any deductions have been made.

Net pay is the amount received by the employee after any deductions have been taken away. This figure is particularly important because it represents the actual income the worker receives.

Statutory deductions

These are compulsory deductions enforced by law:

- *Income Tax* – deducted from each wage payment through the PAYE (Pay As You Earn) system;
- *National Insurance* – weekly contributions to the state welfare scheme (e.g. health services) taken from each payment of wages.

Voluntary deductions

These are deductions that the wage earner can decide whether or not to have deducted automatically from their wages, for example:

- union membership fees;
- contribution to company social club;
- payments to private pension schemes;

- private medical schemes (e.g. BUPA) payments;
- transfers to the state savings scheme (SAYE – Save As You Earn).

Save As You Earn (SAYE)

The National Savings Bank SAYE service offers a form of regular saving that aims to not only give a return on the investment, but also to offset the effect of inflation and price rises by linking the interest paid to the retail price index. In other words, the interest paid is enhanced by any general increase in retail prices.

In this scheme the saver agrees to make monthly payments of a fixed amount (between £4 and £20) over a period of five years. At the end of the five-year contract period the saver can take repayment of his investment. At this time the investment is revalued to take into account any changes in the general index of retail prices between the time of the initial investment and the month of repayment.

Alternatively, at the end of the five-year contract period, the saver has the option to leave his savings invested for a further two years without making any further payments. At the end of this additional two-year period, the value of the investment is again revalued to take into account changes in the prices index at the time of the repayment. In addition, a bonus, equal to the monthly payments, is also paid.

SAYE contracts can be made in three ways:

1 through a post office by monthly cash payments or by National Girobank standing order;
2 through a commercial bank by standing order;
3 through an employer who participates in the SAYE scheme and deducts monthly payments from the employee's salary.

Payment of wages

A wages or payroll department is responsible for the payment of wages. People employed in this department need an aptitude for work with figures and are often required to be familiar with the use of a computer.

When an employee is paid at a time rate, they will have a time card (clock card) which is kept in a rack near a time clock. As the employee arrives and leaves work they 'clock' on and off by inserting their card into the time clock. The times printed on to the time card are used by the Wages department to establish how much the employee should be paid.

Whether payment of wages is made by cash, cheque or credit transfer, the employee receives a pay advice. This is usually a slip of paper which is filled in by the Wages department, often by computer, so that the employees can see how their net pay has been reached. The pay advice will contain the following information.

- employee's name and work number
- tax code
- national insurance number
- gross pay
- bonus, commission, overtime
- compulsory deductions

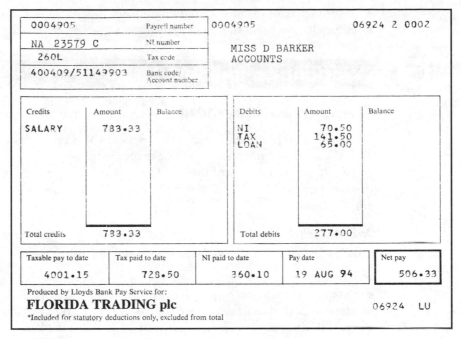

0004905	Payroll number	0004905		06924 2 0002
NA 23579 C	NI number	MISS D BARKER		
260L	Tax code	ACCOUNTS		
400409/51149903	Bank code/ Account number			

Credits	Amount	Balance	Debits	Amount	Balance
SALARY	783.33		NI	70.50	
			TAX	141.50	
			LOAN	65.00	
Total credits	783.33		Total debits	277.00	

Taxable pay to date	Tax paid to date	NI paid to date	Pay date	Net pay
4001.15	728.50	360.10	19 AUG 94	506.33

Produced by Lloyds Bank Pay Service for:

FLORIDA TRADING plc   06924   LU

*Included for statutory deductions only, excluded from total

Pay advice.

- voluntary deductions
- net pay.

Much of the Wages department work of calculating wages and producing pay advices can be assigned to computers. When the worker 'clocks' in and out the time data can be recorded on the time card by punch holes or magnetic ink characters. The data can be 'read' by computer and used to automatically:

- calculate gross and net pay;
- print out pay advice;
- maintain cumulative records for the production of:
  - *Form P45* – statement provided to an employee changing jobs to inform the new employer of the amount of income tax paid to date;
  - *Form P60* – annual certificate or statement notifying employee of gross wages, gross tax, and net wages paid for the whole year.

Fringe benefits

Some firms offer 'invisible' additions to the wages of their employees. These are called 'fringe benefits' or 'perks'. The following are examples of the kind of benefit given by the employer in addition to wages:

- free or subsidised meals (e.g. luncheon vouchers – LVs);
- company car;
- free membership of private health schemes;
- low interest rate loans for house purchase, etc.;
- reduced prices for company products or services;

- assistance with expense of moving house;
- help with payment of private education fees.

6.3 Working conditions

Terms of employment

The terms of employment are the arrangements or agreement between the employee and the employer of what task or responsibilities the employee is expected to carry out, and what reward they will receive for doing so. Information relating to this can be found in the job description, the job specification and the contract of employment.

Job description

This is a broad general statement which may include:

- job title;
- details of duties and responsibilities;
- place or department where work is to be carried out;
- special features or skills/qualifications related to the job;
- supervision and assessment arrangements.

Job specification

This is a detailed statement drawn up from the job description and it contains references to the qualities required of candidates for the job. This will include:

- responsibilities involved;
- qualifications and past experience needed;

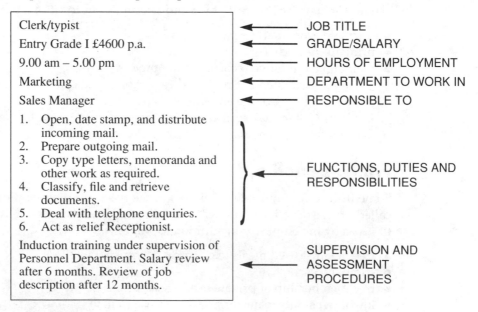

Job description.

- physical fitness required;
- personal characteristics considered important.

Contract of Employment Act 1972

This Act requires employers to give employees particulars of their terms of employment. This contract must either be given to the employee or kept where they have access to it. The contract includes:

- job title;
- hours of work;
- holiday arrangements;
- rate of pay and how frequently paid;
- period of notice to be given by either side;
- person to contact in event of a grievance;
- legal rights such as belonging (or not belonging) to a union.

Hours of employment

One of the most important terms of employment is the hours of work. This refers not only to the total number of hours to be worked, but also what times of the day or night the hours have to be worked.

Although some people work shift work, most people work fixed hours. Consequently, most people are travelling to and from work at similar times. This results in traffic jams and congestion on public transport, and discomfort for travellers. It also means that public transport is not being used economically.

Not everyone finds it convenient to work the same hours as others. Workers sometimes need periods of time when they are not required to be at work. In addition, many businesses have periods of the day when not all members of staff are required to be present. At other busy 'core' times, everyone is needed at the same time.

Flexible Working Time (FWT)

Flexitime, FWT or flexible working time are the names given to a system of arranging working hours so that at 'peak' or 'core' times all members of staff are at work. Outside core time employees are allowed to choose the hours they work, so long as they complete the required number of overall hours in the week.

The working day of the firm is defined in three ways:

1 *Band time* – this is the total period of time the business operates, for example, 8.00 am to 6.00 pm.
2 *Core time* – this is the period of time when all members of the firm are expected to be at work.
3 *Flexible time* – this is the period outside the core time when employees can choose whether they work or not, so long as they complete the total number of weekly hours they are paid for.

To choose their working hours employees first calculate core time. Core time in the above example is 5 days × 3 hours (11.00 am to 2.00 pm) = 15 hours. This leaves 20 hours (35 – 15 = 20) of working which can be chosen from FWT. Before choos-

BAND TIME
8.30 a.m. to 5.30 p.m.

Core time
11.00 a.m. to
2.00 p.m.

Flexible time
8.30 a.m. to
11.00 a.m.

Flexible time
2.00 p.m.
to 5.30 p.m.

Total hours to be worked by employee = 35 hours

Flexible working time.

ing the hours of flexitime, employees will have to take into account the time they wish to use for lunch breaks. Most firms will insist that the employee takes at least a 30 minute lunch break.

Health and safety

The health and safety of employees is a major aspect of working conditions. The duty of employers to provide safe working conditions is often backed up by statutory requirements. The three main Acts which relate to health and safety are the Factories Act 1961, the Offices, Shops and Railway Premises Act 1963 and the Health and Safety at Work Act 1974.

Factories Act 1961

The Act in fact covers more than factories in the normal sense of the word. It includes brickworks, cement works, construction sites, dry cleaners, garages, gas-works, laundries, potteries, printing works, slaughterhouses and many other businesses which use mechanical machinery. The Act includes the following rules:

- work places must be properly lit and well ventilated;
- sufficient toilet and washing facilities must be provided;
- moving machinery must have a fenced surround;
- hoists, lifts, etc. must be properly constructed and maintained;
- floors, passages and stairs must be kept unobstructed;
- floors must not have slippery surfaces;
- fire-escapes must be provided and maintained.

Offices, Shops and Railway Premises Act 1963

This Act represents the principal legislation affecting working conditions in offices. Included within this Act are the following provisions:

- rooms must not be overcrowded (twelve square metres of floor space per person);
- temperature must not fall below 16°C;
- there must be adequate supplies of fresh or artificially purified air;
- suitable natural or artificial lighting;
- suitable and sufficient sanitary conveniences must be conveniently accessible, clean and properly maintained;
- accessible washing facilities with running hot and cold water, soap and clean towels.

Health and Safety at Work Act 1974 (HASAWA)

This Act sets out the duties of both the employer and the employee relating to health and safety.

- The employer's duty can be summed up as the responsibility to provide a safe workplace, including arrangements for hazards such as fire, and the maintenance and safety of machinery and equipment.
- Employees also have the duty to take reasonable care for the safety of themselves and other working colleagues at all times, and to cooperate with the employer on all matters of safety.

Make a note of it

1 Why is it important that people gain satisfaction from their jobs? List six factors that you think make a job satisfying.

2 How can job enlargement and job enrichment help to motivate employees?

3 What is appraisal?

4 Why are wage differentials often the source of envy and discontent between workers?

5 List five factors which influence the supply of people suitable for a particular form of employment.

6 Briefly describe each of the following ways of calculating wages: flat rate; time rate; piece rate; bonus; commission.

7 What is a productivity deal?

8 How does job evaluation assist in establishing rates of pay?

9 Explain the differences between gross pay and net pay.

10 If you have earned a gross wage of £210.28 and must pay deductions totalling £57.36, what will be your net pay?

210.28
− 57.36
= 152.92

11 Give examples and explain the difference between statutory deductions and voluntary deductions.

12 Cash is one way of paying wages. Name two others.

13 What is the purpose of a time card system? How can this system be of help to the Wages department of a firm?

14 List at least six items of information likely to be found on a pay advice.

15 Briefly describe the way that a computer could be employed in the Wages department.

16 Explain the purpose of forms P45 and P60.

17 What are fringe benefits? Give six examples.

18 List the kind of information that is contained in the contract of employment.

19 How does a job description differ from a job specification?

20 Why are hours of employment important to the working conditions of an employee?

21 What is flexible working time? Why is it possible to operate this system for people working in a restaurant, but very difficult to adopt for a school?

22 'The Factories Act 1961, the Offices, Shops and Railway Premises Act 1963 and the Health and Safety at Work Act 1974, all aim to protect working conditions, but they each have differences in their application.' Explain this statement.

Structured Questions

1 The newspaper article on page 105 is related particularly to 'personnel professionals'. These are people who work in the Personnel department of a company.

   (a) What do you understand by the term stress in relation to working? (1)
   (b) Why have the new responsibilities of personnel professionals contributed to their stress? (2)
   (c) What do you understand by the term 'redundancy programme'? (2)
   (d) Why would a redundancy programme result in stress for personnel professionals? (3)
   (e) Briefly describe two forms that industrial action could take and say why such action would contribute to the stress of workers in a Personnel department. (4)
   (f) What is a 'staff evaluation' and grading scheme' and why can this contribute to stress levels for personnel professionals in particular? (4)
   (g) One way that a personnel department might be involved in business strategy is through public relations work. What does this involve? (4)

Personnel stress

THE MOST stressful activity for personnel professionals is the closure of a plant or the announcement of a redundancy programme. The second most stressful situation is the firing of a senior executive.

This is in contrast to the threat of industrial action, which rates only as a 'fairly stressful' situation. These are the findings of a recent survey in Personnel Today.

The survey asked the heads of personnel departments in some of Britain's largest companies to name the areas of their work which they found most stressful. A second survey, also looked at the new responsibilities which personnel departments are facing.

The responsibilities identified reflect the profession's increasing involvement in corporate activities, with 58% of those questioned noting their increased involvement in business strategy.

In the traditional area of trade union negotiations, however, 24% felt that they are now much less involved.

New responsibilities have included the use of computers and the administration of company pension schemes. The latter has become especially complex following changes in legislation.

Another major area has been the introduction of new staff evaluation and grading schemes, and employee share or profit-related pay. The introduction of such schemes now involves 59% of those asked.

"The findings of this latest survey reflect the changing business environment in which the personnel professional is working," explains Helena Sturridge, editor of Personnel Today.

"Their growing responsibilities have brought with them the need to cope with a number of stressful situations, and to manage a workforce in a far more sophisticated nature than ever before."

Source: *Executive Post.*

2 Refer to the newspaper article on page 106 and answer the following questions.

(a) Why would a management consultant be particularly useful to a small firm? (1)

(b) What service would a management consultancy give its clients? (2)

(c) Briefly say what an executive is and give two contrasting examples. (3)

(d) What is executive leasing and how does it differ from management consultancy. (3)

(e) Executive leasing is often used for handling 'one-off' assignments. Give three examples of 'one-off' assignments where an executive might be leased. (3)

(f) Why does executive leasing demand people with 'proven experience at middle or senior management level'? (4)

(g) State one advantage of executive leasing from the point of view of the executive. (4)

3 Refer to the pay advice illustrated on page 99 and answer these questions.

(a) Name the employer and the employee related to the pay advice shown. (1)

(b) Give one reason for giving employees a payroll number. (1)

(c) What do the letters NI shown stand for? (1)

(d) What is the purpose of showing a bank code and account number? (2)

Dramatic Leap in Executive Leasing Now Seen as a Credible Professional Career

There has been a dramatic recent increase in the number of firms offering management consultancy services. These services are particularly useful for smaller firms with insufficient funds to employ suitable management executives.

This trend has been accompanied by the development of executive leasing: the engagement of an executive for a limited period to fill a particular short-term gap; for example, handling a 'one-off' assignment, or bridging a gap between one senior executive leaving and a successor starting.

Executive leasing offers one of the best ways of handling specific but short-term problems.

Executive leasing is now increasingly seen as a credible professional career, but success requires the executive to have had proven successful experience at middle to senior management level.

(e) This pay advice shows two statutory deductions from pay. What are they? (2)

(f) How much is this employee allowed to earn tax free in a year and how can you tell this from the pay advice? (3)

(g) List three possible voluntary deductions the employee could choose to pay. (3)

(h) Use information contained on this pay advice to help you explain the difference between gross pay and net pay. (3)

(i) This pay advice relates to just one calendar month of employment. Assuming that the employee's rate of pay and monthly deductions do not change, what would be the figure for gross pay and net pay for a 12-month period? Show all calculations. (4)

4 Look at the following job description and answer these questions.

(a) What is the purpose of a job description? (1)

(b) Say, in no more than 25 words, what work a sales representative does. (2)

(c) Most job descriptions include details of hours of employment but this one shows none. Give two possible reasons why no hours are included in this description. (2)

(d) Why do you think this company holds its annual sales conference at weekends? (2)

```
┌─────────────────────────────────────────────────┐
│                 JOB DESCRIPTION                   │
│                                                   │
│   Job title:          Sales Representative        │
│   Salary:             £10 000 P.A. + 10% commission │
│   Car allocation:     Grade C                     │
│   Department:         Marketing                   │
│   Responsible to:     Sales Manager               │
│   Duties and responsibilities:                    │
│                                                   │
│       1.    Visit existing customers to obtain orders and │
│             offer advice                          │
│                                                   │
│       2.    Make contact with new potential customers and │
│             solicit orders                        │
│                                                   │
│       3.    Submit monthly sales analysis reports │
│                                                   │
│       4.    Attend bi-monthly sales meetings at Head │
│             Office (Saturday a.m.)                │
│                                                   │
│       5.    Participate in annual sales conference weekend │
│             at various venues.                    │
│                                                   │
│   Supervision procedures: Induction training initially │
│   supervised by Sales Manager for two months. Further two │
│   months supervision by Senior Sales Representative. │
│   Commission at half rate during this induction period, │
│   thereafter at full rate. Review of Job Description and salary │
│   after 12 months.                                │
└─────────────────────────────────────────────────┘
```

(e) Give three examples of the sort of advice a sales representative might
     give to customers.   (3)

(f) What do you understand by 'induction training'?   (3)

(g) This sales representative sold £32 000 of the company's products
     during the first four months of employment, and a further £25 000 in
     sales in the following two months. How much commission would the
     person receive in the first six months, and what would be their total
     gross earnings for the period? Show all calculations.   (3)

(h) In what ways could both the employee and the employer gain from
     payment by both a basic wage and commission rather than by basic
     wage alone?   (4)

Extended Answer Assignments

1 Use personal interviews with workers in a variety of occupations to examine to
   what extent job satisfaction is important.

2 Make a comparative study of wages for different occupations in the same
   industry giving reasons for differences that exist.

3 Make a comparative study of wages for the same occupation in different industries giving reasons for differences that exist.

4 What evidence can you find that indicates the effectiveness of legislation on equal pay for women in your locality?

5 Interview a cross-section of office workers and people involved in some form of production. Find out how informed they are about the aims of their employers. Comment on your finds.

6 In many organisations there are often people who are keen to be promoted, and there are others who are not interested in advancement. Interview a cross-section of people in employment with the aim of establishing why these attitudes exist.

7 Visit your local Job Centre. Identify at least three contrasting job vacancies which illustrate wage differentials. Give a detailed explanation of the reasons for the different wage levels.

8 Obtain an example of a completed P45, P60 and P2 and clearly explain the function of each, identifying the purpose of particular data on each form.

7 Industrial relations

7.1 The importance of industrial relations

People are not only the most important resource of an organisation, they are also the most costly resource. It might, therefore, be considered almost impossible to avoid at least some conflict between the employer and the employee. The employees will want to achieve the highest pay they can, while the employer will want to minimise the firm's wage costs. The term 'industrial relations' is generally used when statements are made which refer to the extent to which conflict or peace exists in industry, as well as between employers and employees.

7.2 Trade unions

Trade unions are associations of people who join together in their common interest to regulate the relations between employees and employers.

Unions are important from the point of view of workers because they enable them to pay a small subscription each, which the union then uses to employ skilled officials to act on the workers' behalf. Unions are also important to employers because they enable them to have discussions and negotiations with a small number of people rather than many.

Trade union aims

Trade unions aim to secure for workers:

- improved wages and reduced working hours;
- improved working conditions;
- full employment and national prosperity;
- job security;
- benefits for members who are sick, retired or on strike;
- improved social security schemes such as unemployment, sickness benefit and pensions;
- a say in government;
- participation in company decision processes;
- a reasonable share in the wealth of the country;
- improved public and social services.

WHITE-COLLAR UNIONS
This is the most rapidly expanding form of trade union. They represent white-collar workers, particularly supervisors and managers

CRAFT UNIONS
These are the earliest form of unions; they tend to be small unions representing skilled crafts or trades, although they are increasingly admitting semi- and unskilled machine operators. The TUC encourages the formation of larger industrial unions

TUC

GENERAL UNIONS
These are unions which represent several different types of workers and particularly semi- and unskilled workers

INDUSTRIAL UNIONS
These developed mainly from amalgamations of smaller unions. They are unions which represent all workers in a particular industry

There are different types of unions, classified according to the type of workers they represent. In many countries trade unions have joined together to form congresses or councils. In the UK the Trades Union Congress is an example of this type of 'union of unions'.

Trades Union Congress (TUC)

The TUC is the central body of the trade union movement. It is the representative voice of the many member trade unions, and consequently the government often discusses industrial policies with the TUC and attempts to obtain its co-operation. The TUC tries to promote the aims of the unions and to encourage support for them.

Although the TUC is an important part of the industrial scene, people often over-estimate its powers. The TUC's powers are in fact very limited. The real power in the TUC lies with the member unions and a democratic process which produces overall union views and policies.

Most of the main unions are associate members of the TUC, and the amount of power each union has within the organisation is determined by the size of its membership.

At the TUC Annual Congress, which usually takes place for one week in September, the General Council is elected to carry out TUC policies and work throughout the year. It is responsible for most of the main decisions and actions, whilst taking into account the wishes of the associated unions.

Each member union can send a number of delegates with voting power to the Annual Congress. The number of delegates is related to the size of the union's membership. The Annual Congress provides an important public platform for the unions to discuss important issues affecting the economy.

Criticisms of trade unions

One of the main criticisms of trade unions is that the typical member does not actively participate in its activities until there is some crisis or conflict which affects them personally. During the absence of active interest by the majority of the union's members, those with more positive and sometimes extremist political views can move into positions of influence and control in the unions. In such circumstances, the union could be open to abuse by persons using conflict situations for their own political ends.

7.3 Collective bargaining

The main function of trade unions is to obtain improved wages and working conditions for their members. Sometimes the employer reaches a satisfactory wage agreement with individual employees, but wage settlements are often the result of collective bargaining. This refers to talks between representatives of employers and trade unions to decide pay rates and conditions of employment.

The union represents a group of workers and negotiates a settlement on their behalf with an employer or a group of employers. It is just as much in the interest of the unions as it is in the employers to reach a speedy settlement, because both sides can only benefit if there is continuity in working.

Although pay is one of the main topics of collective bargaining, many other issues can be involved, including:

- hours of work
- holiday entitlement
- sick pay
- pensions
- maternity leave
- working conditions
- training
- promotion prospects
- redundancies
- recruitment.

Although negotiations between employers and employees may not reach an agreement, there are other possibilities to solve the deadlock.

Conciliation

Conciliation is where a third party is appointed (sometimes by the government) to try and help find a solution acceptable to both sides. The Advisory, Conciliation and Arbitration Service (ACAS) is particularly used to attempt to bring the two sides of a dispute nearer together. The work of ACAS is examined in more detail later.

Arbitration

This is where both sides of a dispute request that the dispute goes before an arbiter. Both sides agree to accept the verdict of the arbiter.

A typical union structure.

 7.4 | **Restrictive practices**

Restrictive practices are the methods or weapons used by the unions in an industrial dispute. The following are some of the most used methods.

Strike

- *Official* – on advice, in consultation or with union approval and backing, workers cease work (withdraw their labour). Under these circumstances the union may provide strike pay from the funds contributed by members.
- *Unofficial* – sometimes called a 'wildcat' strike, the workers cease work without union backing.

Demarcation dispute

A demarcation dispute is one where 'who does what' is in question, and is often a dispute between unions. This is a situation where one group of workers objects to another group doing particular work. Often this sort of dispute is the result of differences in rates of pay between one group of workers and another. It may be that one group of workers is doing work thought to 'belong' to another group, and for a lower rate of pay.

Overtime ban

Overtime provides a convenient way for employers to obtain extra working hours without taking on additional employees. When an overtime ban is in force the workers refuse to work additional hours.

Work to rule

Workers follow the rules and regulations of the company exactly. By adhering strictly to the rules in this way work is slowed down and productivity is reduced.

Go slow

This is similar to a work to rule. The workers do their work thoroughly, but at a slower pace than normal, causing a fall in output.

Closed shop

A closed shop means that all workers in a firm belong to one union and they refuse to work with anyone not a member of that union.

Picketing

In order to maximise the effect of their industrial action, a group of workers on strike may stand outside the firm's entrance and try to persuade other workers not to 'cross the picket line', i.e. not enter the premises.

Sit-in

Workers occupy the premises ensuring that no goods enter or leave, and preventing the operation of the firm. Sometimes, such as when a factory is threatened with closure, the sit-in becomes a 'work-in'. Workers occupy the factory and keep it in operation without the presence of the management.

Blacking

Union members may refuse to work on or move certain machines or equipment, or refuse to work with other people or groups. Someone who goes against the union's wishes is sometimes called a 'blackleg'.

7.5 Employers' organisations

From the foregoing description of the ways in which trade unions organise their activities, it can be seen that a large and powerful union could easily put a small firm at a disadvantage. For this reason firms also need to get together and form associations to protect and promote their interests. By combining in this way the employers are able to match the power of the trade unions. In addition, employers' associations can act as a single voice for many employers. They also provide a means of industrial research and the communication of ideas and information.

Confederation of British Industry (CBI)

The CBI is the major employers' association in Great Britain and it is the opposite number of the TUC. The CBI represents employers in a similar manner to that in which the TUC represents the trade unions.

Although they disagree on many issues, the CBI and the TUC are frequently in consultation with each other and their combined co-operation on many matters related to industry results in useful contributions to industrial policies and plans.

Like the TUC, the CBI has some permanent staff led by its Director General. Also similar to the TUC, the real power of the CBI lies with its members and this is also focused at the Annual Conference.

Advisory, Conciliation and Arbitration Services (ACAS)

ACAS is a body available for use by both the employers and employees. The function of ACAS is to conciliate (pacify) and arbitrate (mediate) on matters related to industrial relations. It is managed by a council of nine members, three of whom are independent of it, three are appointed in consultation with the CBI and three are appointed in consultation with the TUC.

Where the parties to a dispute are in a 'deadlock' position, some progress may be made with the help and consultation of a third 'outside' party such as ACAS. In such circumstances an officer of ACAS examines the issues involved and tries to conciliate the parties.

Another avenue that can be explored through ACAS is to seek arbitration, that is to allow a third party to act as a kind of referee. ACAS will provide arbitration facilities, but only if both parties to the dispute agree to go to arbitration, and both also agree to accept the conclusions reached.

The Employment Act 1988

The Employment Act 1988 gives union members rights which they can use to prevent abuses of union power against them. Members of some unions already had similar rights in their union's rules, but this law now guarantees all union members the same rights.

- Union members can restrain their union from calling them to take industrial action without support for the action from a properly conducted secret ballot.
- Union members have the right not to be unjustifiably disciplined by their union, e.g. for deciding to honour their employment contract and go to work or cross a picket line rather than take part in industrial action.
- Industrial action to enforce or maintain any kind of closed shop is unlawful and dismissal from employment for not being a member of a union is not acceptable.
- Postal voting subject to independent scrutiny is required for many of the situations where union members are required to make decisions.

7.6 Role of the government

The activities of the government obviously affect the lives of workers in a variety of ways, not only through their success or otherwise in managing the economy, but also through the laws which are brought into being. Some of these laws may be seen by trade unionists as being against the interest of their members, especially those laws which aim to place restrictions on what a union can do. Consequently, the unions see part of their responsibilities as to try to prevent such laws from coming into existence. This of course brings the union movement into direct conflict with the government and can contribute to a deterioration in industrial relations.

Traditionally, the trade union movement has always supported the Labour Party and, generally speaking, the movement has always been suspicious of the Conservative Party. Although there do appear to be more conflicts between trade

These protest notices are all related to general issues pressure groups might wish to influence. Design some notices that might be used to influence businesses.

unions and Conservative governments, this is not always the case, and there have been occasions when Labour governments have not been able to rely on the full backing of the trade unionists.

While we have acknowledged in this chapter that trade unions aim to improve conditions of work for their members, unions cannot do this without taking into account government policy. Workers can only hope to achieve full employment and choice of occupation and place of work, if the government is able to plan the economy. For this reason, governments have an important role to play in industrial relations by producing imaginative ideas, and communicating them in a way that is open, honest and clear.

Enlisting the co-operation of the unions in implementing government policies has become an important feature of modern society. This entails involving the trade union movement in matters of economic policy formation, primarily through consultation. It is in this aspect of government that the roles of the CBI and the TUC can prove valuable.

7.7 ▶ Pressure groups

Pressure groups are voluntary organisations which seek to encourage the government, local council, or some other organisation to recognise their views and respond to them. They try to influence the decision-making process by demonstrating the strength of their feelings.

Perhaps one of the most well-known pressure groups in Britain are trade unions. The TUC acts on their behalf to influence the government's thinking on issues that concern trade unions (particularly those connected with pay and working conditions). The TUC also acts in a similar way as a pressure group on employers. The CBI acts on behalf of employers and tries to influence the government from their point of view.

Pressure groups are not all formal ones such as those examined so far. Sometimes an informal group will form spontaneously, perhaps due to a passing situation, e.g. a no waiting system in the local town.

Although pressure groups are often portrayed in the media as trying to influence local or central government, they do at times try to influence business also. Apart from workers trying to influence pay awards, the general public may try to put pressure on businesses to protest about issues such as advertising techniques, building expansion, or use of certain raw materials.

Governments and businesses are subjected to pressure from groups of people or organisations who are trying to influence policies to be adopted. Sometimes continual pressure is put on the government, industry or specific businesses to acknowledge or make concessions to the views of the pressure groups. The pressure may be exerted through the press or TV propaganda, or it may be less formally organised.

Firms face pressure from groups both internally and externally. Internal pressure sometimes comes from groups of shareholders trying to influence company policy. However, the main pressure on firms tends to be external – that is consumer pressure.

The most basic form of consumer pressure is the opportunity customers have to take their custom elsewhere, although where the firm is in a monopolistic position (e.g. supply of electricity or gas) this possibility may be limited.

The Consumers' Association plays an important role as a pressure group. The group obtains funds from members who buy the magazine called *Which?* The funds are used to test a variety of products and to publish comparative reports in the magazine. These reports are frequently quoted in the press and on TV and radio and consequently they influence producers and traders. The Association also publishes books of consumer-related interest.

Some television and radio programmes also act as watchdogs to expose firms who are guilty of malpractice. Many newspapers and magazines also publish details of investigations carried out by their 'Consumer Watchdogs'.

Many of the national organisations providing domestic supplies and services who are in a largely monopolistic position are subject to the scrutiny of consumer councils. For example, the Post Office Users' National Council investigates complaints about the postal service, and there are similar councils for other large domestic suppliers and state-owned industries.

Trade unions and the CBI also act as pressure groups. They not only represent the interests of their members, but they also put forward views on a wide range of issues such as trade, education and consumer affairs. Other organisations such as the AA and the RAC represent the interests of motorists.

There are also environmental pressure groups who represent those who are particularly concerned about the environment. Currently the organisation called Greenpeace is gaining a lot of attention worldwide in its attempts to get government and industry to recognise the need to protect the environment.

Make a note of it

1 What do you understand by the term 'industrial relations'?

2 To what extent would you say that it is inevitable that employers and employees will come into conflict?

3 What is a trade union?

4 List the aims of trade unions. What part does the TUC play in putting across the aims of the unions to others?

5 What is the Trades Union Congress? Why do you think that the government often discusses industrial policies with the TUC?

6 Describe the organisation and functions of the TUC.

7 Give a brief description of the four main types of trade union in the United Kingdom.

8 What are the main criticisms of trade unions?

9 What is the main function of trade unions?

10 Say what you understand by the terms 'collective bargaining', 'conciliation' and 'arbitration'? What is the relationship between these terms?

11 What are restrictive practices? Why are they adopted?

12 Explain the difference between an official and an unofficial strike.

13 Shop stewards are ordinary full-time workers who are elected by a group of union members to represent them to the union and also to the management. Bearing this in mind, why do you think that it is often shop stewards who call a 'wildcat' or unofficial strike?

14 What is a demarcation dispute?

15 Trade unions use a variety of methods to try and persuade employers to agree to wage claims. Explain how the following methods operate:
   (a) overtime ban
   (b) work to rule
   (c) go slow
   (d) sit-in
   (e) blacking.

16 Two controversial aspects of trade union activity are:
   (a) picketing, and
   (b) the closed shop.
     Describe these two forms of action. Why do you think they are controversial? Do you think they should be allowed? Give reasons for your answer.

17 Why do employers need representatives just as much as employees?

18 Describe the functions of the Confederation of British Industry. Explain the relationship and similarities between the CBI and the TUC.

19 What is the function of the Advisory, Conciliation and Arbitration Service (ACAS)?

20 Explain the role of the government in industrial relations.

21 What is a pressure group?

22 Why are pressure groups important to consumers?

Structured Questions

1 Refer to the article about firefighters on page 120.

   (a) Who are 'public sector workers'? (1)
   (b) Why would the Chancellor of the Exchequer want to interfere in the pay awards of public sector workers? (2)
   (c) Why should possible action by the firefighters concern local businesses? (2)
   (d) Explain what you understand by 'industrial peace'? (2)
   (e) What is the function of shop stewards? To what extent can they contribute to industrial peace? (3)
   (f) Describe two forms of industrial action that firefighters could take other than striking. (4)
   (g) In what ways can bodies outside of those involved in an industrial dispute help in resolving the differences that exist. (6)

119

FIREFIGHTERS FIRE THE FIRST SHOT

The country's firefighters have fired the opening shot in the dispute by public sector workers who are incensed by the Chancellor of the Exchequer's decision to restrict the wage rises of public service employees. Local businesses have expressed concern over possible loss of fire cover.

The Fire Brigades Union is on the brink of calling a strike over pay for the first time in 15 years.

The union was meeting employers today in London in a last ditch bid to hold on to a pay formula which has kept the industrial peace since 1977.

But the government wants to scrap that agreement for a year and pin firefighters' wages to a public sector pay ceiling of 1.5 per cent.

If today's talks reach stalemate an immediate ballot and then a strike is on the cards, and shop stewards will begin to organise local action.

2

Today many workers in the same, or similar, trades join a trade union. The union tries to obtain better wages and improved working conditions for all of its members. This saves each employee struggling individually with their employers. This is called 'collective bargaining'.

Union officials representing the employees meet representatives of the employers at a national level. Any agreement they reach applies to everyone in the union or group of unions in the whole country.

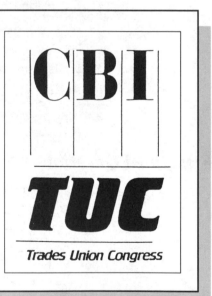

(a) What do the letters CBI stand for? (1)
(b) Define the term 'collective bargaining'. (2)
(c) Describe three of the peaceful ways in which trade unions can try to obtain better wages and working conditions for its members. (3)
(d) Describe four benefits of belonging to a union. (4)

(e) How does the function of the CBI differ from that of the TUC? (4)

(f) In what ways does 'collective bargaining' benefit both the worker and also the employer? (6)

3 The following questions are all related to restrictive practices referred to in this chapter.

(a) What do you understand by the term restrictive practices? (2)

(b) Why can restrictive practices cause damage to businesses? (2)

(c) What part do shop stewards play in restrictive practices? (2)

(d) Describe four main kinds of restrictive practice that workers might take. (4)

(e) Explain the difference between an official and an unofficial strike. (4)

(f) In taking industrial action groups of workers would choose different times of the year to maximise the effect. How would airline pilots and teachers differ in the time of the year they would choose to implement action? Give reason for your answer (6)

4 (a) What is a trade union? (1)

(b) What are the advantages of belonging to a trade union from the point of view of workers? (2)

(c) 'Shop stewards represent their union members but they are also employed by the firm'. Explain this statement. (3)

(d) Briefly describe the four main types of union and explain the types of worker they represent. (4)

(e) Explain the contribution that conciliation and arbitration can make in an industrial dispute. (4)

(f) 'A productivity deal is a means of giving workers the improved pay or working conditions they seek without sacrificing the profitability required by the owners of the firm'. Explain this statement with particular reference to the importance of productivity deals to both the employee and the firm. (6)

Extended Answer Assignments

1 Collect at least four newspaper articles containing reports of industrial problems. In each case describe the influence that trade unions might have on the event in question. Comment whether their involvement is likely to improve or worsen the situation.

2 What contribution do you feel trade unions make to the economy of our country?

3 Describe the work of trade unions. Considering the fact that they have similar aims why are there sometimes disputes between unions? Give examples from the current press to illustrate your answer.

4 Design a questionnaire that can be used to find out the views of the general public of trade unions. Use your questionnaire to survey a representative sample. Present your findings in the form of a report.

5 Approach one of the major trade unions and obtain details of the services and benefits they provide for their members. Design and detail your own leaflet that could be used to attract workers to join the union.

6 Take any current national issue that appears likely to lead to industrial unrest. Describe in detail the steps you would take as an employer to try to deter your employees from taking strike action which would damage your business.

7 An industrial tribunal is an independent body dealing mainly with the claims of unfair dismissal and other alleged breaches of employees' rights. Write a summary of two industrial tribunal cases reported in the press or obtained from a tribunal. What other support is there for employees who feel they have a grievance against their employers?

8 The marketing department

What is marketing?

Marketing refers to all the processes involved in selling goods or services in the most efficient and profitable manner. It begins with an examination of what people want from a product or service *(market research)*. This is followed by an assessment of how to produce the product or service *(product development)* that will satisfy that requirement, and at the same time make a profit in the process. The next stage is to develop a *marketing strategy* that will get the product to the appropriate market at a competitive price. This will involve creating an advertising campaign that is backed by selling and distribution procedures.

The following flow chart shows the way that the marketing process is developed.

Marketing in this sense is a two-way process. It connects those who produce goods and services with potential buyers. It also finds out what products and services consumers want and relays the information to the producers. This enables them to make the right things available.

Marketing is a two-way process.

Marketing concepts

Marketing concept refers to the typical business goal of satisfying customers' wants and trying to make a profit in the process.

We say that a business is pursuing a *sales concept* when it tries to sell something before learning what the customer wants. Sometimes it suits a producer to operate in this way. For example, if a manufacturer is well equipped to produce a particular product he or she might go ahead and manufacture and rely on their salesforce to persuade the consumer to buy.

By following a *marketing concept* a business will firstly find out what customers want and then try to meet this demand. What the customer wants is known as the *customer concept*, i.e. the business may well do what the customer wants, although it might prefer to do otherwise. For example, a store might stay open until late in the evening to please its customers, even though this adds considerably to its wage bill.

The way that a business finds out what the customer wants is by *market research*. This is the systematic and continuous evaluation of all the factors involved in the transfer of goods and services from the producer to the ultimate consumer. It is particularly concerned with the reaction of consumers. (See also Chapter 9.)

Sales is a support system for marketing. In other words, sales is a marketing strategy which facilitates exchange. Therefore, a major part of the work of a marketeer is to choose the best possible methods of sales to match the products being marketed. For example, the sales strategies for a new flavour soft drink would differ from the sales strategies for a property. Market research plays an important role in the development of sales strategies.

8.2 ▶ The marketing department

A firm's *marketing department* is concerned with selling its products or services. This can mean disposing of products the firm has produced, but more often it is a case of identifying what customers want *(customer concept)* and then arranging to meet the need that exists, hopefully making a profit in the process.

There are many ways to organise a marketing department and its structure will be influenced by the size of the firm. In a large company it would be possible to split the department into several subdivisions, each with a specific marketing func-

Typical structure of a marketing department in a large company.

tion. In a small organisation a few members of staff may have to incorporate several of these functions into their duties.

The functions of a marketing department

The marketing department will be controlled by the marketing director or a senior manager. This position entails carrying out sales policies decided by the board of directors, and supervising the work of all the people employed in the department, including the company's *sales representatives* whose job is to visit potential customers and obtain orders.

All documentation related to sales of the firm's products will be dealt with either directly or indirectly by the marketing department. This will include sending out mail shots (sales leaflets), dealing with customers' enquiries and orders, arranging for despatch of goods, and initiating the sending out of invoices and statements of account (see Chapter 12).

A major part of the work of the marketing department is to choose the method of sales to be employed. This will vary according to the product or service being marketed. For example, the method of marketing a new chocolate bar will differ from that used to sell a valuable antique.

The way that products are to be distributed will be given careful consideration. This will involve decisions with regard to which channels of distribution will be used and whether trade will be directed through wholesalers and retailers, or by direct marketing such as by mail order.

The marketing department will obviously be involved in advertising the firm's products. Where the firm is large it may have a separate advertising department. This department will carry out the instructions of the marketing department, and will also offer advice on marketing strategies, including market research. These aspects of marketing are covered in more detail later in this book.

8.3 ▶ Marketing mix

Those directly involved in marketing generally follow the *customer concept* defined earlier; that is, they try to see things from their customers' point of view. Where a business wants to influence a specific group of customers (e.g. teenagers) they are its *target market*. A business will often have many target markets, e.g. one for each of its products or services, and it may well approach each target market in different ways.

Once a business has identified its target market it will select what it considers is the most appropriate marketing mix. The *marketing mix* is a collective term that is used to refer to the whole range of marketing activities, techniques and strategies that a firm uses to reach its target market. The variables of a marketing mix can be easily remembered by referring to the 'four Ps' – *product, price, place* and *promotion*.

Product

Obviously the product, good or service, or even an idea, plays an important role in marketing. There is little point in trying to market something that the con-

The four Ps that make up the variables of the marketing mix enable the seller to reach the target market.

sumer doesn't want. For this reason, the needs of the consumer must be focused on.

Packaging is clearly linked with the product. Packaging is the outer wrapping of or container for the goods. Packaging not only presents the product in an attractive way but it also gives details about the contents, any potential hazards, the correct usage, etc. In this respect packaging:

- protects the product;
- promotes the product;
- preserves the life of the product;
- prevents health hazards that could result from improper use of the product;
- makes it more convenient for the consumer to handle the product;
- improves the general appearance of the product.

An old established product in a new and improved package usually enhances the marketing potential of the product.

Branding is another important aspect of the product. Branding refers to giving a good a distinctive name, term, symbol or even a design to enable it to be recognised easily.

A *brand name* (or trade mark) is that part of branding which represents the actual letter, letters, word or group of words which make up the name of the good. The brand name differentiates one product from another similar or dissimilar product. It is a registered symbol or name which can only be used by the firm.

Packaging presents the product attractively and also gives details about the contents.

A brand name has to be short, descriptive and easy to pronounce, and it must appeal to the target market.

Price

No matter how attractive a product is, a crucial factor in the success of the marketing strategy will be the price. It is important to the seller because it incorporates profit, and it is important to the consumers because it affects their ability to purchase what they want. Price determination is examined later in this chapter.

Place

Those involved in marketing a product have to ensure that it reaches a place where consumers can conveniently make purchases. Getting the item to this convenient place is called *distribution*. This involves wholesalers, retailers, importers and exporters. These aspects of distribution are dealt with in Chapters 10 and 11. Distribution also depends on transportation which is dealt with in Chapter 13.

Promotion

This refers to the ways in which consumers are made aware of the availability of the product or service and the qualities it has. Advertising is the most important aspect of product promotion and this is dealt with in Chapter 9.

Sales promotion is any activity that supplements advertising and other aspects of visual promotion. The following are just a few of the strategies used in sales promotion. You should find out about the form these take:

- trading stamps
- loss leaders
- free gifts/gift tokens
- competitions
- product demonstrations
- free samples
- exhibitions.

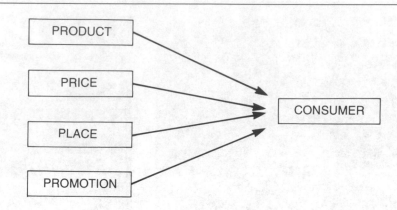

The strategies involved in the marketing mix are aimed at meeting the needs and desires of the consumer.

From the foregoing it will have been seen that the marketing mix aims to get the right product to the consumer at the right price and to a convenient place where it can be bought. The consumer is made aware of what is available through product promotion. All the strategies involved in the marketing mix are aimed at meeting the needs and desires of the consumer.

8.4   Product lifecycle

In addition to deciding on the marketing mix a firm must consider how sales might develop. All products move through identifiable stages which are referred to as the *product lifecycle*. Understanding this cycle assists the preparation of a sound marketing plan.

Pre-launch

This stage consists of all the developmental work undertaken before the product is put on the market. During this time the decision has to be taken whether it is worthwhile to pursue the new development. Once it has been decided to proceed, a considerable amount of capital is consumed with no income being earned. The time between the design of a product and its production is known as the *lead time*.

Introduction

In the early stages of marketing sales tend to be low but large amounts of capital continue to be consumed. It is some time before breakeven (see Chapter 16) stage is reached and the product begins to show a profit.

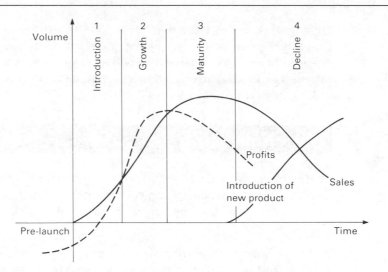

Most products have a lifecycle similar to that shown by this graph which plots a product from its introduction through to its decline. The production and marketing sections of the firm have to be aware of the position of products in their lifecycle in order to maximise profits, and to plan the introduction of replacement products at the appropriate time.

Growth

If all goes well, sales and profits are steadily rising. Marketing becomes more economically viable as an increasing volume of cash comes in from customers. This is a time for vigorous advertising to promote maximum demand for the product.

Maturity

During this crucial period the rate of sales growth begins to slow down. The advent of this is often signalled by prior falling off of profits. The product reaches its ceiling and begins to decline. This is a crucial period for the business because it is important to recognise the signal to improve the product or find a new one.

Decline

This is the period when sales volume shows a market fall. It reveals that the product has lost its appeal or competitive edge. If steps have not already been taken to improve the product it will probably now have to be withdrawn in order to avoid making a loss.

Product range and product mix

From the foregoing examination of the product lifecycle you will realise that if a firm markets only a single product it is at a considerable risk. In fact most products are not marketed on their own but are part of a range of products. For example, a firm might produce a *range* of cake mixes, etc. Many small firms commence their business in this way. A large firm will have a *product mix* which consists of several different products, each with its own range, e.g. cake mixes, biscuits, crisps, instant sauces, dessert toppings, etc.

8.5 Merchandising

Merchandising is an important marketing technique. It refers to the display of goods so that potential customers can conveniently see them and be influenced to buy. The following are just some of the methods of merchandising used by sellers of goods:

- eyecatching window displays, including special offers;
- use of in-house displays to reduce the number of employees needed to sell the goods;
- careful layout of premises that allows customers to get near to goods and move into other parts of the store;
- packaging design that presents goods attractively;
- opportunity for customers to inspect goods closely and perhaps touch them;
- clear labelling and price marking to reduce the need for customers to ask questions;
- eye-level shelf displays for high priority goods.

Packaging and branding are important features of merchandising. Whilst producers will be required to comply with certain regulations relating to information (e.g. contents, weight, etc.) that must be shown on their products, they will also want to put them in containers that will appeal to the consumer.

Branding refers to giving a product a distinctive name that will be easily recognised and identified with the item in question. This is of considerable advantage in advertising a product, because if the brand name is easily recognised then less expense is involved in trying to make the public aware of the qualities of the product.

An obvious example where merchandising is particularly apparent is in self-service stores, but you should not think of merchandising only in respect of retail trade. Merchandising is used by any business that displays goods rather than just keeping them inside their premises.

8.6 Price determination

All free markets involving many buyers and sellers operate according to the laws of demand and supply. That is, if the demand for goods and services increases faster than the supply of them, prices rise. If the supply increases faster than the demand, prices fall. In other words, the price of goods and services is determined by the interaction of the forces of demand and supply and this of course has a direct influence on production.

Demand

The demand for any commodity is the amount that consumers are prepared to purchase at a given price in a given period of time. For each price the demand is different. Usually the lower the price the higher the quantity demanded, and vice versa, although there are exceptions. *Giffen goods* is a name given to those essential and relatively cheap goods for which demand is likely to increase following a rise in price. The term 'Giffen' is given after a nineteenth-century economist of that name who noticed that when the price of bread increased, consumers bought more of it, being unable to afford to buy other more expensive alternatives such as meat and fruit.

The table below shows a possible demand schedule for a fictional commodity at various prices. A demand schedule can also be shown graphically as below right by plotting the data on a demand curve.

This demand schedule and demand curve only refers to an individual consumer, but market demand consists of many people. A market demand curve is obtained by summing the demand curves of all individuals, so we can expect the market demand to behave in a similar way to individual demand.

Both the individual demand curve and the market demand curve express a relationship between the demand for a commodity and the price of it, but there are other determinants of demand:

● price of the commodity;

An individual's demand schedule and demand graph for chocolate bars at various prices. The point x on this demand curve indicates that at a price of 30p the person would be likely to buy three bars.

- price of other commodities;
- income of the buyers;
- population or number of buyers;
- buyer's scale of preferences, i.e. how much the buyer values or prefers the items he or she wants in comparison with other commodities.

If one of the conditions of demand changes the demand curve moves to a new position. For example, a rise in income or purchasing power could increase market demand and shift the demand curve to the right (D to D_1). On the other hand, if one of the determinants causes a fall in market demand the curve moves to the left (D to D_2).

Supply

Supply is the amount of a commodity that producers are willing to put on to the market at various prices in a given period of time. For each price the amount supplied is different. Alternatively, we could say that the supply curve shows the price that is necessary to persuade the producer to provide output. Usually the higher the price the more of the commodity the producer will want to supply and vice versa, but in the same way as in the case of demand, there are some exceptions to this.

A supply schedule and graph can be constructed similar to those used to plot demand. Unlike the demand curve the supply curve usually slopes upwards to the right.

Price

Price is the charge assigned to something, or the *exchange value* for a product or service. The demand for a product or service will be influenced by the price of it.

From our examination of supply and demand so far, it should be clear to the reader that buyers want to buy at the lowest price they can, whilst sellers want to obtain the highest price they can for their goods. Whilst these may at first seem conflicting interests, closer examination shows that it is a combination of demand and supply that determines price.

When any two forces balance each other they are said to be in *equilibrium*. Under the conditions of a perfect market the price of a commodity is determined by the interaction of supply and demand. This can be made clearer by looking at a combined demand and supply schedule which is also expressed graphically for simple observation.

Price	Quantity demanded	Quantity supplied
£5	100	500
£4	200	400
£3	300	300
£2	400	200
£1	500	100

Market for teddy bears – amount demanded and supplied at various prices during one week.

As shown in the table above it is only at the price of £3 that the number of teddy bears the consumers wish to buy is equal to the amount of teddy bears the producer is willing to supply. This is called the *equilibrium price*, which is the only price at which the amount willingly demanded and the amount willingly supplied are equal.

In the diagram it can be seen that the equilibrium price is at the intersection of the demand and supply curves. We can also see that if the price is above the equilibrium price, there is an excess of supply and insufficient demand. The result of this is that the price falls towards the equilibrium price. Alternatively, if the price is below the equilibrium price there is insufficient supply and excess demand. This results in the price rising towards the equilibrium price.

Our examination of the laws of demand and supply in this section has been very elementary although sufficient for our purposes. However, it should be understood that in reality the interaction of demand and supply is often more complex. The *economist* is particularly interested in investigating this interaction in greater depth.

8.7 Competition

Competition enhances the efficiency of the economic system. Competition is a major factor in the determination of price.

There are two main types of competition – perfect or pure or free competition, and imperfect competition.

Perfect competition

Perfect competition results from a market situation in which the products of the marketplace are homogeneous, are well known to the participators in the market, and where 'breaking into' the market on the part of both buyers and sellers poses little or no problem. In other words, no one buyer or seller dominates. The competitiveness of the market eventually forces costs and prices to settle at the lowest possible levels, while production will climb to its peak.

Imperfect competition

This market situation results when there are very few producers of goods and services in the marketplace. In other words, there is less evidence of rivalry and excessive exchange in the marketplace. In this atmosphere, monopoly and oligopoly are usually at work.

Monopoly

A *monopolistic* situation results when a single organisation controls an entire line of products and is, therefore, able to determine the selling price. However, the seller is unable to fix both the price and the quantity supplied; he fixes prices at the highest level that he thinks the market will tolerate.

In all EC member countries governments closely monitor monopolistic situations, i.e. when the price of the product is set by a single firm.

Oligopoly

Oligopolistic situations result when a few large suppliers dominate the marketplace. There are many examples of such situations in the UK. The products being marketed are generally homogeneous, e.g. soap powder. Prices are usually tightly structured. The aim is to reduce or even prevent the level of competition that could arise.

Cartels

Cartels are also members of the imperfect market. A cartel consists of a number of firms within a particular industry such as the petroleum industry (OPEC). The firms agree on aspects such as pricing, production levels, sales and the division of the markets.

Government intervention

Governments are sometimes obliged to intervene and protect consumers from the imperfections in the working of the price system. There are two basic methods of government intervention that are used:

1 *Control of prices* through taxation or subsidies. Taxation increases production costs, whereas subsidies reduce them.
2 *Control of demand* by rationing, which is an attempt to influence production and consumption by regulating effective demand.

8.8 Public relations

All businesses care about what the public thinks of their company and will use a variety of ways to try and influence the public to have a high regard for the firm and its employees. The extent to which the public have a good impression of a business is called public relations or 'goodwill'.

In a large company it will be possible to employ a specialist called the *public relations officer (PRO)* who has the responsibility of promoting a good public image.

In a smaller business this role would have to be carried out by the owner or a responsible senior employee. But the promotion of public relations is really the responsibility of all employees.

Good public relations may be promoted in direct ways such as making donations to charities, giving away free samples and gifts, operating prize-giving competitions, using famous personalities to endorse the company's goods, etc. These and many other methods are deliberately used to encourage the public to look on the business in a favourable way.

There are also many indirect ways that companies promote their public image, and often these will draw on the help of all employees. For example, potential customers will be influenced by the manner in which employees talk to them on the telephone or at the shop counter. They will also be influenced by the way that their enquiries or complaints are dealt with.

Many companies take particular care with the way that they handle after-sales services because they recognise that this is a vehicle for good public relations. They try to ensure that when a customer has a complaint about a purchase made it is turned to the seller's advantage by showing courtesy and a willingness to put things right quickly.

 ## 8.9 Trade associations

Chambers of commerce

Chambers of commerce are voluntary associations of business people. They are sited in towns and cities where commerce is particularly active. Their members come from a wide range of businesses, for example retailing, finance, transport. In other words, a chamber of commerce will consist of people from different types of business. They help to develop and expand business in their locality, and also abroad. They give their members advice on a wide range of matters including legislation, customs regulations, recovery of bad debts and many other important aspects of trading practice.

Chambers of commerce also exist in many overseas countries and today have an important role to play. Through their links with the chambers of commerce in this country they can supply useful information and many contacts for businesses both at home and abroad.

Chambers of commerce also take an interest in education and training for employment. A difficulty faced by educationalists is identifying what skills commerce and industry want students to leave school or college with. The answer to this question can be obtained in part through chambers of commerce and manufacturers' associations.

Manufacturers' associations

A manufacturers' association has many similarities with a chamber of commerce, but in this case each association consists of people from a similar business, for example the Association of British Travel Agents. These organisations provide an ideal forum for the exchange of information between members, and on occasions a common body for carrying out wage negotiations with trade unions.

Such associations have a number of aims but an important one is the formation of codes of practice that are to be followed by their members. In this respect the trade association acts as a focal point for dealing with consumer complaints, as well as promoting goodwill for all their members.

It is not unusual for trade associations to sponsor research and technical information projects for the mutual benefit or all their members. Similarly the trade association may undertake publicity campaigns at home or abroad aimed at creating trade for all members.

Make a note of it

1 You are employed by a major company that manufactures a range of soft drinks. Briefly describe the process the company would be likely to follow in marketing a new drink.

2 Why is marketing said to be a 'two-way process'?

3 Explain the difference between 'sales concept', 'marketing concept' and 'customer concept'.

4 Describe the functions of a marketing department.

5 What sort of things do you think help a business in identifying its 'target market'?

6 What is meant by 'marketing mix'?

7 Describe the stages involved in a product's lifecycle.

8 How does 'product range' differ from 'product mix'?

9 What is merchandising?

10 List at least six merchandising techniques used by the seller of goods.

11 What are branded goods?

12 What do you understand by demand? What are the determinants of demand?

13 Use the following information to produce a demand graph:

Price per unit (pence)	Quantity demanded at each price (kilos)
45	1
40	2
35	3
30	4
25	5

14 With the aid of a simple diagram explain the effects of changes in demand on the demand graph.

15 List the factors that determine demand.

16 Use simple diagrams to describe the effect of changes in demand on a demand curve.

17 What do we mean by the term 'supply'?

18 What do you understand by price?

19 How does supply and demand help to identify 'equilibrium price'?

20 How does perfect competition differ from imperfect?

21 How does monopoly differ from oligopoly?

22 Briefly describe the work of a public relations officer.

23 Why is public relations an important aspect of a firm's operations?

24 What part do trade associations play in business?

Structured Questions

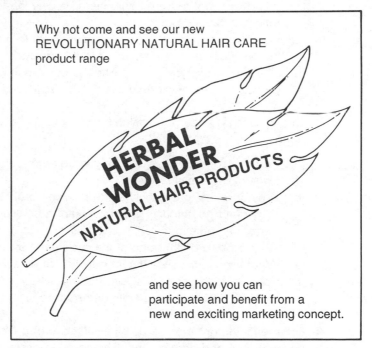

1 Look at this part of an advertisement placed by Herbal Wonder in a trade magazine. It aims to get those in the hairdressing trade interested in the manufacturer's new range of products. Answer these questions related to the advertisement.

   (a) The advertisement refers to a 'product range'. Name four different items that might be included in the range. (2)

(b) State four different places to sell this company's products, bearing in mind the target audience. (2)

(c) How could 'branding' assist the marketing of the product range? (3)

(d) Name three different marketing occupations that would be involved in the process between the completion of production and eventual purchase by the consumer. (3)

(e) Briefly describe four different ways in which the final consumer public might be made aware of this producer range. (4)

(f) What factors would be likely to influence trade customers to purchase Herbal Wonder's products? (6)

2 Read the newspaper article on page 139 'Why is fruit and veg so dear?' and answer the following questions.

(a) Give one possible economic reason why some traders are destroying fruit and veg. (1)

(b) In what way can destroying products affect retail prices? (1)

(c) Use information from the newspaper article to show that the wholesale price of fruit and veg has generally fallen. (2)

(d) Some aspects of this article clearly show that fruit and veg prices have fallen. So what reasons could there be why the fall in prices is not yet reflected in the shops? (4)

(e) Describe the work of the 'middlemen' likely to be involved in the purchase and distribution of fruit and veg. (4)

(f) The supermarket chains say 'shop prices are inflated by transport, processing and packaging costs'. Discuss the validity of this statement. (8)

3 The following questions are related to the chart of a product lifecycle shown on page 129.

(a) Describe some of the work likely to be done during the 'pre-launch' stage of a product lifecycle. (2)

(b) Why does the 'pre-launch' stage show no profit being made? (2)

(c) Why do large amounts of capital tend to be used during the early stages of marketing? (3)

(d) Why is the 'growth' stage of the cycle the most profitable stage? (3)

(e) What factors influence the introduction of a new product? (4)

(f) How would the profit lifecycle of salt be likely to differ from that of pop records? You may use simple diagrams to illustrate your answer. (6)

4 Refer to the diagram of the possible structure of a marketing department shown on page 124 and answer the following questions.

(a) Why is the diagram shown not likely to be typical of a small company? (2)

(b) How do home sales differ from overseas sales? (2)

(c) What work is carried out in the costing section of a marketing department? (3)

WHY IS FRUIT AND VEG SO DEAR?

Consumer Affairs Consultant

From the dockside to the supermarket, everyone is saying: 'It's not our fault'.

THE GREAT MYSTERY of the fruit and vegetable markets is why are the prices so high to the consumer, when everyone in the trade is saying that profits have been cut to the bone, and competition is higher than it has ever been?

If tomatoes and other salad products are being imported so cheap that some traders are actually destroying some of their imports, why is it so dear in the shops?

Import prices have halved in less than two months, with tomatoes now about 24p a lb. In Superstores yesterday they were selling at 89p.

Cucumbers are just 12p at the dockside … and 68p in the supermarket.

When our Consumer Affairs Consultant tried to discover the answer yesterday, everyone – from shopkeepers to the importers – denied that it was their fault.

Supermarket chains say shop prices are inflated by transport, processing and packaging costs. Supermarket prices are set months in advance.

A Superstore spokesman said: 'Our prices are coming down. Tomatoes have been reduced by 10p a lb in the past two months and we are continually reviewing our prices. In fact we are doing so almost daily'.

Two months ago 1 cwt of imported potatoes sold to the trade in Southampton for £4.48. Yesterday the same quantity fetched only £2.20.

At Manchester bananas have been selling wholesale at around £28 per cwt – less than half of the price six weeks ago. It's a similar story in London.

Fruit and veg goes through a complex chain of middlemen between the grower and the supermarket shelves. For example, bananas are picked on the plantations in, say, the Caribbean, in the green state. They are then transported in refrigerated ships and come in through our docks.

Importers sell them into the wholesale markets, and the wholesalers sell on to the retailers. Sometimes the product may pass through more than one wholesaler before it reaches the retailer. From the wholesalers the bananas eventually end up on the shop shelves, in the yellow condition that most consumers prefer. Timing is a crucial factor in all aspects of the fruit and veg trade.

(d) Why is market research an essential feature of marketing? (3)

(e) In what way can the structure shown be said to be illustrative of the 'marketing mix'? (4)

(f) Explain how the development, sales and marketing sections of this hypothetical marketing department are interrelated. (6)

5 Read the following newspaper article and answer the questions below.

BUYING FROM YOUR OWN HOME

Television shopping is about to arrive in some European countries. For one hour, every Saturday morning, families will be able to shop from their TV screens.

Each product will have a four minute slot. During this time viewers can telephone using one of 200 lines, free of charge. They will be able to order a product over the telephone and pay by quoting their credit card number.

The 'Armchair Shopping Show' will follow the pattern of successful shopping shows running in the United States of America.

In the UK, mostly branded name products will be sold, with nothing costing below £200, and presented in an interesting and informative way. Typical items will include clothes, washing machines, cameras, and other goods.

The idea began with the Homes Shopping Network, in America, a 24 hour show. The American show started from nothing in 1986 and by 1990 had a turnover of $4 billion a year.

(a) What is meant by the following terms used in the newspaper article:
  (i) 'branded name products';   (2)
  (ii) 'turnover of $4 billion a year'.   (2)
(b) In what way is television shopping likely to be convenient for
    consumers?   (2)
(c) What marketing techniques are likely to be used by the seller?   (4)
(d) How will the producers of goods advertised on the 'Armchair Shopping
    Show' benefit?   (4)
(e) What factors will determine whether the 'Armchair Shopping Show' is
    a success or not?   (6)

Extended Answer Assignments

1 Visit two different types of local businesses, such as a food store, a clothing store or a furniture store. Compare the merchandising techniques that each use and comment whether differences that exist are related to the nature of the products or are differences in technique.

2 Choose a product or service that is of interest to you. Visit four different stores that sell the product or service. Make a comparison of the way each store markets the product or service.

3 Name a product or service that you purchased recently. Describe the marketing technique that you know helped you to make your choice of purchase.

4 Assume that a major company is planning to build a large sports complex and has asked for your help. You are required to identify different groups of people that would be likely to pay to use the complex, and indicate the features or facilities that should be included in the sports complex so that it will appeal to each of these groups of people.

5 Describe a promotional plan that could be used to market your school or college in order to make as many people as possible aware of the good features of it. How could you evaluate the effectiveness of your plan?

6 Use a particular product, such as a car, and explain why the marketing price demands observation of the product lifecycle.

7 Construct a demand curve to illustrate an analysis of the demand for a particular good or service.

9 Market research and advertising

Market research

In Chapter 8 we learnt that the marketing concept requires a firm to be aware of the customer's needs, to try and meet those needs, and to attempt to make a profit in the process. Market research assists the firm to meet the goal of the marketing concept by helping the process of finding out what the customer wants – in other words, market research has the effect of identifying the appropriate marketing strategy that will reach the target audience.

Market research investigates what consumers are buying or are likely to buy in the future. The research is normally carried out before launching the advertising campaign. Thoroughly carried out, market research can help to direct advertisers to the most economic and effective way to run their campaign. Sometimes market research is carried out after the product is already well established in order to assess and improve advertising and evaluate product performance.

The aims of market research

Market research has three broad aims:

- *to find out what the public wants* so that the business does not waste resources producing goods or services that are not required.
- *to assess likely volume of demand* to ensure that over-producing does not occur;
- *to discover what will influence consumers* – product name, style and colour of packaging, best target audience, price range, effective hidden persuaders, etc.

In order to achieve these aims the marketeer needs to be aware of the following factors that influence consumer behaviour.

- *Choice.* Where there are several competitors in the market consumers will have several alternatives to choose from. For this reason the marketeer is forced to be competitive.
- *Taste.* People differ in their preference for goods and services and, therefore, the marketeer has to identify these preferences.
- *Tradition.* In some circumstances there may be a long-standing tradition that influences consumer behaviour. For example, some products (e.g. scents) have traditionally been associated with members of only one of the sexes.
- *Income.* The amount of money a person earns clearly affects their ability to purchase. Consequently some highly priced products and services will only be purchased by the higher paid wage-earner.

- *Brand loyalty*. Marketeers often try to create loyalty for their products with consumers. The hope is that the customer will stay with their existing product because it has satisfied them for some time. Conversely, this brand loyalty also makes it difficult for the marketeer to woo the consumer away from a product that they are satisfied with.

The importance of market research

Market research provides a marketeer with information which will help with decisions about where to sell a product or service, how to sell it, which customers need the product and exactly what they want, how to price the product, how to promote the product, who the competitors are in the market place and the size of the market.

The person responsible for market research has to be able to answer a number of appropriate questions in order to come up with useful information which can aid marketing decision-making in the firm.

Those carrying out market research find out the information they need by asking a cross-section of the public (from all age groups and social backgrounds) a number of carefully designed questions. The questioning is carried out in a variety of places.

In the street, shop or home the researcher will have a set of prepared questions. The answers to many of these questions can be quickly recorded by ticks in boxes marked Yes or No. The telephone is increasingly being used for research in the home.

Questionnaires are also circulated in shops or homes. A carefully constructed questionnaire must be:

- easy to understand;
- simple to answer, perhaps by ticks;
- capable of useful analysis (frequently by computer).

Sampling

- Members of the public may be invited to try the product or compare one or more examples and make constructive observations.
- Test marketing may be carried out by selling the product in a small sample area in order to assess likely demand prior to commencing full-scale production.

9.2 Types of market research

The following are some of the market research strategies used by marketeers.

Experiments

A product may be developed and marketed in one or two limited geographical areas. During this process data would be collected, tabulated and analysed. The findings would then be used in deciding whether the *pilot* experiment suggests that it would be worthwhile embarking on large-scale production and distribution.

MARKET RESEARCH QUESTIONNAIRES

The questions used in surveys have to be carefully constructed to ensure that the data collected is of constructive use. The questions may require:

- **a direct response**
  'YES' ☐   'NO' ☐   'DON'T KNOW' ☐
  e.g. Have you ever read the magazine Which?

- **a scale of responses**
  Strongly agree ☐   Agree ☐   Disagree ☐   Strongly Disagree ☐
  e.g. Do you think smoking should be banned in public places?

- **a range of answers**
  e.g. Which of the following forms of transport have you used in the past week?

Method		How many times?
Bus	☐	☐
Rail	☐	☐
Taxi	☐	☐
Own car	☐	☐

Please indicate your hobbies, sports and interests.

Hobbies and Interests

☐ 1 Cooking   ☐ 4 Knitting   ☐ 7 Issues of Collectables/
☐ 2 Gourmet Foods ☐ 5 Photography   Special Editions etc.
☐ 3 Gardening   ☐ 6 Dressmaking   ☐ 8 Home Computing

How many magazines do you buy a month?   ☐ 9 Listening to Music
☐ 11 0   ☐ 12 1 - 3   ☐ 13 4 - 6   ☐ 14 7+   ☐ 10 Reading Books

Sports and Activities

☐ 15 Fishing   ☐ 18 Cycling   ☐ 21 Running/   ☐ 23 Snow Skiing
☐ 16 Tennis   ☐ 19 Horse Riding   Jogging   ☐ 24 Sailing
☐ 17 Squash   ☐ 20 Golf   ☐ 22 Shooting   ☐ 25 Water Skiing
        ☐ 26 Please tick if you normally include your sports and
             activities as part of your holidays.

Clothing & Fashion

☐ 27 Ladies Fashion   ☐ 29 Winter/Thermal   ☐ 30 Womens Clothes
☐ 28 Mens Fashion   Underwear   Size 16+

☐ 31 Please tick if you have ever bought anything for your Leisure via
     mail order.
☐ 32 Please tick if you were satisfied with the purchase.

What do you drink?   **Are you interested in buying?**   ☐ 5 Home Brewing Kits
☐ 1 Beer   ☐ 3 Spirits   ☐ 4 Wine by mail order   ☐ 6 Cigarettes/Cigars   ☐ 7 A Pipe
☐ 2 Wine   **Do you smoke?**
        ☐ 8 Please tick if you would like to stop smoking

A manufacturer of chocolate bars wants to produce a high energy snack bar. Draft out a questionnaire that could be used to find out what would be an appropriate target audience, and the characteristics that should be incorporated into the bar and its packaging to help it sell well.

Observations

Observation is perhaps the most widely used form of market research. The observations may be *formal* or *informal*.

Using the observation approach the researcher watches how people behave or respond to certain situations. For example, does change in packaging design have the effect of improving sales?

Guidelines to be followed during the observations would be set out by the researcher, and appropriate notes made during the period. The information collected would be passed on to the researcher's firm for analysis and decision-making.

Surveys

Sometimes we encounter market research personnel in supermarkets, our communities, in airport buildings, and other public places. These people use questionnaires, personal interviews, or telephone interviews based on carefully constructed questions to establish the views of consumers.

It is of course impossible to survey every consumer and, therefore, a sample is used. This sample has to reflect the whole population. So, the *representative sample* includes both sexes, a variety of age groups, country and town dwellers, and people that are poor as well as those who are not.

The main ways of conducting surveys are:

- *By post.* This is by far the easiest method but it has the disadvantage that many people will not bother to complete and return the questionnaires.
- *By personal interview.* This is the most common method, but it can be expensive because it is very labour-intensive.
- *By telephone.* This approach is becoming increasingly common although it sometimes has a counter-effect on consumers who are 'put off' the product because they object to being disturbed in their homes.

9.3 Market research in action

The market research team

Market research is carried out by specialists called *market researchers*. In a large organisation several such specialists will be used to form a team.

The market research team must ensure that the research is relevant to the needs of the firm as well as the needs of the consumer. Research must be accurate and timely, too, if it is to really achieve the desired result. For example, suppose an organisation that produces clothing for teenagers learns from its research findings that certain types of T-shirts will be popular among teenagers during the summer months. To meet the demands of the teenagers, the T-shirts must be produced to the required specifications in terms of style and colour, they must be produced in sufficient numbers in time for the summer, and they must be delivered to places where the buyers can gain access to purchase them.

If a business is not large enough to employ its own market researchers it can hire the services of a market research agency which is a firm that specialises in this work.

Sources of information

The sources from which a market researcher collects information can be classified as primary or secondary.

Primary data is usually drawn from original sources. In other words, none of the data has been collected previously by someone else. This type of data can be collected through experiments, observations and interviews, as described earlier.

Secondary data refers to information that is already in existence in a form different from that the researcher intends to use, but which may be useful to managers in the decision-making process. In other words, secondary data has already been gathered previously by someone else and the researcher's intention is to access the data and make use of it. A firm's files, annual reports, manuals, and brochures, among others, are rich sources of secondary data for the market research team.

Secondary data also includes items such as government statistics, reference books, newspaper articles and even the sales literature of competitors. Because the researcher does not actually have to go out into the field to collect this data first-hand it is often referred to as *desk research*.

Research procedures

The following are typical examples of procedures followed by professional researchers:

1 Identify the problem to be solved or information to be obtained.
2 Set limits to the problem. Focus on one or a few manageable things.
3 Draw on current knowledge (of the product or of the market).
4 Seek out new knowledge. (Current knowledge might be inadequate, irrelevant, or just out of date.)
5 Consider all possible solutions to the problem set (through careful examination of current and new knowledge).
6 Attempt to make suggestions for alternative solutions to the problem set.
7 Select the best solution to the problem. This should always be related to the situation or the environment of the target market.
8 Try out the identified solution, e.g. experiment with a sample/trial run.
9 Evaluate and adjust where necessary.

9.4 ▶ Functions of advertising

The main functions of advertising are as follows:

● to announce new products;
● to highlight the unique features of a product;

- to build a firm's image around its products;
- to highlight special events – concessions, sales, late openings;
- to increase market share by stimulating demand;
- to educate consumers about the products.

The purpose of advertising

It would be pointless for a business to develop a product or service if there was no way to tell consumers about it. Advertising is a means of communication – it is used to make consumers aware of the goods and services that producers and traders have to offer. An advertisement is a message that uses words, pictures or sound to:

- *inform* potential buyers of the availability of goods and services;
- *persuade* people to buy or behave in a particular way.

Informative and persuasive advertising

Informative advertising gives detailed information about the goods or services available and leaves consumers to decide, without persuasion, if they wish to purchase. An informative advertisement will contain useful details such as specification, sizes, colour and material. This type of approach can also be employed in public relations and image creation.

Persuasive advertising uses a variety of techniques to persuade people to buy a product or service, irrespective of whether they need it or not. These persuasive techniques are sometimes referred to as 'hidden persuaders'.

Examples of informative advertising.

Advertising's 'hidden persuaders'

One of the ways an advertiser may use an advertisement to promote sales is to persuade the consumer that the advertiser's product will make the consumer better off in some way. Some of the factors to which this type of advertisement appeals are far from obvious and, therefore, they are sometimes called *hidden persuaders*, for example:

- *sex appeal* – the product is claimed to make the user attractive to the opposite sex;

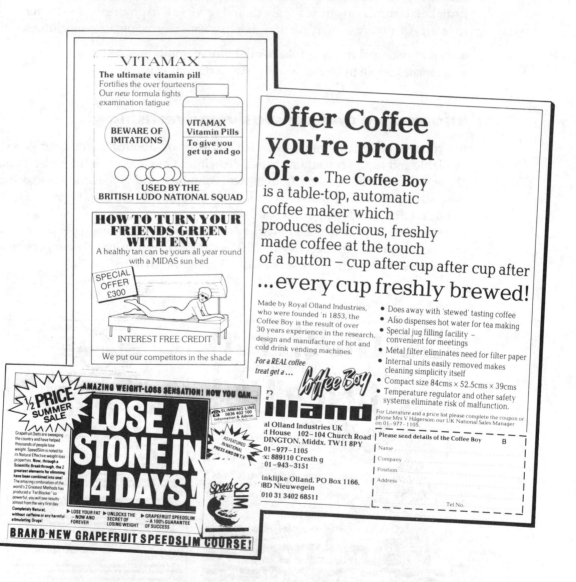

Look at these examples of persuasive advertisements. Notice how they attempt to try and convince the consumer that they are better than alternatives from other producers. Can you recognise any hidden persuaders?

- *ambition* – the advertisement implies that those who use the product will be successful;
- *personality appeal* – famous personalities are shown using the product to give it an acceptable image;
- *social acceptability* – the advertisement implies that by using the product the consumer becomes more acceptable to others;
- *work simplification* – the product is claimed to make a task easier to carry out;
- *health* – the advertisement suggests that the use of the product contributes to good health.

9.5 Forms of advertising

Advertising media

There is a wide variety of ways in which an advertisement may reach the public, but not all of the ways are suitable for every advertisement. There are many media through which advertising may take place, each of which has a varying degree of effectiveness and cost.

- *Television and radio* are very expensive but are the most effective method of reaching a large audience.
- *National press* reaches a wide area, but is expensive and, therefore, mainly used by large companies.
- *Local newspapers* offer cheaper advertising rates for cover of a limited area. 'Free' local newspapers rely on advertising to meet costs.
- *Magazines or journals* have a more limited circulation but reach a 'selected' audience, offer greater scope for colour advertisements and have a longer life than newspapers.
- *Cinemas* reach a relatively small audience but can be effective, particularly in advertising local shops etc.
- *Posters and hoardings* provide eye-catching signs, sited in public places or on public transport.
- *Point-of-sale* methods provide eye-catching shop counter or window displays to influence the consumer to buy on impulse.
- *Exhibitions* attract large numbers of people who already have at least some interest in the product. Exhibitions also enable specialists in a field to meet and compare products and experience.
- *Circulation* by leaflets (the *mail shot*) can be an effective medium but is very labour-intensive, or costly with regard to postage.
- *Word-of-mouth* (i.e. personal recommendation) is sometimes encouraged by firms carrying out a *whispering campaign* by giving away free samples which they hope the users will talk about favourably.

The marketeer has to decide which of the media is most appropriate for the product or service they are trying to sell. Often a combination of the forms of advertising described above will be incorporated into the seller's advertising campaign.

The advertising campaign

An advertising campaign is all of the processes a firm employs to sell its goods or services. The campaign will be based on a clearly defined plan, much of which will be formed as a result of the market research described earlier.

Some firms are large enough to have their own advertising department, others may decide it is preferable to employ an advertising agency to carry out an advertising campaign on their behalf. Whichever is the case, the advertiser or agency will have to take many factors into account. The following questions must certainly be answered if the campaign is to be effective.

- Which groups (the *target audience*) of the public is the campaign intended to reach?
- How much money is available to be spent on the campaign?
- How extensive is the campaign intended to be – countywide, countrywide or worldwide?
- Which techniques will catch the attention of buyers?

Some of these questions, such as the amount of money to be put into the campaign, can only be answered by the advertiser. Others can be solved through market research.

Advertising agencies

Advertising agencies are businesses which specialise in assisting others with their advertising needs: a service for which they are paid.

The extent of the work that an agency will undertake for its client will depend on how much the client wishes to spend on advertising its product. The agency may work in conjunction with the client's own advertising department, providing advice on how to conduct the campaign, or alternatively it may be employed to organise the complete advertising campaign.

It takes the work of many skilled people to formulate a single advertisement, and the formulation of a complete campaign for a large national company is a vast undertaking. An agency handling such a campaign will employ people with specialist skills associated with marketing.

Apart from market research, an advertising department or an advertising agency would be concerned with artwork and space-buying.

Artwork

This involves the formation of the pictorial display of the advertisement, and includes the creation of wording to go with the advertisement. *Brainstorming* is a typical technique employed in this regard which involves the free expression of ideas until the most suitable wording and visual display is formed.

Space-buying

This is the process of hiring the most appropriate space to display the advertisement. This must be not only the most effective but also the most economically appropriate. For example, although television is one of the most effective forms of advertising it is far too expensive for selling a few inexpensive items.

9.7 Is advertising wasteful?

There is no real answer to this question because it depends on one's personal point of view. Some people argue that advertising benefits the consumer in a variety of ways, whereas others suggest that it causes an added expense to be met by the consumer. What do you think?

Arguments for advertising

- It makes consumers aware of the range of choice available.
- It encourages healthy competition between suppliers.
- It promotes demand and makes mass production possible.
- Mass production provides employment and also keeps prices down.
- It helps to pay for sports events and concerts.
- It contributes towards the cost of newspapers and magazines.
- It brightens up town centres with colourful displays.

Criticisms of advertising

- The cost of advertising has to be incorporated into the price of goods or services.

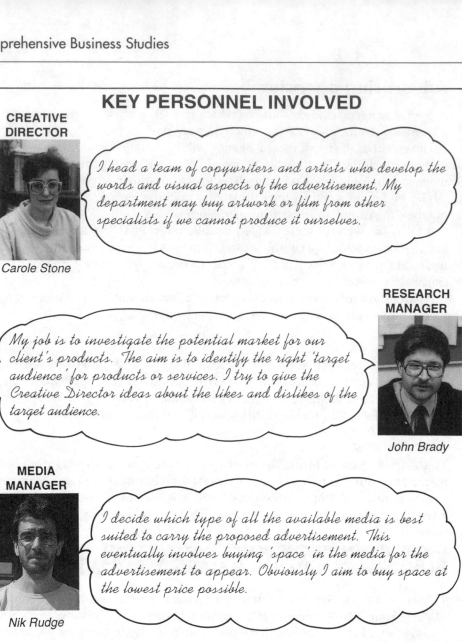

KEY PERSONNEL INVOLVED

CREATIVE DIRECTOR

I head a team of copywriters and artists who develop the words and visual aspects of the advertisement. My department may buy artwork or film from other specialists if we cannot produce it ourselves.

Carole Stone

RESEARCH MANAGER

My job is to investigate the potential market for our client's products. The aim is to identify the right 'target audience' for products or services. I try to give the Creative Director ideas about the likes and dislikes of the target audience.

John Brady

MEDIA MANAGER

I decide which type of all the available media is best suited to carry the proposed advertisement. This eventually involves buying 'space' in the media for the advertisement to appear. Obviously I aim to buy space at the lowest price possible.

Nik Rudge

ACCOUNT MANAGER

Whilst I am after the client's money, I do have a wider role. Each of our clients is referred to as an 'account'. Part of my job is to personally supervise all of the work involved in the account. I will be the main point of contact for clients.

Aileen Killick

How an agency can help in the planning of an advertising campaign.

- Most advertising aims to persuade people to buy whether they need the commodity or not.
- 'Hidden persuaders' appeal to emotions and prejudices.
- Some advertising encourages unsociable habits and behaviour.
- Some advertising misleads by making exaggerated claims.
- It encourages people to be wasteful and discard older but satisfactory products for new ones.

9.8 Consumer protection

The need for consumer protection

All firms, people, businesses and even governments are consumers, although we usually refer particularly to individuals when talking about consumers. We have seen earlier in Chapters 1 and 2 of this book that the aim of production is to make things that can be used by consumers. In fact it has been said that 'The sole end and purpose of all production is the consumer.' We have also seen in this chapter that advertising aims not only to inform us about goods and services, but also to persuade us to buy them.

With the growth of large-scale production and the increased spending power of many people, the motivation for firms to obtain and maintain a larger share of the consumer market has risen considerably. This has been further encouraged by technological changes which have not only revolutionised products and the way they are manufactured, but also the manner in which they are marketed.

At one time the attitude of the law in relation to the protection of consumers was *caveat emptor*, or 'Let the buyer beware'. In other words, consumers were expected to protect themselves. Today consumers are protected in a number of ways by legislation and government agencies, but it is still important for consumers to help protect themselves by shopping wisely.

Traders cannot deprive consumers of their rights without facing the risk of legal action. Obviously traders need to know the rights of their customers and the responsibilities that they have to treat them fairly in order to meet their own legal obligation. In addition, the trader has similar rights against his suppliers as his customers have against him, so long as he has not agreed to give up those rights.

Consumer law

The following are some of the most important British laws that aim to protect the consumer and guide the businessperson.

Food and Drugs Act 1955 (enforced by public health inspectors)
- Forbids the sale of unfit food.
- States hygienic conditions for production and sale of food products.
- Regulates labelling and description of items.
- Provides minimum standards in food composition (e.g. meat content of sausages, pies, etc.).

Weights and Measures Act 1963

- Requires quantity of pre-packed goods to be shown on the container.
- Makes short weight or false measurement an offence.
- Certain goods must be sold in 'prescribed quantities' (e.g. milk).

Resale Prices Act 1964

- Suppliers are not allowed to impose a minimum price at which their goods must be sold, but they can suggest a manufacturer's recommended price (MRP).
- Suppliers cannot refuse supplies to a retailer who sells below the recommended price.
- Books, maps and medicines are exempt from this Act.

Trade Descriptions Act 1968

This Act makes it an offence punishable by fine or imprisonment to falsely describe goods or services offered for sale. The Act applies to verbal or written descriptions.

Unsolicited Goods and Services Act 1971

This Act makes it illegal to demand payment for goods or services that have not been ordered. Should unsolicited goods be delivered the consumer has two clear courses of action:

1 They can write to the firm giving the name and address from where the goods can be collected. If the trader fails to collect the goods within thirty days they belong to the holder.
2 Alternatively, if unsolicited goods are not collected by the trader within six months, they become the property of the holder.

Fair Trading Act 1973

This Act established a permanent Office of Fair Trading which is a government body with the broad function to keep watch on trading matters in the United Kingdom and protect both consumers and business people against unfair practices.

Prices Acts 1974 and 1975

These Acts gave the government the power to:

- subsidise food;
- regulate food prices;
- require shopkeepers to display prices in a way that does not give a false impression.

Consumer Credit Act 1974

The purpose of this Act is to control all forms of credit services. It includes regulation of credit and hire agreements, licensing of lenders, advertisements, breaches of agreements, extortionate charges and credit referencing. The Act protects the consumer in the following ways:

- All businesses involved with credit or hire agreements are required to obtain a licence from the Office of Fair Trading.
- Consumers can ask a court to reduce unfair or 'extortionate' rates of interest.

- Individuals can ask to see the contents of files referring to them held by credit reference agencies which supply information about the financial standing of people. The individual can ask for wrong information to be corrected.
- All relevant information must be brought clearly to the notice of the borrower. Advertisements offering credit should not be misleading and must advise the consumer of the annual percentage rate (APR), i.e. the true annual rate of interest.
- Compensation may be claimed for goods that are faulty.

Types of credit covered by the Act are as follows:

- *personal credit agreements* – bank loans, overdrafts, personal loans, pawnbrokers, etc.;
- *credit token agreements* – credit cards, chargecards, cash dispenser cards, etc.;
- *hire purchase (HP) agreements* – contracts for the hire of goods for a fixed period of time with an option to purchase for a nominal sum at the end of the period of repayment by regular instalments;
- *credit sales agreements* – similar to HP but goods become the property of the buyer immediately the deposit or initial payment has been made;
- *consumer hire agreements* – these relate to true hire arrangements rather than sales because the items rarely become the property of the person hiring them.

Restrictive Trade Practices Act 1976

This Act aims to safeguard the consumer against the practice of agreements between companies to limit production in order to keep prices artificially high, and to exploit a monopolistic position.

Consumer Safety Act 1978

This Act regulates the sale of goods which may be potentially dangerous, for example toys, electrical goods, cooking equipment, heaters, etc.

Sale of Goods Act 1979

This Act covers all goods (including food) bought from a trader to a shop doorstep seller, and sales by mail order. The seller has three main obligations. Goods must:

1 *Be of 'merchantable quality'*. This means that goods must be reasonably fit for their normal purpose, bearing in mind the price paid, the nature of the goods and how they were described. Thus a new item must not be damaged and it must work properly.
2 *Be 'as described'*. They must correspond with the description given by the seller, or in accordance with labels on the item or the packing.
3 *Be 'fit for any particular purpose made known to the seller'*. If you ask for plates that are 'dishwasher safe' and the seller assures you that they are, he has broken his contract with you if they are not.

Note: In the case of private sales only obligation 2 applies.

Supply of Goods and Services Act 1982

This Act applies the terms of the Sale of Goods Act to goods supplied as part of a service, e.g. faulty taps provided by a plumber, and where goods are hired or exchanged instead of actually being purchased. The Act also provides that a person providing a service must do so:

- with reasonable skill and care;
- within a reasonable time;
- for a reasonable charge.

Although there is still a need for the 'buyer to beware' when making purchases, modern marketing methods and trends sometimes make it difficult for the consumer to judge fairly the quality and value of purchases. Pre-packed goods are difficult to examine before they reach home. And how can the purchaser (or even the retailer) of a complex computer or hi-fi system know if the equipment is sound?

It is for these reasons that the manufacturer as well as the retailer has responsibilities to the consumer under the Sale of Goods Act.

Consumer Protection Act 1987

This Act makes it an offence to give a misleading price indication for any goods, services, accommodation or facilities. This also applies to 'special offers' which turn out to be false.

Government agencies providing consumer protection

Department of Prices and Consumer Protection

This government department promotes legislation aimed at the protection of consumers, and administers laws related to this. The department also encourages the formation of consumer advice centres and citizens' advice bureaux.

Office of Fair Trading (OFT)

The OFT:

- publishes consumer advice information;
- encourages industries to form associations and codes of practice;
- investigates and prosecutes traders who persistently commit offences;
- checks on fitness of traders who provide credit or hire agreements;
- makes suggestions for changes in consumer law.

Ministry of Agriculture, Fisheries and Food (MAFF)

MAFF administers the law relating to milk production, fisheries, slaughterhouses and the meat trade, and the composition and labelling of food.

Department of Health

This department is concerned with the production and distribution of medicines and also hygiene.

Local Authorities

- *Trading standards (consumer protection departments* investigate local complaints about quality description, and the weights or measures of goods supplied.

- *Environmental health departments* deal with complaints related to impure food and food production or selling premises.
- *Consumer advice centres* set up by local authorities deal with consumer problems.

Independent agencies providing consumer protection

Consumers' Association

- A non-profit making association financed by members' subscriptions.
- Carries out comparative tests on goods and services.
- Publishes results in the association magazine *Which?*
- Publishes books on consumer-related matters.

Citizens' Advice Bureaux

Give confidential advice on legal and consumer matters, on a voluntary basis.

British Standards Institution (BSI)

Publishes a series of standards intended to ensure products are fit for the purpose for which they are intended.

- The *kite mark* is awarded to products meeting the required standard.
- The *safety mark* is given to products which pass BSI safety standards.

Design Council

Examines products of British manufacture and issues its own level to those which are judged to demonstrate a high standard in all aspects of design and performance.

Professional and trade associations

Many trade and professions have set up associations to formulate and administer codes of practice which include procedures for dealing with consumer complaints.

Media support for consumers

Media such as television, radio and the newspapers play a valuable part in consumer protection today by investigating complaints, comparing goods and services and evaluating and recommending 'best buys'.

When things go wrong

Of course, things go wrong, and it may not always be the fault of the seller. Before setting off to the shop to complain about faulty goods the consumer should ask three simple questions

- Was it a fault I should have noticed when buying?
- Was it something I was told about?
- Am I expecting too much from something cheap?

If the answer to all three questions is 'No', then the consumer has a reason to complain. They should take along proof of purchase (e.g. receipt), and they should remember to act in a reasonable manner because most respectable traders will want to put things right.

If they have no success at the shop the consumer can write to the organisation's head office. They should keep copies of all correspondence. Should they still not be satisfied they may well then need support from some other agency described earlier.

Make a note of it

1 In what way does market research help a firm to achieve a marketing concept?

2 What kind of decisions does a market researcher hope to be able to make from data collected?

3 Briefly describe the factors that influence consumer behaviour.

4 Where is market research carried out?

5 Describe some of the strategies used by market researchers to gather information.

6 Why is it often important that a market researcher uses a 'representative sample'?

7 Explain the difference between 'primary data' and 'secondary data'.

8 What is the aim of advertising?

9 How does 'informative' advertising differ from 'persuasive' advertising?

10 What are 'hidden persuaders'?

11 Briefly describe the various advertising media.

12 What do we mean by the term 'advertising campaign'?

13 What is the function of an advertising agency?

14 List the arguments for and against advertising.

15 Why is consumer protection so important today?

16 What does *caveat emptor* mean and why is this less relevant today?

17 List three aspects of consumer protection contained in the Food and Drugs Act.

18 In which way does the Weights and Measures Act aim to protect consumers?

19 What do the letters MRP stand for? What is the relevance of these letters to consumer law?

20 Briefly describe the purpose of the Trade Descriptions Act.

21 What are the two courses of action open to someone who has received unsolicited goods?

22 Name the important body established by the Fair Trading Act.

23 'The Consumer Credit Act is the main safeguard for those who buy on credit.' Explain this statement.

24 List and briefly describe the types of credit covered by the Consumer Credit Act.

25 Briefly explain the purpose of the two following consumer protection Acts:
   (a)   Restrictive Trade Practices Act;
   (b)   Consumer Safety Act.

26 The Sale of Goods Act states that goods must be 'of merchantable quality', 'as described', and 'fit for the purpose'. Explain these phrases.

27 Your friend has recently bought a pair of shoes that are now found to be faulty. Give three suggestions on how she should go about getting the matter put right.

28 State one function of the Office of Fair Trading.

29 Which government department is concerned with the production and distribution of medicines?

30 Briefly describe the work of three types of local authority departments which help to safeguard the interests of consumers.

31 Give a brief description of the contribution that the Consumers' Association makes to consumer protection.

32 The 'kite mark' and 'safety mark' are both symbols that the consumer should look for. Why is this so?

33 In what way do professional and trade associations contribute to consumer protection?

34 In spite of the fact that many of the media rely on advertisers for much of their income, they still try to promote consumer awareness. Give two examples of how they do this.

35 What questions should the consumer ask before they are sure they have a case for complaint?

160

Structured Questions

1 Consider the advertisement on page 160 from the Peterborough Development Corporation.

    (a) Who do you think paid for this advertisement?   (1)
    (b) Who is the target audience for this advertisement?   (2)
    (c) What is the aim of the advertisement?   (2)
    (d) The advertisement says that 'Peterborough's overheads are amongst
         the lowest in the country.' What does this mean?   (3)
    (e) In what ways do you think that this could be said to be an example of
         informative advertising?   (3)
    (f) State four claims that the advertisement makes as benefits of moving to
         Peterborough.   (4)
    (g) This advertisement was produced by an agency called Deighton and
         Mullen. Briefly describe how this type of agency assists an advertiser.   (5)

2 Lazy Bones Ltd is a manufacturer of household electrical goods. They have decided to produce a new product aimed at the busy working housewife – a remote-controlled vacuum cleaner. The head of the product development department has been instructed to produce a prototype with electronic sensors to prevent collisions with furniture, etc.

   A name for the new cleaner has yet to be decided; this will be the subject of a brainstorming session. The advertising campaign will be decided following market research and pilot marketing.

    (a) Define the term 'prototype'   (1)
    (b) What is the purpose of a prototype?   (2)

(c)   What is a 'brainstorming session'? (2)
(d)   Describe the kind of market research that would be carried out:
   (i)   before the new cleaner goes onto the market; (3)
   (ii) after the cleaner goes on sale to the public. (3)
(e)   List four contrasting questions that could be included in a market research questionnaire to help the development of an advertising campaign for this new product. (4)
(f)   If the market research clearly shows that there is a need for the planned cleaner, why will there still be a need for an advertising campaign? (5)

3 Read the following information about marketing and then answer the questions on page 163 which ask you to relate market research to this information.

WHAT IS MARKETING?

'Marketing is the management process responsible for identifying, anticipating and satisfying customer requirements profitably'

Don't think – as many people do – that marketing is just the smart 'in' word for selling. Selling is a vital, indispensable component of marketing, but only one of several other activities. Marketing thinking and planning begins at or even before, the drawing board and ends only when the company has made certain that the customer is really satisfied with the products or service provided. Because marketing affects so many of the company's resources and activities, it is essentially a team effort.

Good marketing is the end product of a well-led management team fully embracing the marketing concept. The marketing manager is responsible for the marketing plan and the basic information and guidance about prospective markets, their behaviour, size and potential for each product or service supplied by the company.

The Marketing Spectrum

▶ RESEARCH: Identifying, analysing and predicting customer needs.
▶ PLANNING & DEVELOPMENT: deciding on who, what, when and how to meet these needs via new or existing product or service development.
▶ PRICING: setting an acceptable and profitable price level.
▶ PACKAGING: matching physical requirements with visual image.
▶ PROMOTION: generating product awareness and influencing customers' purchasing decisions, e.g. advertising, public relations.
▶ SALES: choosing the most efficient and effective sales approach.
▶ DISTRIBUTION: evaluating the most efficient way of getting the product to your customer, whether directly or indirectly.
▶ AFTER SALES: providing a comprehensive customer care service.

The Marketing Spectrum comprises a number of different functions, many of which are undertaken by specialists. It is the role of the Marketing Manager to co-ordinate the efforts and advice of these people and, based on a view of the situation overall, decide on future action.

Source: *The Chartered Institute of Marketing (UK).*

(a) What does market research tell a business? (1)

(b) In what way would you say that market research helps a firm to set an 'acceptable and profitable price level'? (2)

(c) How would market research help a producer to 'match physical requirements with visual image'? (3)

(d) Describe two examples of ways that market research can help a business to choose 'the most efficient and effective sales approach'. (4)

(e) 'Marketing thinking and planning begins at or even before the drawing board. . .' How does market research contribute in this respect? (4)

(f) 'Good marketing is the end product of a well-led management team fully embracing the marketing concept.'

   (i) What do you understand by the phrase 'marketing concept' in the manner in which it is used here? (4)

   (ii) Give examples of other wording included in this information that can be directly related to the marketing concept. (2)

4 Answer the following questions about the two advertisements shown below.

(a) 'These two advertisements are aimed at different target audiences.' Explain this statement. (2)

(b) Which of the advertisements shown do you think is probably involved in marketing by mail order? Give a reason for your answer. (2)

(c) What is the significance of the MOPS sign on the bag advertisement? (2)

(d) Which of the advertisements is 'persuasive' and which is 'informative'? Give reasons. (4)

(e) Using any parts of these advertisements as examples, explain how market research could have indicated to the advertiser that it would be advantageous to word the advertisement in the manner shown. (4)

(f) In what way would you say that the Tingle After Shave advertisement uses 'hidden persuaders' to encourage the consumer to buy? (6)

Extended Answer Assignments

1 You are the advertising manager of a firm that is developing a new soft drink. Describe the way that you would formulate an advertising campaign to promote the launch of your product into a highly competitive market.

2 Advertising is wasteful of resources and causes an increase in the costs of goods. Discuss this statement.

3 Sometimes market research takes the form of 'desk research', that is finding out information about a potential market by referring to reference sources readily available to anyone. Describe the application of some specific reference sources available to market researchers.

4 Using specific examples of marketing techniques employed by companies with which you are familiar, explain why advertising is important to industry, commerce and the consumer.

5 Using a selection of advertisements to assist you, explain why you consider there is a case for consumers to have some protection against the claims of advertisers.

The home market

The chain of distribution

In Chapters 8 and 9 your attention was drawn in various places to the need to distribute goods so that they reach the intended customer. We could divide the target market into two broad categories:

- sales to local markets – *home trade;*
- sales to overseas markets – *foreign trade.*

In this chapter we will concentrate on home trade. We will turn our attention to foreign trade in Chapter 11.

The chain of distribution for home trade links the producer with the consumer through two main *intermediaries* – the *wholesaler* and the *retailer*. Both of these traders are part of *tertiary production* because they add to the value of goods.

Producer ⟶ Wholesaler ⟶ Retailer ⟶ Consumer

The wholesaler buys in very large quantities from the producer, thus helping to make mass production possible. If the retailer can order a great enough quantity they may buy direct from the producer, bypassing the wholesaler.

Spot the difference!

Wholesale trade

Producers need to sell their products in large quantities to enable them to carry out mass production and enjoy economies of scale. But many retailers cannot buy in the large quantities that the producers and manufacturers want to sell. Wholesalers bridge the gap between producers and retailers by buying in large quantities and selling in smaller, more convenient lots, to the retailer. The retailer in turn sells individual items to the consumer.

The wholesaler's premises are usually a large warehouse divided into sections dealing with specific commodities, and operating on organisational lines similar to a large supermarket.

Retailers may visit the wholesaler to choose their purchases. Alternatively, orders may be telephoned in, or passed to the wholesaler's representatives on their periodic visits to the retailers, and delivered in due course by the wholesaler's own delivery vehicles.

Part of a wholesale warehouse.

Types of wholesaler

There are two basic forms of wholesaler:

- *General* wholesalers operate from large warehouses sited for convenient access from many local towns. They will allow retailers credit and will also deliver goods to their shops.
- *Cash and carry* wholesalers do not allow credit and do not deliver goods. Retailers come to warehouses, select goods, pay for them and provide their own transport.

Sometimes wholesalers will specialise in a particular aspect of trade. For example, one might specialise in supplies in hair care products, whilst another might specialise in clothing and footwear.

10.3 Functions of wholesalers

Acting as an intermediary

The wholesaler is positioned between the producer and the retailer. For this reason he is sometimes referred to as a *middleman* or *intermediary*.

Producer ——→ Wholesaler ——→ Retailer

But there are exceptions where the producer will sell direct to the retailer, or even straight to the consumer, bypassing both the wholesaler and the retailer.

Breaking of bulk

The wholesaler will buy in large quantities from the producer and sell in smaller lots, usually to the retailer.

Taking on risks

The wholesaler will predict market trends and buy ahead of demand.

Warehousing

By storing goods the wholesaler saves space for both the producer and the retailer.

Offering credit

The wholesaler may supply goods and allow the retailer to pay at some later date (*trade credit*). This gives the retailer the opportunity to possibly sell the goods before he or she has paid for them.

 10.4 Services provided by wholesalers

For the producer

- *Reduces transport costs.*
- *Advises producer* of current market trends.
- *Finishes goods* by grading, packing and branding.
- *Makes mass production possible* by ordering in large quantities and therefore reducing production costs.

For the retailer

- *Offers choice* of products from many producers.
- *Supplies small quantities* to suit retailers' needs.
- *Locally situated* providing quick access to goods and open until late in the evening.
- *Advises* latest trends and 'best buys'.
- *Pre-packs goods* ready for the retailers' shelves (graded, labelled, priced, weighed).

PRODUCERS

RETAILERS

PRODUCERS

RETAILERS

WHOLESALER

(a) **Without wholesaler**. *We can see how the wholesaler saves in transport costs if we take a simple example of four different producers each supplying their produce to four retailers without the use of a wholesaler. Each producer would need to make four journeys to supply each retailer.*

(b) **With wholesaler**. *If we now introduce a wholesaler between the producers and the retailers each producer now only makes one journey to the wholesaler and the wholesaler makes one journey to each retailer.*

Elimination of the wholesaler

Wholesalers are sometimes referred to as 'leeches' because they increase the price of goods, *but:*

- Their functions still have to be carried out by others if they are eliminated.
- They help smaller retailers to exist and, therefore, encourage competition.
- They make mass production possible and so reduce overall costs.

However, there are many ways in which the wholesaler is being eliminated. Sometimes the producer will bypass the wholesaler and sell directly to the retailer such as in the following circumstances:

- if the retailer is part of a large multiple chain, he or she can buy in large quantities and deal direct with the producer;
- when after-sales service is particularly important, for example servicing of washing machines, televisions, cookers.

The producer sometimes omits both the wholesaler and the retailer as illustrated in the following examples:

- products made to specific requirements, for example fitted furniture;
- mail-order firms selling direct by catalogue, agents, advertisements;
- very large, expensive items such as machinery for industry are sent directly to the firm(s) which desire them.

Retail trade

The retailer is a trader who provides goods and services to the consumer. They are positioned either between the producers or manufacturers and the consumer, or between the wholesaler and the consumer. In other words, the retailer is the last link in the chain between the producer and the consumer.

The retailer buys in large quantities from the wholesaler and sells in small, convenient quantities to the consumer. If the retailer can order a great enough quantity he or she may buy direct from the producer.

The functions of retail trade

Today we live in a society in which specialisation plays a major part. Most of us concentrate on carrying out our particular specialism and rely on others to satisfy most of our needs. For each of us to be able to specialise in this way requires an intricate pattern of distribution between producers and consumers. This involves a whole range of intermediaries such as banking, insurance, transport, advertising and the many other aspects of commercial activities that are dealt with in other parts of this book. Here we shall concentrate on retail trade which is the final and important link between producers and consumers.

The retailer is the last stage in the passage of goods from the producer to the consumer. In this position the retailer performs a number of important functions:

- *Outlet.* The retailer performs a valuable service to the producer by providing him with an outlet for his products, thus saving the producer from the need to market his own goods.
- *Stocks.* The retailer holds stocks which the consumer can purchase locally in small, convenient quantities.
- *Choice.* The consumer is able to choose from the variety of products of different producers offered by the retailer.
- *Information and advice.* The retailer's expert knowledge and experience enable him to advise and inform customers on quality and suitability of products.
- *Feedback.* The retailer provides a feedback of consumer responses to wholesalers and producers. This helps the producer to become aware of what the consumer market wants, and also helps to ensure that consumers' requirements are satisfied.

10.7 Types of retail outlet

Door to door

Traders involved in this form of selling generally deal in sales of minor items of goods or services.

- *Pedlars* carry goods from door to door on foot.
- *Hawkers* use some method of transport.
- *Mobile shops* are vehicles adapted to serve as travelling shops, for example the ice cream van or soft drink seller.

Market traders

These operate from stalls in open or covered areas, sometimes in streets or areas specially kept for markets. They are often able to keep prices very low because they avoid expenses *(overheads)* such as electricity, high rent, shop fittings, etc.

Independent shops

This category of retailer is not attached to a large organisation, and for this reason they are referred to by a variety of names, including 'sole trader', 'corner shop', 'unit shop' and 'convenience shop'.

This type of shop is owned by a sole trader or small partnership and is typical of the small shop sited away from town centres. This type of retailer often specialises in offering a single commodity or service, for example the baker, butcher, confectioner, newsagent, etc. There are advantages and disadvantages to this type of retailing:

Advantages:

- gives personal attention to customers;
- saves customer from need to travel into town;
- owner has thorough knowledge of the business;
- sometimes allows customers credit.

Disadvantages:

- cannot buy in very large quantities;
- prices often higher than larger shops;
- carries a limited range of stock;
- difficulties in running shop if the owner is sick.

Small retailers such as the independent shop are facing considerable difficulties in larger towns where they have to face up to the competition of large organisations that tend to be more cost-effective.

Multiples (chain stores)

Multiples are chains of shops trading under a single name of common ownership. They are generally controlled from a central headquarters and tend to be sited in town centres and shopping precincts. Examples of multiples are, Woolworths and Tesco.

The multiple shop enjoys many advantages over smaller retailers:

- Their large size enables them to bypass wholesalers and buy in large quantities direct from the producer.
- A single national advertisement can cover all branches nationwide.
- They have the resources to rent or buy stores in prime central sites with large car parking space.
- They can afford to attract customers with *loss leaders* (goods sold at below cost price).

Supermarkets

A supermarket is a large self-service store. A self-service store is defined as a supermarket when it has more than 200 square metres of shopping area and three or more checkout points. Such stores are often organised as multiples.

These shops deal particularly in pre-packed, priced products. Loss leaders are frequently used to attract custom, and customers serve themselves. The provision of shopping trolleys reduces the customers' awareness of the weight of their purchases and encourages *impulse buying* (unplanned purchases).

Because supermarkets are often organised in multiples they usually enjoy the advantages mentioned earlier. They also benefit from economies of scale, for example being able to employ specialist staff such as butchers, bakers and fishmongers. In addition, they save in staff because the customers do much of the work by serving themselves.

Although this type of shop has many advantages over other retailers it faces some disadvantages:

- large premises in prime areas are expensive;
- pilferage (stealing) levels are high;
- customers receive little personal contact;
- shopping trolleys are stolen.

Department store

This type of shop is sometimes called a 'shop of shops' because it is divided into commodity departments. Each department is operated like a single shop responsible for its own profitability.

Department stores tend to be comfortably equipped with carpets, lifts and a restaurant. Merchandise is attractively displayed, and credit facilities (sometimes interest free) are given to suitable customers. Some have introduced their own charge cards.

Advantages:

- customers can shop in comfort;
- wide variety of goods available under one roof;
- shop assistants give personal service;
- sited in towns and convenient to transport and car parks.

Disadvantages:

- large central sites are expensive;
- cannot compete with prices of multiples;
- comfortable surroundings can be a drain on profits;
- labour-intensive compared with some retailers.

Hypermarkets

These are a very large form of supermarket with a shopping area in excess of 5 500 square metres. They offer a very wide range of goods in many specialist departments similar to the divisions in a department store, or parts of the hypermarket complex may be rented out to other approved traders.

Hypermarkets are usually one of many in a chain. They are frequently sited on the outskirts of towns where sites are cheaper. Good parking facilities are provided and some late night trading.

Mail order

Products are sold in a variety of ways through the mail order method:

Section of a mail order catalogue.

- through advertising in the press, radio or on television, inviting potential customers to buy by post;
- through direct selling with customers choosing articles from a catalogue at home;
- through part-time agents selling to friends from catalogues in return for a commission.

Advantages:

- interest-free credit often given;
- buying in comfort of home;
- goods chosen at leisure.

Disadvantages:

- prices often dearer than shops;
- difficult to assess quality from a catalogue;
- can be inconvenient to return unsuitable goods.

Vending machines (automats)

These retail outlets are open 24 hours a day and provide a wide variety of products such as hot and cold snacks, confectionery, drinks, petrol, etc. Vending machines are sited in busy public places and they sometimes suffer as a result of vandalism.

Catalogue shops

A catalogue shop (e.g. Argos) publishes a comprehensive catalogue detailing all the products they have for sale in a similar manner to a mail order catalogue. The catalogues are given away free to prospective customers.

Customers who see an item they are interested in buying visit the shop to see a sample. If they like the product the customer can then make the purchase direct.

Telephone order trading

Salespersons use the telephone to contact potential customers to try and persuade them to buy the company's products.

Sometimes the telephone canvasser will already have knowledge of the person's interest, perhaps because they have replied to an advertisement. But sometimes the canvasser will have just approached the customer by chance. The latter is sometimes referred to as *cold selling*.

10.8 ▶ Patterns in retailing

The following are just some of the many trends that are increasingly apparent in retail trade.

Shopping precincts

Sometimes called malls or shopping centres, these are shopping areas shut off from traffic, well served by public transport, road links, car parks and an information centre.

Loss leaders

This refers to popular products being sold at below market price (and sometimes below cost price) to encourage customers to enter the shop. Once in the shop it is hoped they will buy other things on impulse.

Branded goods

Producers and retail multiples use a distinctive trade or brand-name to allow easy identification of their goods. Sometimes large retailers will buy products from manufacturers and have their purchases 'branded' with their own names.

Brent Cross shopping centre.
Photo courtesy of Hammerson Group Developments

Branded goods enable consumers to identify purchases quickly.

Free gifts

Items such as tumblers, ashtrays and pens are sometimes given away free with purchases.

Credit facilities

Many retailers offer suitable customers credit facilities, sometimes without charging interest. Some of the larger retailers have introduced their own chargecards which allow customers to buy and pay later in instalments.

Company logos.

Franchise shops

A franchise agreement is made between an entrepreneur (business person) and a franchise house. The agreement allows the entrepreneur to use the name of a well-known company and the exclusive right to market their products within a specified area. This form of business is particularly evident in the fast food *(takeaway)* trade.

Logos

Many large firms now use logos (symbols) with the company title on their products to assist easy recognition.

Competitions and lotteries

Some traders give lucky numbers or competition tokens with each purchase.

Bar codes

A bar code consists of a pattern of vertical lines that a computer can 'read'. Producers and large retailers are increasingly giving each shelf item a bar code. As customers leave through the checkout area, the bar-coded items are automatically totalled by the point-of-sale terminal (POS) computer link to produce an itemised bill for the customer. The same data transfer method can also be used to automatically update stock records and to decide when the retailer needs to order more stock.

Selling on credit

Selling on credit means allowing a buyer the use of goods while paying for them later, perhaps over a period of time by regular instalments. There are a variety of forms that selling on credit may take.

Trade credit

Trade credit occurs where the seller allows the buyer to have goods and pay for them after an agreed period of time. For example, a producer or wholesaler may allow the retailer to have supplies and pay for them at the end of the month. This

ISBN 0-273-03913-X

9 780273 039136

Example of a bar code.

allows the seller the opportunity to resell the goods before he has even paid for them, thus increasing the scope of his business.

Hire purchase agreement (HP)

This is a contract for hiring goods for a fixed period with an option to purchase them for a nominal sum (e.g. £1) at the end of the period.

An initial deposit is paid, which consists of a percentage of the purchase price, and a number of equal weekly or monthly instalments are repaid over a given period. Interest is charged for the credit given.

The goods purchased do not become the property of the buyer until the last instalment has been paid. The item purchased must not be sold until the last repayment has been made because the seller or finance company remains the rightful owner until the last instalment has been paid.

The seller can repossess the item if the buyer defaults on repayments.

Credit sale agreement

This is also a deposit, instalment and interest system similar to a HP agreement, but the buyer becomes the owner of the goods immediately the agreement has been made.

In the case of a credit sale agreement, if the buyer defaults on the repayment the seller or finance company does not repossess the goods but can sue for repayment of the debt.

Note: Most retailers do not finance HP and credit sales agreements themselves but use companies that specialise in this kind of finance.

Interest-free credit

The buyer is allowed to pay for purchases by regular instalments but is not charged any interest.

Credit cards

The holder of a credit card can use it to make purchases up to a set amount without paying cash. The trader claims the money due for the purchases from the company that has issued the credit card.

The cardholder is presented with an account from the issuer of the credit card. Payment of the outstanding amount can be made at once in full, or at some later time. Interest is charged on the outstanding balance.

Charge cards

Some retailers have introduced their own form of credit card for use in their stores. These allow approved customers to make purchases and charge these to their personal account which will be repaid later. The system is frequently linked to an instalment system operated by the firm, sometimes providing interest-free credit.

10.10 Mark-up and profit margin

Both of these terms refer to ways of looking at the differences between a trader's cost price and his selling price.

- *Mark-up* refers to the percentage profit which is added to the cost price by a trader to establish his selling price. For example, if an article has a cost price of 80p and it is to be sold for £1, the mark-up is:

$$\frac{20}{80} \times 100 = 25\%$$

- *Profit margin* is the percentage of the selling price which is the seller's profit. For example, on an article with a cost price of 80p which is sold for £1, the profit margin is:

$$\frac{20}{100} \times 100 = 20\%$$

10.11 Setting up a retail business

The following factors need to be taken into account when setting up a retail business.

How will the capital required be raised?

- Savings of owners.
- Borrowing from a bank or other institution.
- Contributions from partners.
- Selling shares privately or publicly.

What type of business is to be established?

- *Sole trader* – one owner running the business with or without employees to assist.
- *Partnership* – with one or more partners which enables responsibilities to be shared, but also means ownership and profits are shared.
- *Limited company* (private or public) – shareholders providing capital in return for a share of the profits and some say in the operation of the business.

Do the owners or assistants have the necessary skills?

- A thorough knowledge of the products to be sold.
- The ability to manage a business – accounts, stock records, cash flow, profit margins, wages, advertising, taxation, etc.
- The personality and temperament necessary to deal with employees and customers.

Where will the shop be sited?
Site costs vary considerably. A central or busy site may be good for trade, but will also be expensive. The entrepreneur needs to be sure that there is sufficient demand (or not too much competition) to support the shop in a chosen position.

What safeguards have to be applied?

- *Insurance* – public liability, employers' liability, fire, theft, plate glass, vehicles, fidelity bonds, bad debts, business interruption.
- *Health and safety laws* – the need to ensure that the business has complied with legal requirements to protect health, safety and welfare of employees and customers.

Make a note of it

1 List the functions of wholesalers.

2 Why is the wholesaler sometimes referred to as an intermediary?

3 In what way can the wholesaler be said to 'break bulk'?

4 Why is trade credit useful to the retailer?

5 List the services that the wholesaler provides:

   (a) for the producer;

   (b) for the retailer.

6 How does the wholesaler reduce transport costs?

7 In what way does the wholesaler help to make mass production possible?

8 Why is the wholesaler sometimes called a 'leech'?

9 Give three reasons why wholesalers are important even if they do cause an increase in distribution costs.

10 Give an example of a product that the wholesaler might grade or pack on behalf of the retailer.

11 Describe two circumstances in which the producer might sell direct to the retailer.

12 Give three examples where the producer might bypass both the retailer and the wholesaler.

13 What are the main ways in which general wholesalers and cash and carry wholesalers differ?

14 Describe the functions of the retail trade.

15 Explain the difference between a pedlar and a hawker.

16 What are 'overheads'?

17 List the advantages and disadvantages of being a sole trader.

18 What are chain stores and how are they generally controlled?

19 Name four examples of multiples.

20 List the advantages the multiple store enjoys over smaller retailers.

21 'All supermarkets are self-service stores, but not all self-service stores are supermarkets.' Explain this statement.

22 Give three examples of the economies of scale gained by operating as a multiple shop.

23 What are the main disadvantages faced by supermarkets?

24 Why is a department store sometimes called a 'shop of shops'?

25 List the advantages and disadvantages of department stores.

26 What is a hypermarket?

27 List three methods of mail order selling.

28 What are the advantages and disadvantages of buying by mail order from the point of view of the customer?

29 Make a list of ten items you can think of that are sold through vending machines.

30 What is a catalogue shop?

31 Describe telephone order selling.

32 Briefly describe the features of a shopping precinct.

33 What are 'branded' goods?

34 Describe two techniques used by shops to encourage people to enter their premises.

35 What are franchise shops?

36 How does trade credit benefit the retailer?

37 Explain a hire purchase agreement.

38 What is the advantage to a customer of buying on interest-free credit?

39 Briefly describe the use of the credit card system in retail trade.

40 Give three examples of credit cards.

41 Explain the terms 'mark-up' and 'profit margin'.

42 Describe three factors it is necessary to take into account when setting up a retail business.

43 Why is the siting of a shop very important?

44 Describe two legal requirements that need to be observed by the shop owner.

Structured Questions

1 Look at the diagram below and answer the following questions.

(a) What is the name given to the series of lines that many shop products have on their labels? (1)

(b) Where would a point-of-sale terminal be found in a shop and why would it be placed in this position? (2)

(c) How does the use of point-of-sale terminals help to reduce queues in supermarkets? (3)

(d) How do computers help to reduce staffing levels in the retail trade? (3)

(e) In spite of their many advantages some shoppers are not happy about the introduction of point-of-sale terminals. Why do you think that is the case? (3)

How a point-of-sale terminal improves supermarket efficiency. The illustration above shows a bar code reader being used. State one other method of reading a bar code.

(f) Explain how point-of-sale terminals help shops to improve their efficiency. (4)

(g) Although computerised stock records are automatically updated, periodic manual stocktaking is also necessary. Explain why manual stocktaking has to be undertaken occasionally. (4)

2 (a) What is the name given to the computer terminal at the checkout point of a supermarket. (1)

(b) What advantages does an itemised receipt have over conventional supermarket receipts? (1)

(c) What is the purpose of a bar code? (2)

(d) Why does a computerised checkout system result in fewer mistakes? (2)

(e) Write out the following list in the correct order of sequence of supermarket operations:
  - stock record updated
  - itemised receipt produced
  - bar code read by reader device
  - products taken off shelf by customer. (2)

(f) The above illustration shows a bar code reader being used to read a bar code. State one other method of reading a bar code. (2)

(g) Although point-of-sale terminals increase the efficiency of shops many do not have this facility. Give two possible reasons why some shops do not have them. (2)

(h) Briefly describe two jobs that supermarket personnel do not have to do if computers are used in the store. (4)

(i) Details of purchases can be input to the computer by keyboard or a bar code reader. Briefly compare the two methods. (4)

3 Read the article on page 184 and answer the questions which follow.

(a) Name the site of Argyll's latest distribution centre. (1)

(b) Draw a flow diagram to show the chain of distribution used by Presto's to get most of their grocery stock. (2)

(c) What are 'short life' products? Give examples. (2)

(d) What effect will the new distribution centres have on employment in the distribution sector of the economy in general? (3)

(e) Explain the advantages that having its own distribution centre has for:
  - Presto's
  - Presto's customers. (6)

(f) In the light of this type of distribution expansion what is the prospect of independent grocery retailers surviving? (6)

4 (a) What is 'interest-free credit' and why do some retailers offer this facility? (3)

(b) State three essential features of a hire purchase agreement. (3)

(c) Give examples of types of goods which are (i) often and (ii) rarely purchased from a retailer on long-term credit and say why this is so. (6)

GIANT DEPOT NO 3 MAKES ITS DEBUT

JUST after *Argyll Express* went to press this month, Argyll's third new distribution centre opened, at Welwyn Garden City, Herts. Last year, depots at Bristol and Wakefield were completed and the new chain of three giant purpose-built distribution centres now forms a vital link with Argyll's existing centres at Felling, Abbotsinch and Portrack. The total depot network offers 1½ million square feet.

By March 1987, the new national network will be supplying 60 per cent of all Presto's grocery stock. The aim, by March, 1988, is to supply more than 70 per cent; eventually, 100 per cent of groceries, together with short-life products, will be delivered to the door by the company's own ordering and supply service.

The key advantage of an Argyll own-distribution system is control – over what needs to be delivered and when – to keep all the supermarkets well-stocked every day of the trading week.

Presto has had numerous food manufacturers supplying direct to its stores, a confusing and often 'clogged' system. Says Laurence Christensen, distribution director:

"Presto stores' hectic 300 deliveries a week should fall to around 25."

Double

While delivery numbers plummet, jobs opportunities rise. With between 300 and 400 new vacancies created in the three new centres, the employee figure for the whole division will double. Argyll has given backing of £21 million to distribution development, a hefty and determined commitment.

Wakefield, Bristol, Welwyn and a dedicated third party depot at Bathgate, due to come on-stream next January, will together provide 842,000 sq ft of space. Wakefield centre, which opened in July last year, houses 4,000 different product lines and can deliver a phenomenal 300,000 cases of goods every week. That's typical of the performance the company can expect from its modern, computerised network.

The system is already proving its worth. It is reliable and efficient, easing the pressures on store staff and pleasing customers, who will always return to shop again in a well-stocked and well-run store.

Source: *Argyll Express*, 1987.

(d) Explain how a credit sale agreement differs from a hire purchase agreement. Which do you feel is more beneficial for a retailer to offer their customers? (8)

5 Rudge Wholesale Foods Ltd supplies a range of groceries to retailers over a 25 mile radius of their warehouse. Today their sales representative has been given the list on page 185 of 'special offers' for this week.

(a) Who pays the cost of delivering items ordered from Rudge Wholesale Foods Ltd? (1)

(b) What sort of service might a sales representative offer a customer other than selling them goods? (2)

(c) Why are several items (e.g. mixed vegetables) listed more than once and at varying prices? (2)

Rudge Wholesale Foods Ltd		Price list (canned products)		
		Price per case		
Description	*Item No*	*1–50 Cases*	*51–100 Cases*	*101+ Cases*
Carrots	18004	£5.00	£4.50	*£4.00*
Carrots	18017	£10.00	£9.50	*£8.00*
Peas	18107	£5.50	£5.00	*£4.50*
Peas	18108	£11.00	£10.00	*£9.00*
Baked Beans	18300	£4.80	£4.30	*£3.80*
Baked Beans	18302	£9.60	£8.60	*£7.60*
Mixed Vegetables	18614	£3.60	£3.20	*£2.70*
Mixed Vegetables	18615	£3.80	£3.40	*£3.00*
Mixed Vegetables	18616	£7.60	£6.80	*£6.00*
Raspberries	18701	£12.00	£11.00	*£10.00*
Sliced Peaches	18902	£11.00	£10.00	*£9.00*
Peach Halves	19001	£10.00	£9.00	*£8.00*

Trade Discount 25%   Terms: 5% 7 days

Carriage paid   2½% 28 days

Special offer – one week only

(d) Explain the meaning of 'Trade Discount 25%'.   (3)

(e) What is trade credit and how is it indicated on the price list?   (4)

(f) How much would a retailer pay for the following order, assuming that they pay for the goods immediately they are delivered? Show all calculations.

    59 cases peach halves

    12 cases raspberries

    15 cases sliced peaches   (8)

6 (a) Why does a small retailer tend to deal with a wholesaler instead of dealing direct with producers?   (2)

(b) Give two examples of items that a consumer might buy direct from a producer.   (2)

(c) State ways in which a wholesaler might contact potential customers.   (4)

(d) Give a brief comparison of the methods of the wholesaler and retailer in the purchase and selling of goods.   (4)

(e) Explain the difference between the following types of wholesaler: general, cash and carry.   (8)

7 The following questions are all related to the things that an entrepreneur would need to take into account when setting up a retail business.

(a) What is a retail business?   (1)

(b) What is an entrepreneur?   (1)

(c) Name the type of business organisation that would be appropriate for two people setting up a small corner shop.   (1)

(d) State two possible ways that the necessary capital could be raised.   (2)

(e) Give three examples of the knowledge or skills the owner or manager of a shop must have. (3)

(f) What considerations would be taken into account when choosing a site for a shop? (6)

(g) Describe three safeguards that the owners of a shop must observe in the interests of the staff and customers. (6)

Extended Answer Assignments

1 Discuss the view that wholesalers should be eliminated because they cause an increase in the cost of goods.

2 Take any local retail business with which you are familiar and explain the sort of factors that the owner would have needed to take into account in setting it up.

3 To what extent would you say that there is genuine competition between retail outlets in your town?

4 Make a survey of the types of retail outlet in your town. Show the results of your survey in a colour-coded box diagram. What observations can you make about your findings?

5 Conduct a survey of local high street consumers that clearly identifies which retail outlets are visited most frequently. What reasons can you suggest for your findings?

6 To what extent have small retailers been affected by larger organisations in your locality? Provide evidence to support your views.

The international market

The importance of international trade

The reasons countries trade

The overseas market is important to businesses and to countries as a whole. It is important to businesses because it provides potential additional income from the sale of goods and services. It is important to countries because it is by selling overseas that the home country can earn money to buy things from other countries. By doing this the quality of life of all the countries involved can be improved.

Because the trading referred to here takes place in an overseas market it is often called 'foreign trade'. Foreign trade is the buying and selling of goods and services between different countries of the world.

- *Imports* are bought from other countries and result in an outflow of funds.
- *Exports* are sold to other countries and result in an inflow of funds.
- *Visible trade* refers to the import and export of goods (e.g. food, machinery, vehicles).
- *Invisible trade* is the importing and exporting of services (e.g. tourism, transport, insurance and banking).

Countries are in many ways like a big family or a household. Both have to earn money to spend on things they need (e.g. food, shelter, clothing) and things they want (luxuries). Countries earn money by selling their products and services overseas (exporting) and they spend their money buying from other countries (importing). The result of this can be a better way of life for the population.

If people in a household – or countries – earn more than they spend, they can build up a surplus, become wealthy, and generally have a better standard of living. If people or countries spend more than they earn, they get into debt, and generally this leads to a poorer standard of living.

Differences between countries in the form of climate or natural resources mean that they have to trade in order to obtain goods which they cannot produce themselves, or do not find it economic to produce. One country may have natural deposits of oil or gas while another may have metal deposits not found in many other countries. By each country concentrating on the production of those goods for which it has a comparative advantage, greater output is achieved more cheaply, which is in the best interests of all people. This is an extension of specialisation or division of labour that economists refer to as following the *principle of comparative costs*.

The principle of comparative cost advantage, simply put, states that when a country is able to produce a variety of products, it will concentrate on those for which the

Table 1

	Costs per unit	
	Computers	Sugar
Country A	600	80
Country B	500	100

Table 2

	Costs per unit	
	Computers	Sugar
Country A	600	200
Country B	500	100

In what ways does Britain's trade with other countries contribute to the food we eat?

The principle of comparative costs.

comparative costs of production are lowest. Take Table 1 above as an example:

The table uses a hypothetical situation in which the two countries involved trade only in two goods, computers and sugar. Country A is more efficient at producing sugar than Country B, because it can produce it more cheaply. Country A is therefore said to have an absolute advantage in sugar; similarly Country B has an absolute advantage in computers. If the two countries trade freely with each other, Country A will specialise in the production of sugar and export it, while Country B will specialise in the production and export of computers. This is to the mutual advantage of both countries.

It can also be mutually advantageous to trade even if a country does not have an absolute advantage in any commodity. Table 2 above helps to clarify this:

In this second table it can been seen that Country B has an absolute advantage in the production of both computers and sugar. However, Country B has a comparative advantage only in the production of sugar: a unit of sugar in Country B costs one fifth of a computer, so sugar is relatively cheaper in Country B. Country A, on the other hand, has a comparative advantage in the production of computers.

From this it can be seen that it is to the mutual advantage of countries to specialise in producing and exporting commodities for which they have a comparative advantage and to import commodities from other countries where production is comparatively cheaper.

Sometimes the comparative advantage one country has over another is not the result of natural resources but is one that has been developed. For example, a country may have developed the expertise to produce a particular commodity that other countries require, for example micro-electronic components. Countries will participate in international trade in order to obtain the specialisms of others, and so gain access to a wider variety of goods. Thus by participating in foreign trade each country enhances the way of life of its people.

The UK needs to import because:

- We are not self-sufficient in foods.

- We do not have a climate suitable for producing all our needs.
- We need raw materials, some of which are only found overseas.
- We enjoy the benefits to be gained from international specialisation.

The UK needs to export (mainly manufactured goods) in order to obtain the foreign currencies required to pay for imports, and also to satisfy our desire for foreign produce. Imagine how boring our diet would be without tea, coffee, oranges and the many other products the UK buys from other countries.

Balance of trade

In the same way that every family has to budget to ensure it spends only what it can afford, so every country must also keep its spending within the limits of its income.

The family may keep a record of its income and expenditure, and countries will also record the difference in value between its imports and exports. The difference between the value of goods a country imports and exports is recorded in the *balance of trade*. Because goods can be seen they are collectively called 'visibles'.

When exports exceed imports the balance is said to be *favourable* because a *surplus* has been created which has resulted in a net flow of funds into the country.

When imports exceed exports the balance, or *trade gap*, is said to be *adverse* (unfavourable). A *deficit* (loss) has been created which has resulted in a net outflow of funds. The UK frequently has an adverse balance of trade.

Balance of trade figures (£ million)

1	Visible exports	+ 48 440	
	Visible imports	− 47 322	
	Balance of trade	+ 1 118	surplus
2	Visible exports	+ 47 322	
	Visible imports	− 48 440	
	Balance of trade	− 1 118	deficit

Balance of payments

In our trade with other countries the UK buys and sells a number of services. Because these services cannot be seen in the same way as goods they are collectively called *invisibles*. More than one-third of the money the UK earns abroad comes from 'invisible' trade, and this is frequently sufficient to make up for the balance-of-trade deficit mentioned in the previous section.

The balance of payments is a statement of the difference in total value of all payments made to other countries and the total payment received from them. This balance includes both visible and invisible trade, and it shows whether the country is making a profit or a loss in its dealings with other countries.

- A *favourable* balance of payments is when there is net inflow of capital. The country has earned more than it has spent.

- An *adverse* balance is when there is a net currency outflow. The country has spent more than it has earned.

The balance of payments comprises the current account and the capital account. The *current account* records trade in goods and services. The *capital account* records flows for investment and savings purposes.

Balance of payments figures (£ million)

1	Visible exports	+ 48 440		
	Visible imports	− 47 322		
	Balance of trade		+ 1 118	surplus
	Invisible exports	+ 25 650		
	Invisible imports	− 23 120		
			+ 2 530	surplus
	Balance of payments on current account		+ 3 648	surplus
2	Visible exports	+ 47 322		
	Visible imports	− 48 440		
	Balance of trade		− 1 118	deficit
	Invisible exports	+ 25 650		
	Invisible imports	− 23 120		
			+ 2 530	surplus
	Balance of payments on current account		+ 1 412	surplus
3	Visible exports	+ 48 440		
	Visible imports	− 47 322		
	Balance of trade		+ 1 118	surplus
	Invisible exports	+ 23 120		
	Invisible imports	− 25 650		
			− 2 530	deficit
	Balance of payments on current account		− 1 412	deficit

Correcting a balance-of-trade deficit

A recurring balance-of-payments deficit situation is worrying for any country because it means that there is a sustained outflow of funds – the country is spending more than it earns.

A current account deficit can only be tolerated in the short term. A persistent current account deficit must be dealt with eventually because other countries will not tolerate continually having effectively to lend to the deficit country.

The following are *temporary measures* that a country can take to correct an adverse balance-of-payments problem, but these are not satisfactory in the long term because often they only delay tackling a more deep-seated problem:

- borrowing from the International Monetary Fund (IMF);
- obtaining loans from abroad;
- drawing on gold and currency reserves;
- selling off foreign assets.

The best way to solve a deficit problem is to increase exports. Governments can help to achieve this by offering incentives to firms involved in exporting goods. These incentives may take the form of tax relief and extended or special credit facilities, or *subsidies* on home-produced goods to make them cheaper.

There are a variety of other strategies that a country may use in an attempt to combat a persistent balance-of-payments deficit. These include devaluation, deflation, exchange control and import control.

Devaluation

Devaluation means lowering the value of a currency in relation to other currencies. This makes imported goods more expensive and exports cheaper. For example, if Britain's currency is devalued by 10 per cent overseas buyers will now only have to pay 90 pence for items that previously cost them £1. Conversely, you will have to pay £1.10 for imported goods which prior to devaluation cost £1.

Deflation

If people's income, or its spending power, is reduced this can lead to a reduction in imports because people will buy fewer goods, including imports. Deflation can be achieved by wage rise controls, restricting credit and hire purchase, increasing interest rates, and increasing taxes.

Exchange control

The central bank may take direct action to reduce outward flows of currency by placing limits on the amounts of foreign currency that can be bought. By refusing requests for foreign currency the central bank reduces the supply of domestic currency on the market, thus raising the price of the currency.

Import control

The two main methods of restricting imports are by the use of tariffs and quotas. A *tariff* is a duty or tax imposed on imports to increase their cost and discourage purchase. A *quota* is a numerical limit put on the numbers of a commodity which can be imported. Both of these methods are dealt with later in this chapter.

Methods of selling abroad

11.4

The channels for selling abroad can be grouped into two broad categories: (a) selling from the UK, and (b) selling from an overseas base.

Selling from the UK

There are several ways in which an exporter can sell abroad without going overseas. Advertising in foreign journals or circulating catalogues, brochures and other sales literature can be effective, although some items are not easy to describe and more direct contact is necessary. This can be achieved through contact with the agents of overseas buyers visiting the UK.

Where a firm is not large enough to operate its own export department it may use an *export house* which is a firm that specialises in securing orders from abroad. The export house may act as a merchant or an agent:

- *Merchant* – the export house actually buys the goods from the producer and then markets the goods overseas, accepting the risk of loss.
- *Agent* – the export house may market the goods on behalf of the seller from whom it receives a commission.

Selling from an overseas base

The firm may send its own representatives overseas to make direct contact with potential customers. Alternatively, the exporter might employ an agent already based overseas and willing to seek contracts for sales in return for a commission.

Whichever of the foregoing approaches is employed, the representative or agent will be helped by trade fairs and exhibitions which provide a useful meeting place for buyers and sellers involved in international trade.

11.5 Difficulties faced by exporters

We have already recognised that it is important for a country to export in order to pay for its imports, but companies that engage in foreign trade face a number of difficulties. Some of these are also experienced in home trade, others are particularly evident in overseas trade. The main problems can be summarised as follows:

- *Language* – the exporter needs to be conversant with the language of the country to which he intends to export.
- *Differences in measurements*, weights and sizes also have to be taken into account by the exporter.
- *Suitability* of products, regulations, safety standards, etc., may differ in some foreign countries.
- *Import regulations* – the exporter must observe and be familiar with the import regulations of other countries.
- *Damage* to goods during their long journey to the customer.
- *Packaging* may need to be stronger than that used for home trade.
- *Transport* will be more difficult to organise than for home trade and the method chosen must be efficient and economic.
- *Documentation* and payment arrangements can be complicated in overseas trading.
- *Agent* – it may be necessary to find a suitable agent to act on behalf of the exporter to make contracts for the sale of goods.
- *Payment defaults* by overseas customers are more difficult to sort out than those in home trade.
- *Exchange rate* fluctuations can adversely affect the market price of exports.
  (a) A *rise* in the value of the pound results in a fall in the cost of imports, and a rise in the price of exports.
  (b) A *fall* in the value of the pound results in a fall in the cost of exports and a rise in the price of imports.

Aids to exporters

Department of Trade

This is a branch of the Department of Trade and Industry. It operates a number of divisions and sub-departments and publishes journals aimed at information, helping and encouraging exporters. Help given includes:

- assessment of potential overseas markets for products;
- provision of details of current import regulations abroad (e.g. tariffs and quotas, etc.);
- advice on financial standing of potential overseas customers;
- introductions to prospective customers;
- issue of UK export licences when necessary;
- organisation of and/or assistance with international trade exhibitions or fairs;
- ECGD (*see* below).

Export Credits Guarantee Department (ECGD)

This part of the Department of Trade plays an important part in helping exporters by providing the following on a non-profit basis:

1 *Insurance* against non-payment of debts by foreign importers due to:
   (a) importer being unable to pay
   (b) export restrictions by UK government
   (c) political restraints (e.g. war or diplomatic relations) on payment.
2 *Grants* or low-interest loans to assist exporters in meeting initial expense of exporting.

Consular officials

UK government officials who are based overseas collect information useful to exporters, and give local help to traders while they are abroad. Foreign officials based in the UK are also a source of advice and information.

Banks

The banks provide help for exporters with:

- short and long-term loans;
- financial advice;
- arranging documentary credit.

Free trade restrictions

If every country specialised in the things it does best, and then its products were freely traded anywhere in the world, all countries would gain maximum benefit.

In fact, free trade between countries is difficult to organise. Countries sometimes use a variety of techniques in order to restrict free trade between countries. The following are the methods most frequently used.

Subsidies

A government may give finance towards the cost of the home-produced product to enable it to be sold at a lower price abroad.

Tariffs

These are a tax or custom duty imposed on imported goods to raise the price of foreign goods to the home consumer and thus protect the home market. There are two methods of imposing tariffs, which are collected by HM Customs and Excise Department:

- *Specific duties* are a set price for each item imported.
- *Ad valorem duties* are calculated as a percentage of the value of the imports.

Note: The importer can place goods in a *bonded warehouse* under Customs supervision until they are able to pay the duty due, or until the goods are re-exported.

Quotas

A quota is a limit on the quantity of a product allowed to enter the country during a year. An import licence must be obtained before goods subject to quota restrictions can be imported.

Exchange controls

Sometimes a country will restrict the availability of foreign currency to importers, thus restricting their ability to pay for imports.

Embargo

This is a straightforward government ban on trading between one country and another.

11.8 Reasons for trade restrictions

There are four main reasons why a country may decide to impose trade restrictions.

(a) *To protect home producers.* Infant (newly formed) industries may need protection until they have become sufficiently established to be able to compete fairly. Other industries may require protection because they are important to future national security.

(b) *To resist 'dumping'*. 'Dumping' means selling goods at a loss abroad. Some countries will dump goods abroad either to reduce supplies at home or to increase their share of the market overseas. This kind of action can be very damaging to some industries in the country where the goods are being dumped.

(c) *To safeguard jobs*. Even when goods are brought into a country fairly and competitively it may threaten a particular industry. Under such circumstances the importing country may feel it necessary to introduce trade restrictions.

(d) *To correct a balance-of-payments deficit*. A continuous balance-of-payments deficit cannot be ignored. One way in which a deficit can be rectified is by reducing imports by imposition of import control.

11.9　Free trade

Free trade exists when no tariffs, quotas or other restrictions to trade exist between countries. Free trade is important because it encourages countries to specialise in producing the goods and services they are best at supplying, and where they have a 'comparative advantage'. Specialisation between countries, each exporting the goods and services in which it has a comparative advantage, raises the standard of living in every country. The result of this is that all countries simultaneously benefit.

There have been varied attempts by some groups of countries to reduce restrictions to free trade. The following describe some of these.

General Agreement on Tariffs and Trade (GATT)

GATT became operational in 1948 and it seeks to encourage the reduction of trade barriers between countries and to promote free trade. Countries which are members (including the UK) meet in Geneva to try and reach agreements leading to a reduction of trade barriers. Customs unions have been set up by members, aimed at removing tariffs between members. The European Free Trade Association and the European Economic Community are examples of customs unions.

Member countries of the EC impose common low trade barriers to member countries and higher barriers to non-members. Most of the internal barriers were supposed to have been removed by 1 January 1993.

THE EUROPEAN COMMUNITY

Total population – 341.7 million
Total Gross Domestic Product – £3067bn
Total Exports from Community – £688602m
Total Imports to Community – £681795m

FRANCE
Population – 55.9 million
Gross Domestic Product – £594bn
Exports
  (inside EEC) £71400m
  (outside EEC) £47600m
Imports
  (inside EEC) £69440m
  (outside EEC) £42560m

UNITED KINGDOM
Population – 57.1 million
Gross Domestic Product – £464bn
Exports
  (inside EEC) £47500m
  (outside EEC) £47500m
Imports
  (inside EEC) £63440m
  (outside EEC) £58560m

ITALY
Population – 57.5 million
Gross Domestic Product – £444bn
Exports
  (inside EEC) £38324m
  (outside EEC) £28911m
Imports
  (inside EEC) £41351m
  (outside EEC) £31195m

GERMANY
Population – 77.9 million
Gross Domestic Product – £960bn
Exports
  (inside EEC) £118360m
  (outside EEC) £96440m
Imports
  (inside EEC) £88400m
  (outside EEC) £81600m

NETHERLANDS
Population – 14.8 million
Gross Domestic Product – £161bn
Exports
  (inside EEC) £53036m
  (outside EEC) £17679m
Imports
  (inside EEC) £44339m
  (outside EEC) £23875m

IRELAND
Population – 3.5 million
Gross Domestic Product – £20bn
Exports
  (inside EEC) £8457m
  (outside EEC) £2971m
Imports
  (inside EEC) £6286m
  (outside EEC) £3400m

BELGIUM
Population – 9.9 million
Gross Domestic Product – £105bn
Exports
  (inside EEC) £50487m
  (outside EEC) £11083m
Imports
  (inside EEC) £44946m
  (outside EEC) £16624m

SPAIN
Population – 39.1 million
Gross Domestic Product – £197bn
Exports
  (inside EEC) £14610m
  (outside EEC) £7526m
Imports
  (inside EEC) £18933m
  (outside EEC) £14283m

GREECE
Population – 10.0 million
Gross Domestic Product – £21bn
Exports
  (inside EEC) £1546m
  (outside EEC) £870m
Imports
  (inside EEC) £3393m
  (outside EEC) £2080m

LUXEMBOURG
Population – 0.4 million
Gross Domestic Product – £5bn
Exports and Imports included with Belgian figures

PORTUGAL
Population – 10.4 million
Gross Domestic Product – £23bn
Exports
  (inside EEC) £4479m
  (outside EEC) £1742m
Imports
  (inside EEC) £6479m
  (outside EEC) £3338m

DENMARK
Population – 5.2 million
Gross Domestic Product – £73bn
Exports
  (inside EEC) £8860m
  (outside EEC) £9221m
Imports
  (inside EEC) £8809m
  (outside EEC) £8464m

The EC gives member countries privileged access to a very large market.

Aerial view of the Commission building in Brussels.

The electorate of the EC member countries elect European MEPs to serve in the European Parliament. The functions of the European Parliament are:
(a) to advise the Council of Ministers on Commission proposals;
(b) with the Council of Ministers, to determine the Budget for the Community;
(c) to exert some political control over the Council and the Commission.

The European Court of Justice hears cases involving Community laws from all member countries. For example, firms can be prosecuted in the European Court for operating restrictive trade practices. The Court is made up of judges from each Community country.

European Free Trade Association (EFTA)

EFTA was formed in 1957. Common tariffs are charged between member countries, but members are allowed to impose whatever restrictions they wish on non-members. *Members* are Austria, Iceland, Norway, Finland, Sweden, Liechtenstein and Switzerland. Britain was at one time a member of EFTA but left to become a member of the EEC (European Economic Community) in 1973. Denmark and Portugal were also EFTA founder members who subsequently left to join the EC.

European Community (EC – 'Common Market')

The EC (originally the EEC) was formed by the Treaty of Rome in 1957, by six countries: France, Luxembourg, Belgium, the Netherlands, Italy and West Germany. Later, Denmark, Ireland, Greece and the United Kingdom became members. More recently Portugal and Spain have joined to bring membership to twelve countries.

Aims of the EC
- To raise the living standards of people in member countries.
- To promote freedom of movement of labour, capital and services between member countries.
- To encourage close co-operation between members in matters of commerce, farming, finance, social services and legal systems.

● Reduction of trade restrictions between members, and establishment of a common tariff policy to non-members.

Organisation of the EC

(a) *The Commission* – the European civil service. Headquarters in Brussels (Belgium). Members appointed by governments of member countries to carry out daily administrative tasks.

(b) *European Parliament* – meets in Strasbourg (France) six times a year. Each member country has seats in proportion to its population size. Representatives are directly elected by the electorates of member states.

(c) *Council of Ministers* – the ultimate decision-making body. It consists of one minister from each country. Meets periodically. Depending on the issue under discussion in the Council of Ministers, a proposal may be adopted by a majority vote, a qualified vote, or by unanimity.

(d) *European Court of Justice* – safeguards the principles and laws of the community. Considers complaints and cases from member countries, private and public industries and individuals.

Make a note of it

1 Define the terms 'imports' and 'exports'.

2 Explain the term 'principle of comparative costs'.

3 Give one result of following the above principle.

4 Give two examples why international trade is important to all countries.

5 Why does Britain in particular need to import?

6 Define 'balance of trade'.

7 What are 'visibles'? Give three examples.

8 Explain each of the following terms:
   (a) trade gap
   (b) surplus
   (c) deficit.

9 What are 'invisibles'? Give three examples.

10 Explain the following statement. 'Balance of trade is related to visible trade, but balance of payments includes both visible and invisible trade.'

11 Why is it important to have a favourable balance of payments?

12 Briefly describe ways in which an exporter can sell abroad without going overseas.

13 Explain the difference between the work of merchants and agents.

14 List eight problems, other than fluctuation in exchange rates, that are faced by exporters. Describe four of these problems in detail.

15 Clearly explain how fluctuation in exchange rates can affect the price of both imports and exports.

16 List the aid given by the Department of Trade to exporters.

17 How does the ECGD help exporters?

18 List the main ways in which banks assist exporters.

19 What are tariffs? Describe the two ways that tariffs are collected.

20 What is the function of a bonded warehouse?

21 What is a quota?

22 Why might a government subsidise home produced goods?

23 What is an embargo?

24 Describe the four main reasons countries impose trade restrictions.

25 What is the main aim of GATT?

26 Name the countries which are members of EFTA.

27 State one way in which EFTA differs from the EC.

28 List the member countries of the EC.

29 What are the aims of the EC?

30 Briefly describe the ways in which the UK and other countries have a say in the operation of the EC.

Structured Questions

1 Study the following data and answer the questions on page 201 related to it:

THE BENEFITS OF FOREIGN TRADE

All countries gain advantages from trade with other countries. These advantages benefit both industry and consumers.

Businesses can benefit from the opportunities they gain for increased specialisation and greater economies of scale. Another advantage of foreign trade is that the increased competition that comes from abroad encourages home-based producers to become more efficient.

However, a major benefit for consumers is that they are able to choose from a wider range of goods and services.

(a) Give two examples of specialisation that are in evidence in international trade. (2)

(b) In what way can international trade provide opportunities for greater economies of scale? (2)

(c) How does competition from abroad encourage home-based producers to become more efficient? (3)

(d) List three items which consumers in your country could not buy without foreign trade. (3)

(e) Why is it more difficult for businesses to trade overseas than at home? (4)

(f) Suggest three ways that your country could encourage more overseas tourists to visit it. (6)

2 Refer to the following data and the information in Chapter 12 related to bills of exchange and answer the questions that follow.

> Daly Designs have received an order for £500 000 of the products that they manufacture. The order has come from the Koh Trading Company in India, whom Daly Designs have never traded with before.
>
> Daly Designs estimate that they will make £200 000 profit on the deal. It will take them four months to produce and deliver the goods, and they will give their usual '28 days to pay terms'. Consequently, Daly Designs cannot hope to obtain the £500 000 payment in less than five months from the receipt of the order. They cannot afford to operate on this basis.

(a) Clearly identify the buyer and the seller involved in the case referred to here. (1)

(b) How much are Daly Designs expecting that it is going to cost them to produce and deliver the order referred to here? (1)

(c) Briefly describe two difficulties Daly Designs face in trading with a firm in another country that they would not encounter in home trade. (4)

(d) Although the prospect of an order valued at £500 000 will obviously be attractive to Daly Designs, accepting it is clearly going to cause the company a cashflow problem. Explain this statement using information from the data given to illustrate your answer. (6)

(e) One way to overcome the cashflow problem would be for Daly Designs to raise a bill of exchange. Explain how this could solve the problem, including mention of the possibility of 'discounting' or 'negotiating' the bill. (8)

3 Read the following article and then answer the questions below.

1992: Opening doors to Europe

December 31, 1992 was a red-letter day for every business man and business woman. For on that date most existing trade barriers between the member countries of the European Economic Community were completely swept away. The 12 EEC countries all signed the Single European Act which is committed to making Europe a unified market of some 322 million people from that date.

This internal market was not expected to just happen overnight. Instead, in the years leading up to 1992, trade barriers were gradually whittled away. By the time the internal market is complete, 300 individual pieces of legislation will have taken place.

Because the situation is continually changing, businesses throughout the Common Market need to be aware of what is happening and how it affects them. This is particularly the case in Britain, which tends to pay less attention to business opportunities within the EEC than the other members. France, for example has invested a lot of money in making business aware of existing opportunities by running a massive television advertising campaign.

Unfortunately, Britain has not in the past felt European; but this is an attitude which must be changed if British business is to benefit from the internal market. This change in attitude has begun to materialise.

European Commission

To ensure that Britain does not linger behind its counterparts, the Department of Trade and Industry launched an awareness campaign in March 1988 to alert businesses to the possibilities in Europe. However, it is generally the smaller businesses which have more difficulty obtaining information about European opportunities. Most small businesses simply do not have the resources to find out what is available.

Adapted from Employment News, *May 1988.*

(a) What do the letters EC stand for? (1)

(b) What other name is the EC known by? (1)

(c) What has been the purpose of the Department of Trade and Industry's awareness campaign? (2)

(d) Name six countries, other than Britain, that are members of the EC. (3)

(e) Why do you think that in the past Britain has paid 'less attention to business opportunities within the EC than the other members'? (4)

(f) What does this article mean when it says that 'most existing trade barriers between the member countries of the EC were completely swept away'? (4)

(g) In what way can the developments commented on in this article be seen as improving marketing opportunities for British businesses? (5)

4 On page 203 is an imaginary advertisement placed in a trade journal by a company specialising in providing support services for businesses interested in trading in overseas markets by exporting or importing. The company is particularly active in promoting export trade.

(a) Briefly explain the difference between importers and exporters. (1)

(b) How would Easy Exports Ltd earn a living? (2)

(c) What do you think a 'profile' is likely to be in the way that the term is used in this advertisement? (2)

(d) What kind of 'trade statistics' might Easy Exports provide its customers? (2)

(e) What do you think are 'non-tariff barriers'? Give two specific examples. (3)

(f) Why might a business not involved in foreign trade be interested in obtaining 'profiles' of exporters, importers, manufacturers and producers? (4)

(g) Describe the sort of 'market research data' that a firm interested in breaking into overseas trade would find useful. (6)

Extended Answer Assignments

1 It is possible for a country to have an adverse balance of trade but a favourable balance of payments. Discuss this statement using imaginary data to illustrate your answer.

2 'Overseas trade is important to every member of our country.' Discuss this statement using specific examples to justify your answer.

3 'Imports threaten home producers and can ruin national prosperity.' Discuss this statement.

4 You are employed by a manufacturer of electrical goods. Explain the process by which you could go about obtaining orders for your company. Describe some of the ways in which the government agencies might assist you.

5 Visit a business convenient to you that is involved in foreign trade and investigate what marketing strategies it uses that are in your opinion different from those used in home trade. Write a report of your findings.

Business documents

12.1 Purpose of business documents

The complete process of supplying goods and services from ordering to payment is called a *transaction*. A variety of documents are raised at various stages in the process and most of these pass between the buyer and the seller. Most of these documents are trading documents, i.e. those that are directly involved in the change of ownership. Others are sometimes used supplementary to trading documents in order to assist the trading process. These supplementary documents are particularly evident in foreign trade.

Businesses need documents to:

- ensure that there is no confusion about what has taken place between the buyer and seller;
- provide a record or proof of that activity at a later date.

12.2 Trading documents

Enquiry

The enquiry may be a letter or a standard form that is sent by the buyer to one or several firms seeking information about products or services available. Alternatively, the buyer may invite any number of suppliers to *tender*, or make an offer to supply. Based on the information received in response to the enquiry the buyer will decide who to purchase from

Quotation

The quotation may take the form of a letter or a standard printed form, a catalogue or price list. It is an offer by the seller to supply at a *quoted* price. The quotation may also contain:

Delivery period
How long before delivery (or despatch) can be executed.

Discount offered
- *Cash discount* ('terms') – offered by seller to encourage prompt payment by buyer.
- *Trade discount* – given to people in the same trade as the seller to enable them to make a profit on resale of goods purchased.

Carriage arrangements

- *Carriage paid* – price includes transport costs.
- *Carriage forward/ex-works* – price does not include transport costs.
- *Promotional material* – catalogue, price list, samples, etc.
- *Estimated cost* – where it is not possible to give a precise price, the seller may give an estimated or expected cost.

12.3 Purchasing

Order

If the prospective customer finds the quotation of interest he will send the seller an official order. This may take the form of a letter, but more often it will be a standard form. The order will convey four pieces of information in particular:

1 number and description of items required;
2 price the buyer is expecting to pay;
3 when delivery is to be executed by;
4 delivery address, which may be different from the address from where the order has originated.

Acknowledgement

When the seller receives the order he will acknowledge receipt and confirm that it has been received safely, that the goods can be supplied by the date they are required, and that the prices stated on the order are acceptable.

Despatch

Advice note

The advice note is sent separate from the goods and its purpose is to advise the buyer that the goods ordered have been despatched, and to specify the method of transport used. If the goods do not arrive within a reasonable period of time the buyer should advise the seller.

Delivery note

This is sent with the goods when the seller uses his own vehicles. The lorry driver obtains a signature on delivery.

Consignment note

This is a document provided by the transporter of goods. The consignor (sender) fills in the form with details of the consignment, e.g. number of packages, details of consignee, etc. The consignment note accompanies the goods during transit and the consignee signs it to acknowledge receipt when it arrives at its destination.

Charging

Invoice

This important document is sent by the seller to the buyer immediately the goods have been despatched advising:

- details of goods despatched
- cost per item
- total cost, including VAT where applicable
- discounts offered, for example, trade or cash discount.

Many trading documents, and particularly those concerned with charging for goods or services supplied, show the letters E & OE somewhere. These letters stand for 'errors and omissions excepted'. The seller puts this on documents to advise the buyer that if a mistake has been made, the right to correct the error at a later date has been reserved.

Pro-forma invoice

The pro-forma invoice is frequently used by the seller to charge a customer for goods in advance of despatch, but it can also be used when goods are sent on 'approval' or on a 'sale-or-return' basis.

```
                         INVOICE                           ──── Serial number of seller's invoice

  Teenwear plc                    Invoice No. 11323
  Heston Way                      Date 12 May 1987      ──── Date of invoice
  BROOKHILL                                             ──── Name and address of seller
  BH9 0JP                                               ──── Name and address of buyer

  ┌ Clobber Boutique ┐
    High Street                  Terms: 5% 7 days            Cash discounts offered
    CRAYSTONE                           2½% 28 days     ──── for prompt payment
  └ C56 0JP         ┘                   otherwise net

  Despatched  4 cartons- Hull Transport   11.5.87       ──── Method of despatch
  Customer's Order No.  CB 1076 dated 3.4.87            ──── Details of buyer's order
  Quantity | Description           | Unit Price | Amount ──── Details of goods ordered

    100      Polka Dot Tights PDT 73        .90    90.00
     20      Unisex Baggy Sweaters BS 96  12.50   250.00
     10      Boy's Jogging Suits JSB 34   18.00   180.00
     10      Girl's Jogging Suits JSG 57  18.00   180.00  ──── Gross invoice total
                                                  700.00  ──── Discount given to traders
              Less 20% Trade Discount         140.00      ──── Net invoice amount
                                                  560.00
              Plus 15% VAT                          78.60 ──── VAT added to net invoice amount
              Total                            £638.60    ──── less the 5% cash discount offered
                                                          ──── Amount to be paid by buyer
              Carriage Paid                                ─── Transport costs to be met
                                                               by seller

  E & O E
```

E & O E Errors & Omissions Excepted – seller reserves right to correct any mistakes at a later date

Statement of account

The statement of account is sent by the seller to the buyer at the end of each month to summarise the trading position since the previous statement was issued, and to request payment of the outstanding balance. It shows all the following:

- the amount outstanding from the previous month's statement;
- the date, value and document number of each subsequent transaction;
- the cumulative balance;
- payments received since the last statement was issued;
- current balance outstanding;
- discounts offered for prompt payment.

Payment for goods and services

There are a variety of arrangements that may be made between the seller and the buyer for payment of goods or services supplied, and these will be influenced by how well the seller knows the buyer. The buyer may pay:

- *In advance:*
  (a) cash with order (CWO); or
  (b) in response to a pro-forma invoice.

STATEMENT OF ACCOUNT

Teenwear p/c

Heston Way
BROOKHILL
BH9 0JP

Date 1st June 19×9

Clobber Boutique
High Street
CRAYSTONE
CS6 LLT

Terms: 5% 7 days

2½% 28 days

Date	Details	Debits	Credits	Amount
1st May	To account rendered April			890.36
9th May	To invoice 10109	180.10		1070.46
12th May	To invoice 11323	639.80		1710.26
20th May	To invoice 13488	83.14		1793.40
22nd May	By credit note 103		46.00	1747.40
28th May	To invoice 1446	360.80		2108.20
29th May	To debit note 112	10.60		2118.80
30th May	To invoice 1555	223.00		2341.80
31st May	By cheque payment		1000.00	1341.80

Amount outstanding £1341.80

E & OE

Amount outstanding from previous statement.

All amounts which increase the buyer's debt are entered in the debits column and added to the cumulative total. All amounts which reduce the customer's debt are listed in the credits column and taken away from the cumulative total.

Amount outstanding to be carried forward to next account.

- *Cash on delivery (COD)*
  The carrier will be expected to collect payment before handing the goods over.
- *On receipt of invoice*
  To gain the benefit of cash discounts offered for prompt payment.
- *Against statement of account*
  Payment delayed until the end of the month to take full benefit of trade credit allowed.

The most common method of payment of debts today is by *cheque* which is used to pay for all or part of the balance of a statement. Where the buyer sends a cheque covering only some of the invoices listed on the statement a *remittance advice note* may also be sent listing the invoices which the cheque is intended to pay.

Correcting mistakes

Two documents are used to effect changes in invoice values, the credit note (usually printed in red) and the debit note (printed in black).

Credit note

This is sent by the seller to the buyer to correct an overcharge or to give a refund. It has the effect of reducing the charge made.

Reasons for issue include:

- an invoicing error has resulted in the customer being overcharged;
- some of the goods have been returned as faulty;
- too few goods were delivered;
- refund on returned packing material.

Debit note

Sent by the seller to the buyer to correct an undercharge. The debit note has the effect of increasing the charge made.

Reasons for issue include:
- an invoicing error has resulted in the customer being undercharged;
- too many goods were sent and the buyer has agreed to keep them.

Value added tax (VAT)

This is a tax levied on some goods and services. It is collected by traders by adding an amount to the purchase price and this addition is passed to the government. VAT is levied as a percentage added to the purchase price after deduction of discounts.

12.6 Foreign trade documents

We have seen in the previous chapter the important part foreign trade plays in providing a country with many of the wants and needs that it cannot economically produce. As with other forms of trading examined in earlier chapters, documentation is raised at various stages in the marketing and distribution of products. The following are the main documents used in foreign trade.

Bill of lading

The bill of lading is used in the shipping of goods and it represents the title to ownership of goods. On it are shown details of the goods, their destination and the terms under which the shipping company agrees to carry the goods. Three copies of the bill of lading are raised.

- One is retained by the exporter.
- One is given to the ship's captain.
- One is given to the importer who has to produce his copy to take possession of the goods on arrival.

```
CANADA MARITIME LIMITED                          BILL OF LADING

SHIPPER                          CARRIER    VES.  VOY. SHIPMENT No.  GRP.    TT
  PITMAN PUBLISHING LTD          CODE NO
                                 9385       E.C.I.
  SOUTHPORT             A/C No.  AGENTS A/C No. CM AGENT      REV.           CANADA
                                                                            MARITIME
CONSIGNEE                                DANGEROUS GOODS CLASSIFICATION
  ERA BOOK CO LTD
  10-16 PORTLAND ST
  KOWLOON                                TEMPERATURE CONTROL IN CENTIGRADE      TO
  HONG KONG           A/C No.     INSTRUCTIONS
NOTIFY ADDRESS (WITHOUT LIABILITY TO CARRIER)

                      A/C No.
PRE-CARRIAGE BY        PLACE OF RECEIPT   EXPORTERS REF.        AGENTS REF.
                                          243 607
OCEAN VESSEL           PORT OF LOADING    ORIGIN OF SHIPMENT    FOR CM USE ONLY
  SEVEN SEAS            FELIXSTOWE
PORT OF DISCHARGE      PLACE OF DELIVERY  FREIGHT PAYABLE AT
  HONG KONG                               MANCHESTER
MARKS & NUMBERS   CONTAINER No.  No. OF PKGS., DESCRIPTION OF GOODS  WEIGHT   MEASURE
  ERA. B.C.                       1 PAL BOX                          500KG   1.030cm
  P.L. 206                        PRINTED EDUC. BOOKS
  HONG KONG
```

Received by the Carrier from the Shipper in apparent good order and condition (unless otherwise noted herein) the total number or quantity of Containers or other packages or units indicated, stated by the Shipper to comprise the Goods specified above, for Carriage subject to all the terms hereof (INCLUDING THE TERMS ON THE REVERSE HEREOF AND THE TERMS OF THE CARRIER'S APPLICABLE TARIFF) from the Place of Receipt or the Port of Loading, whichever is applicable, to the Port of Discharge or the Place of Delivery, whichever is applicable. In accepting this Bill of Lading the Merchant expressly accepts and agrees to all its terms, conditions and exceptions whether printed, stamped or written, or otherwise incorporated, notwithstanding the non-signing of this Bill of Lading by the Merchant.

NON-NEGOTIABLE EXPRESS BILL OF LADING
(SEE CLAUSE 26 OVER FOR CONDITIONS)
CFDS 3f REV 09/84

Freight note

The bill or charge for shipping goods, the freight note is sent to the exporter by the shipping company.

PANDAIR
INTERNATIONAL AIRFREIGHT

Pandair Freight Limited

SHIPPERS AIR FREIGHT INSTRUCTIONS

WE HAVE DESPATCHED TO YOU TODAY VIA:-

☐ YOUR COLLECTION SERVICE   ☑ OUR TRANSPORT   ☐ PARCEL POST

☐ PASSENGER TRAIN TO   STATION (T.B.C.F/TO BE DELIVERED)

FOR AIRFREIGHT TO   →   DESTINATION AIRPORT: MALTA

CONSIGN GOODS TO:	ALSO NOTIFY
M.C.E. BOOKSHOP	PITMAN PUBLISHING LTD
MALTA COLLEGE	SLAIDBURN CRESCENT
MCAST MFIDA	SOUTHPORT
MALTA	
Telex Telephone	Telephone
Consignees Order No: 26307	Shippers Order No: 26307

SPECIAL INSTRUCTIONS (e.g. LETTER OF CREDIT/CONSULAR REQUIREMENTS/H.M. CUSTOMS)

CONSOLIDATION SERVICE REQUIRED
CARGOSPEED ☐
CARGOSAVER ☐
CARGOTHRIFT ☐

For Goods destined for the EUROPEAN ECONOMIC COMMUNITY:-
We Hereby Certify that these goods are in free circulation within the EEC and Authorise PANDAIR FREIGHT LIMITED to issue T2L on our behalf

Signed

I.A.T.A. RESTRICTED ARTICLES REGULATIONS—SEE "RESTRICTED AND PROHIBITED CARGO (AIR)" OVERLEAF.

NO. OF PACKAGES	METHOD OF PACKING	NATURE AND QUANTITY OF GOODS	MARKS AND NUMBERS	MEASUREMENTS (Specify cms or ins)	GROSS WEIGHT (Specify Kilos or lbs)
	EXPORT CARTONS	PRINTED EDUC. BOOKS	M.C.E. BOOKSHOP	19X13X10 .040CM	20 KG
		RESTRICTED/NON RESTRICTED CARGO (Delete Accordingly)			

DECLARED VALUE FOR CUSTOMS   NUD.   DECLARED VALUE FOR CARRIAGE £ NUD. (NOT ACCEPTABLE IN CONSOLIDATION) (IF REQUIRED)

INSURE FOR   (IN WORDS)   £   (IN FIGURES)

AMOUNT OF C.O.D.   (IN WORDS)   £   (IN FIGURES)

CHARGES	PAYABLE BY	
	SHIPPER	CONSIGNEE
AIR FREIGHT		49.50
FOB (Processing)		N/R
INSURANCE		N/R
AT DESTINATION		

DOCUMENTS ATTACHED (Please Indicate)	
COMMERCIAL INVOICES	3
CERTIFICATE OF ORIGIN/CONSULAR INVOICE	N/R
EEC DOCUMENTS (State Type)	N/R
RESTRICTED ARTICLES CERTIFICATE (In Duplicate)	
OTHERS	

SHIPPERS NAME AND ADDRESS

The Shipper hereby declares that the above particulars are correct and that he is aware of and accepts the Conditions of Trading referred to on the reverse side of this form.

Signed on behalf of Shipper

By

Dated

Telephone Number
J168 (Revised August 1983)

Certificate of origin

This is a document certifying the country of origin of goods. This document is sometimes required by the importing country if it has been agreed that the goods of a particular country will be allowed to enter the country at a more favourable tariff rate.

Air waybill

This is used in connection with air transport and it serves as a receipt for goods by an aircraft captain to the sender of a consignment. The air waybill shows details of goods, departure and destination points, and consignor and consignee.

Mitchell Cotts Airfreight

CRN		**HOUSE AIRBILL NUMBER** 7443773

HOUSE AIR WAYBILL
NOT NEGOTIABLE

A/C NO

VAT REGISTRATION No. 321 2294 00	M.A.W.B. No. 13228305	CONSOLIDATION REF No.	Airport of DESTINATION HONIARA	CODE

CONSIGNED TO: SOLOMON ISLANDS – COLLEGE OF HIGHER EDUCATION KUKUM CAMPUS P.O. BOX 923 HONIARA, SOLOMON ISLES

ALSO NOTIFY:

No. OF PACKAGES	METHOD OF PACKING	NATURE AND QUANTITY OF GOODS	MARKS AND NUMBERS	DIMENSIONS OR VOLUME	GROSS WEIGHT SPECIFY KGS. OR LBS.
1	EXPORT CARTONS	PRINTED EDUC. BOOKS	COMPUTER LABELS	19 x 13 x 10 .040cm	20 KG

CONSIGNEE'S ORDER NUMBER: 43642   **SHIPPERS REFERENCE NUMBER:** 43642

DOCUMENTS TO ACCOMPANY SHIPMENT: – INVOICES 3   CON. INV: C. of O.   T.Doc/M.Cert.

SHIPPERS DECLARED VALUE (Specify Currency)
FOR CUSTOMS £230.00   **FOR CARRIAGE**

METHOD OF ROUTING AND CHARGES — Agreed stopping places are those places (other than the places of departure and destination) shown under Air Carriage, and/or those places shown in carrier's timetables as scheduled stopping places for the route. SEE CONDITIONS ON THE REVERSE HEREOF.

INTERNATIONAL AIR CARRIAGE DEPARTURE (Airport of)	(ADDRESS OF FIRST CARRIER)	CHARGEABLE WEIGHT KGS.	RATE CLASSIFICATION	RATES	CODE	PREPAID	CHARGEABLE TO CONSIGNEE zero rated for VAT
TO	FIRST CARRIER	20 KG		1.40	01	YES	
TO	CARRIER				01		
CLEARANCE AND HANDLING				7 50	02		
CARTAGE				2 50	03		
E.E.C. DOCUMENTS					04		
CONSULAR / CERTS. OF ORIGIN					05		
PACKING				1 50	07		
INSURANCE VALUE PREMIUM				N/R	08		
FREE DOMICILE FEE				N/R	10		
SHIPPERS C.O.D.				— —	11		
SHIPPER'S C.O.D. IN WORDS							
C.O.D. FEE					12		
AGENTS DISBURSEMENT					14		
					16		
INCLUSIVE PROCESSING CHARGE							

PAYABLE BY CONSIGNEE

NAME and Address of SHIPPER PITMAN PUBLISHING LTD SOUTHPORT

TOTAL DUE 99

CERTIFICATION
We hereby declare that the goods mentioned herein were despatched as shown below and a copy of this House Waybill was forwarded to the consignee on the same aircraft.

The shipper certifies that the particulars on the face hereof are correct and agrees to the CONDITIONS ON THE REVERSE OF THE SHIPPERS/CONSIGNEES COPY.

_____ AT _____
(date and tax point)   (place)
ISSUING AIR FORWARDER

_____ SIGNATURE OF ISSUING AIR FORWARDER

Carrier certifies above described goods were received for carriage SUBJECT TO THE CONDITIONS ON THE REVERSE OF THE SHIPPERS/CONSIGNEES COPY, the goods then being in apparent good order and condition except as noted herein.

Mitchell Cotts Airfreight (U.K.) Limited,
Galleymead Road, Colnbrook, Slough, Berkshire, England SL3 0EL
Telephone: Slough (0753) 684555
Telex: 847552 Mcair
Telegrams: Mcair Slough

Registered Office: Cotts House, Camomile Street, London EC3A 7BJ
Registration No. 710872 England

1
ORIGINAL – Shipper
THIS IS NOT A TAX INVOICE FOR VAT PURPOSES

We draw your attention to our TRADING CONDITIONS overleaf.

Manifest

A summary of all the bills of lading and cargo a ship is carrying.

Import licence

Issued by the importing government giving permission to bring certain commodities into the country. It can be used to enforce quotas.

Export licence

An export licence is sometimes needed before certain goods are allowed to leave a country (e.g. firearms, works of art, etc.).

Bill of exchange

The bill of exchange is widely used in the settlement of international debt. It is a document made out by the seller of goods (exporter – creditor) requiring the buyer (importer – debtor) to pay a named sum of money on demand, or on an agreed future date (usually three months).

The bill is signed first by the seller, and then by the buyer and returned to the seller. When the buyer has signed the bill it is said to have been 'accepted'.

The use of a bill of exchange enables the importer to obtain credit for a period of time. It also helps the seller because instead of waiting for payment he can:

● sell the bill at a *discount;* or

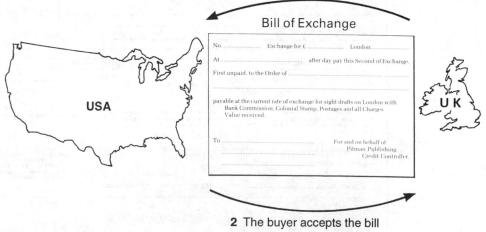

1 A seller in the UK will draw up a bill of exchange sign it, and send it to the buyer.

Bill of Exchange

No. .... Exchange for £ .... London ....

At .... after day pay this Second of Exchange.

First unpaid, to the Order of ....

payable at the current rate of exchange for sight drafts on London with Bank Commission, Colonial Stamp, Postages and all Charges Value received.

To ....
For and on behalf of
Pitman Publishing
Credit Controller.

USA

UK

2 The buyer accepts the bill and signs it and returns it to the seller.

- negotiate it by using it to pay off his own debts, or use it as collateral against a bank loan.

Note: A bill of exchange is drawn up by the seller (creditor) whereas a cheque is drawn up by the buyer (debtor).

Make a note of it

1 What is a transaction?

2 Name the main parties involved in a transaction.

3 Why do businesses need documents?

4 What is the purpose of an enquiry?

5 State three forms a quotation may take.

6 What is an estimate?

7 Explain the difference between a trade discount and a cash discount.

8 Give three examples of promotional material.

9 Explain the difference between carriage paid and carriage forward.

10 State four items of information likely to be found on an order.

11 What is the function of an advice note?

12 Explain the difference between a delivery note and a consignment note.

13 State four items of information found on an invoice.

14 What is the purpose of putting the letters E & OE on a trading document?

15 Give two possible reasons for the issue of a pro-forma invoice.

16 What do the letters CWO and COD stand for?

17 Name the most common method of payment of debts.

18 What is the purpose of a remittance advice note?

19 Explain the difference in function between a credit note and a debit note.

20 What is value added tax?

21 A trader buys goods valued at £400. He is entitled to 25 per cent trade discount. How much will he actually pay for the goods?

22 An invoice value of £200 is subject to an addition of 15 per cent VAT. How much will the buyer actually pay?

23 What is the purpose of a bill of lading?

24 How are the three main copies of a bill of lading distributed?

25 State one way in which an air waybill differs from a bill of lading.

26 Name the document that states where imported goods were made.

27 Explain the difference between an import licence and an export licence.

28 Give a detailed explanation of the function of a bill of exchange.

29 Explain the difference between a 'discounted' and a 'negotiated' bill of exchange.

Structured Questions

1 Look back at the flow diagram on page 206 which shows the documents that pass between the buyer and seller and answer the following questions.

  (a) What is the name given to this complete chain of events which make up a deal between a buyer and a seller? (1)

  (b) Which document would be likely to be accompanied by promotional material? (1)

  (c) At what point in this chain would the customer be asked to pay their outstanding account, and which document would request the payment? (2)

  (d) State three items of information likely to be contained in a quotation. (3)

  (e) Under what circumstances would this diagram show the words 'consignment note' and where would the words appear in the diagram? (3)

  (f) Where in the chain shown would a credit note be most likely to appear? Give three reasons why a credit note might be issued. (4)

  (g) Briefly describe the function of each of the following trading documents: order, acknowledgement, advice note. (6)

2 Look back at the invoice shown on page 208 and answer these questions.

  (a) Name the seller and the buyer involved in this transaction. (1)

  (b) What is the significance of the numbers and letters at the end of each of the addresses shown? (1)

  (c) This invoice has a number (11323). What is the purpose of including this number at the top of the document? (1)

  (d) Explain the meaning of the words 'carriage paid' on this invoice. (1)

  (e) Explain the purpose of the 'unit price' and 'amount' columns. (2)

  (f) Why are there three different dates shown on this document? (3)

  (g) How does the function of an invoice differ from that of a statement of account? (3)

  (h) Explain the method of applying VAT to an invoice using simple figures (but not those shown in the example) to illustrate your answer. (4)

  (i) What would be the net value of this invoice if there was no VAT applicable and the trade discount read 25 per cent instead of 20 per cent? (4)

3 The following questions are all related to the statement of account shown on page 209.

(a) Clearly identify the buyer and the seller on this document. (1)

(b) How frequently are statements of this sort usually sent out? (1)

(c) What purpose does this document serve? (1)

(d) What was the total amount spent by the customer during the period covered by the statement? (1)

(e) What is the implication of the letters E & OE in the left-hand corner of the document? (2)

(f) Why does this document show three months, April, May and June? (3)

(g) What is the meaning of the words 'to account rendered' and what will be the amount shown for the month following this statement? (3)

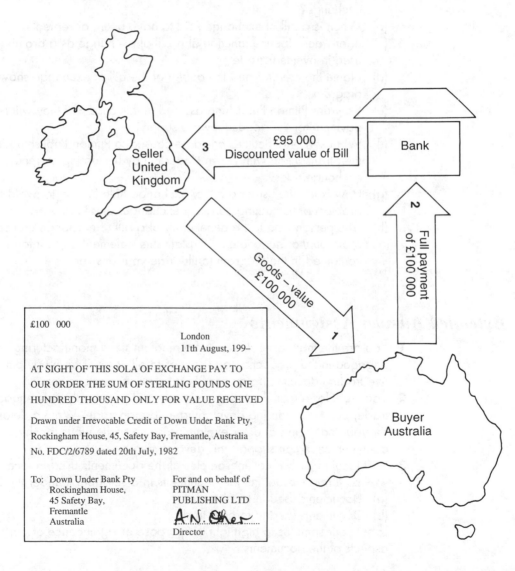

£100 000

London
11th August, 199–

AT SIGHT OF THIS SOLA OF EXCHANGE PAY TO
OUR ORDER THE SUM OF STERLING POUNDS ONE
HUNDRED THOUSAND ONLY FOR VALUE RECEIVED

Drawn under Irrevocable Credit of Down Under Bank Pty,
Rockingham House, 45, Safety Bay, Fremantle, Australia
No. FDC/2/6789 dated 20th July, 1982

To: Down Under Bank Pty
Rockingham House,
45 Safety Bay,
Fremantle
Australia

For and on behalf of
PITMAN
PUBLISHING LTD

A.N. Other

Director

(h) Give four possible reasons for the entry dated 22nd May. (4)

(i) The figure in the amount column is sometimes called a 'cumulative balance'. Why is it referred to in this way, and how are these figures calculated? (4)

4 The UK company Pitman Publishing Ltd have received an order with a value of £100 000 from an Australian company, Down Under Pty. Pitman need some assurance that Down Under Pty are going to make the payment in due course. They would also like to receive the value of the order prior to supplying the goods. The diagram on page 217 shows how they have used a bill of exchange to achieve what they want. Study it and then answer the questions below.

(a) A cheque is usually drawn up by the debtor. Who draws up a bill of exchange? (1)

(b) When is a bill of exchange said to have been 'accepted'? (1)

(c) Briefly describe the function of a bill of exchange as a promissory note used in overseas trade. (2)

(d) Name the *creditor* and the *debtor* of the bill of exchange shown in the diagram (2)

(e) How are Pitman Publishing assured in this case that they will receive payment for the goods they are supplying? (2)

(f) What sort of difficulties could be caused to Pitman Publishing in their transaction with Down Under Pty by fluctuating currency exchange rates? (3)

(g) How could the use of a bill of exchange help Pitman to avoid the problem of fluctuating currency exchange rates? (3)

(h) 'The person who is the beneficiary of a bill of exchange can sell it at a *discount* or *negotiate* it.' Explain this statement using information contained in the diagram to illustrate your answer. (6)

Extended Answer Assignments

1 You are the managing director of a medium-sized manufacturing company engaged in the production and sale of small items of farm equipment. Design five trading documents you are likely to use in your business.

2 You work for a manufacturing company that is currently only engaged in home trade, but is considering developing in foreign trade. Write a detailed report for your managing director explaining some of the ways in which documentation can support this development.

3 Visit local firms and collect samples of the documents used in *local trade* as well as *foreign trade*. Put the documents in a scrapbook under the headings:
(a) Documents used in local trade
(b) Documents used in foreign trade
Label your samples to highlight the purpose or significance of particular aspects of the documents

or

Display the documents you have collected on the bulletin board in your classroom or on a chart. Use appropriate headings and attach labels for a similar purpose to that above.

13 Transport

13.1 The importance of transport

Transport is a form of communication, a means of making contact between two distant points. It provides services that enable workers to go to and from work, raw materials to reach the producer, and finished products to be distributed. An efficient transport system reduces the amount of capital needed to be tied up in stocks, because new supplies can be obtained quickly. It also makes international trade possible, which is one of the important aspects of marketing and distribution discussed in Chapter 11.

Transport plays an important part in the marketing of goods because without transport raw materials would not reach the producer, and the finished articles would not be distributed.

For marketing to be effectively carried out there is a need for a sophisticated transport system which enables goods to reach the right place, at the right time, and in the right condition.

The importance of transport can easily be understood if we examine the distribution of a single product. Consider the transportation involved in the movement of bananas from the Caribbean region to the UK. The fruit must be taken from the plantation to the port where it is loaded onto a special ship with a cooling system to preserve the bananas during the long sea voyage. Upon arrival in the UK the cargo is transhipped onto road or rail transport for the journey to the wholesale produce markets. Subsequently many further journeys are then carried out by wholesalers and retailers before the fruit reaches the consumer. Timing is important at every stage of the journey to ensure that the bananas, which are harvested in a green condition, reach the consumer before the ripening process is complete. Transport is a crucial element in this timing.

In relation to transport, the *consignor* is the person sending cargo and the *consignee* is the person to whom it is being sent. The firm transporting the cargo is often called the *carrier* and cargo is sometimes referred to as *freight*.

13.2 Choice of transport

Each type of transport has its special uses. Some are more suitable for a particular task than others. Consequently, choosing an appropriate method of transport for particular circumstances is one of the skills essential for business success. Transport users will take the following factors into account when choosing the form of transport to use:

This graph shows the costs of various means of transport.
(a) List the cheapest method of transport at each of the points
shown as A, B, C and D.
(b) Which of the points X, Y or Z would you consider to be related
to air transport? Give a brief explanation of your choice.

- the nature of the goods;
- how urgently the consignment is needed;
- the value of each item;
- cost of the transport;
- distance the consignment must be transported;
- the size and weight of the load;
- convenient position of terminals, e.g. station, docks and airport;
- possibility of combining loads to reduce costs;
- the reputation of the carrier.

 ## Methods of transport

Road transport

Road transport carries 60 per cent of inland freight and 92 per cent of passenger traffic. There has been a steady growth in road traffic and this has called for the development of elaborate motorway systems to reduce congestion and maintain traffic flow.

All vehicles in Britain must be insured and those over three years old must pass a Ministry of Transport (MOT) test to show that they are fit for use on public roads.

Advantages of road transport
- Door-to-door service provides maximum flexibility.
- Fast over short distances of less than 200 miles.
- Risk of damage reduced by lack of need for transhipment.
- Can reach places inaccessible to other forms of transport.

221

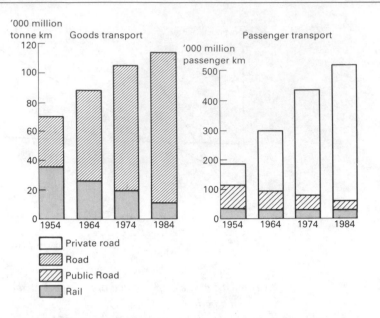

Changes in the transport of goods and passengers by road and rail in Great Britain.

(a) *What general change in trends has taken place between 1954 and 1984 with respect to:*
   (i) *goods transport in total*
   (ii) *goods transport by rail*
   (iii) *passengers travelling privately by road?*
(b) *Give reasons for the trends you have identified.*

- Motorway network speeds up movement and reduces congestion.
- Less tied to a rigid timetable than railways.
- Suitable for speedy direct delivery of perishable goods.
- Other forms of transport rely on road transport to connect with terminals such as airports, stations, docks.

Disadvantages of road transport

- Expensive to operate in large congested cities.
- Subject to mechanical breakdowns.
- Affected by adverse weather conditions.
- Loads are limited in size and weight.
- Some roads unsuitable for very large vehicles.
- Slower than railways over long distances.
- Wastes resources if lorry returns empty.
- Tax on vehicles and fuel must be incorporated into costs.

Rail transport

The railways were nationalised (taken into state ownership) in 1947 and placed under the control of the British Railways Board. Control is delegated through five regions: Eastern, Southern, Midland, Western and Scottish. British Rail also operates some ferry services. The present British government has announced plans to privatise the railways system.

Freightliner service

This is British Rail's high-speed container service which links up with special road and sea terminals.

Standard sizes (ISO) of containers are loaded direct from lorries on to special train bogies, and at their rail destination they are unloaded in a similar manner.

This simplified handling results in:

● improved speed and handling economies;
● simplified and more effective timetabling;
● reduced losses from damage or theft;
● direct links between terminals such as ports.

Freightliner service movements are carried out mainly at night when the lines are clear from other traffic.

Advantages of rail transport

● Easier for passenger travel than road transport.
● Faster than road over distances in excess of 200 miles.
● Less labour intensive than road transport.
● Especially suited for container traffic.
● More economical in fuel use than road transport.

Disadvantages of rail transport

● Routes determined by railway lines and stations.
● Equipment costs are very high.
● Relies on road transport for transhipment.
● Less economic than road movement for journeys of less than 200 miles.

Inland waterways (canals and rivers)

Despite the glorious past of the great canal era this form of transport has largely been replaced by road and rail transport. Its few advantages today are the smoothness of movement and the fact that it is the cheapest form of transport. But these advantages are generally outweighed by the main disadvantage which is slowness. However, there has been a drive to increase the use of canals and rivers by leisure and holiday business.

Sea transport

Shipping is particularly important to Britain as an island because it provides our main link to overseas markets. Transport is also one of Britain's invisible earners, contributing to the balance of payments (*see* Chapter 14).

There are four basic classes of ships: passenger liners, cargo liners, tramps and special freighters.

Passenger liners

Passenger liners are built primarily for passenger (particularly cruising) travel. They carry some cargo, and as they follow fixed routes and keep to a regular timetable delivery dates can be guaranteed. However, high freight costs limit freight use to high value cargoes.

Cargo liners

This type of ship sometimes carries a few passengers, although their main purpose is to deliver cargo. They operate on fixed routes and to a regular timetable. The vessel will sail from a port on time, even if some of the scheduled cargo has not arrived.

Tramp ships

Tramps are ships that have no timetable or set route. They will carry any type of cargo to any port in the world. The vessels are chartered through a charter party agreement (*see* later).

Special freighters

For special cargoes there are a variety of purpose-built ships:

- *container ships* – cellular design vessels for fast load / unload;
- *bulk carriers* – ore and grain;
- *tankers* – oil and other bulk liquids;
- *ferries* – roll-on / roll-off; hovercraft have proved particularly successful.

Sea port requirements

Efficient sea transport operations require the provision of good terminal facilities which enable vessels to 'turn round' quickly. The following are the main requirements of a modern port.

- clear access channel with deep water;
- some protection from rough seas;
- wharves with appropriate lifting gear and equipment such as that necessary for moving containers, etc.;
- warehouses, including specialist storage, such as refrigeration, bonded stores, hazardous cargo;
- supplies of oil, water and other ship's requirements;
- repair facilities such as dry dock;

- customs and immigration facilities;
- good links with road and rail network;
- buildings for offices and commercial services such as banks, restaurants.

Air transport

This is the youngest but most highly technical form of transport. It is constantly expanding in the volume of both passenger and freight it handles. The major British airports are controlled by the British Airports Authority (BAA).

Advantages of air transport

- It is the fastest form of transport.
- Operates to timetables, mostly on direct routes.
- Reduces risk of damage or pilferage.
- Shorter transit time reduces insurance costs.
- Packaging costs reduced.
- Particularly effective over long distances.
- Containers are now being used to speed up cargo loading and unloading facilities.

Disadvantages of air transport

- High operational costs result in high freight rates.
- Weight and size of cargo is limited.
- Sometimes affected by adverse weather conditions.
- Relies on other forms of transport to and from airport.
- Not suitable for short distances.
- Causes noise and pollution.
- Economic use is limited to certain cargoes, for example light weight, high value, urgently required commodities such as drugs, mail or perishable goods.

Airport requirements

In a similar way that a sea port demands facilities that enable it to operate efficiently, an airport also has requirements that must be met if it is to fulfil its functions.

Siting

The siting of an airport is very important. While it would be convenient to site an airport in a country area when land costs are cheaper than in cities, most air travellers are heading for one of the world's major cities where they can link up with other forms of transport. For this reason, an airport has to be sited as near as possible to a major city, but avoiding high rise buildings and causing as little noise and pollution as possible to local residents.

Road and rail links

Road and rail links play an important part in providing easy access to and departure of travellers and freight. If the road and rail links are speedy and efficient they can allow the airport to be sited further away from a city centre. The modern terminal also requires facilities for long- and short-term parking as well as freight storage areas such as a bonded warehouse.

Operational, repair and safety facilities

A wide range of equipment and repair services are necessary to keep aircraft flying. For example, sophisticated radio, radar, computer and other technical equipment and the people to operate them have become increasingly important at busy international airports. In addition, aircraft use vast quantities of highly inflammable fuel. This must be stored safely, and a fleet of tankers and other vehicles are needed to load fuel, luggage and freight on to aircraft. In addition, safety and medical services such as fire engines and ambulances must be permanently ready for action.

Customs and immigration officials

These are needed to regulate the import of goods on which duty must be paid, as well as to check for prohibited items such as drugs or firearms. Immigration officials are also necessary to ensure that those who enter the country have the right to do so.

Terminal buildings and personnel

Terminal buildings containing baggage and freight handling equipment are required to ensure speedy movement of passengers and cargo. Within these buildings there may be incorporated hotel accommodation and commercial services such as banks, post offices, duty-free shops and bars and restaurants. Airports require a variety of personnel to operate the terminal buildings. Security staff have become increasingly important.

Pipelines

Pipelines allow the transport of commodities without using a vehicle. Examples are pipelines for gas, oil and water.

13.4 Containerisation

A container is a large pressed steel box available in two International Standards Organisation (ISO) sizes (20 or 40 ft × 8 ft × 8 ft) capable of carrying twenty or thirty tonnes of cargo. The container is packed at the factory or inland pooling depot and delivered to the container terminal by rail (freightliner) or road and deposited in the container parking area in the dock container terminal.

The containers are moved around the terminal by straddle carriers. The container is loaded precisely into position in the ship's hold by special gantry cranes.

Advantages of containerisation
- Reduced staffing requirements lowers transport costs.
- Damage and pilferage is reduced.
- Packaging and insurance costs are reduced.
- Ship 'turn round' is speeded up considerably.

1

4

2

5

3

1. Containers are packed at the factory by the manufacturer, or the packages are sent to a container pooling depot to be combined with other packages to make a worthwhile economic load.

2. Containers can be taken to and from the container terminal by road transport.

3. The railway Freightliner service moves containers and avoids road congestion.

4. Containers are moved around depots and ports by special vehicles.

5. Containers are loaded precisely into position on trains, ships or lorries by massive gantry cranes.

13.5 Baltic Exchange

The Baltic Exchange is the centre for the following important markets:

- freight market
- air freight market
- grain futures market
- oil and oilseeds market.

Freight market

This market provides a market place for the sale of ships and the chartering of vessels or space on them. Dealing is carried on by three types of specialists.

- *Chartering agents* represent merchants who wish to charter vessels. The agreement is set out in a charter party. 'Voyage charters' cover the hire of a whole ship for a particular voyage. 'Time charters' give the charterer use of the complete vessel for a period of time.
- *Shipbrokers* are agents who represent shipowners and arrange charter party contracts between shipowners and charterers.
- *Independent brokers* act as intermediaries arranging ships for cargo and cargo for ships.

Air freight market

This market operates similarly to the above freight market. It is here that arrangements are made for the charter of aircraft. These arrangements are carried out by classes of specialists with similar titles and functions to those of the sea freight market – charter agents and brokers.

Grain futures market/oil and oilseeds market

These two markets provide facilities for the buyers and sellers of wheat and barley and primary commodities that are used to extract oils (fish, palm, sunflower, rape, linseed, etc.). The term 'futures' is used because these markets allow producers to sell their crop in advance of harvest, thus assuring the future price of their products.

13.6 Transport terminology

- *Air waybill* – used in air transport as a receipt given to the consignor by the aircraft captain.
- *Bill of lading* – a document used in shipping representing:
  (a) a description of the cargo and its destination;
  (b) title of ownership of goods in transit;
  (c) a receipt for goods aboard ship.

- *Charter party* – a contract made between a shipowner and a consignor for the transport of cargo.
- *Consignment note* – accompanies goods being transported by land and is signed by consignee on delivery.
- *Delivery terms:*
  (a) *Carriage forward* – cost of transport to be paid by consignee.
  (b) *Carriage paid* – cost of transport is paid by consignor.
  (c) *Cost insurance, freight* (CIF) – cost of goods includes freight and transit insurance.
  (d) *Franco* – price of goods includes delivery to buyer.
  (e) *Free alongside ship* (FAS) – cost of goods includes delivery to side of ship.
  (f) *Free on board* (FOB) – cost includes freight as far as loading on to ship.
  (g) *Free on rail* (FOR) – transport costs are paid by the seller as far as railway.
- *Freightliner* – a container-carrying train.
- *Freight note* – a bill presented to the consignor by the shipping company for shipping goods.
- *Lloyd's List* – a daily newspaper published by Lloyd's of London listing ship movements.
- *Manifest* – a summary of all the bills of lading and cargo a ship is carrying.
- *Shipping agent* (freight forwarding agent) – companies specialising in deciding the best form of transport and arranging necessary documentation.

Make a note of it

1 Why can transport be looked on as a means of communication?

2 State one reason why transport is important to all countries.

3 List the factors that a business would take into account when deciding which form of transport to use.

4 Why are all vehicles over three years old required to pass an MOT test?

5 Give three advantages and three disadvantages of using road transport as part of the system of distribution of manufactured goods.

6 State one example where road transport would be preferable to rail transport for delivering goods.

7 Why is road transport important to both air and rail transport?

8 The railways were 'nationalised' in 1947. What does 'nationalised' mean?

9 What is the freightliner service?

10 List the advantages and disadvantages of the railways as a means of carrying freight.

11 State one circumstance where rail transport would be preferable to road transport for movement of freight.

12 Name the public corporation responsible for railways in the UK.

13 What is the main disadvantage of canal transport?

14 Why is sea transport particularly important to Britain?

15 Briefly describe the four basic classes of ships including mention of the circumstances or cargo for which each is particularly suited.

16 List the requirements of a modern port.

17 Name the organisation which controls the major British airports.

18 List the advantages and disadvantages of air transport as a means of carrying freight.

19 Give a detailed description of the facilities needed for an airport to function efficiently and safely.

20 List three examples of cargo for which you think air transport is particularly suited.

21 Name the method of transport that does not use a vehicle.

22 What is containerisation and what are the advantages of this system for freight handling?

23 Name the organisation in London which provides facilities for the chartering of vessels to carry cargo.

24 Describe the functions of the three main specialists who deal in the freight market.

25 Give a brief description of the air freight market.

26 What are 'futures'?

27 Explain the purpose of an air waybill and a bill of lading.

28 What is a charter party?

29 Explain the difference between carriage forward and carriage paid.

30 What do the following letters stand for: CIF, FAS, FOB and FOR?

Structured Questions

1 Juicyfruit Ltd is a major producer and distributor of fresh fruit and vegetables. Juicyfruit sells through its own supermarket chain and also to wholesalers who trade with independent retailers. Juicyfruit's own fleet of delivery vehicles play an important part in distributing its products throughout the UK. The diagram on page 231 shows how Juicyfruit can quickly distribute its products to the UK to reach the final consumer within 24 hours.

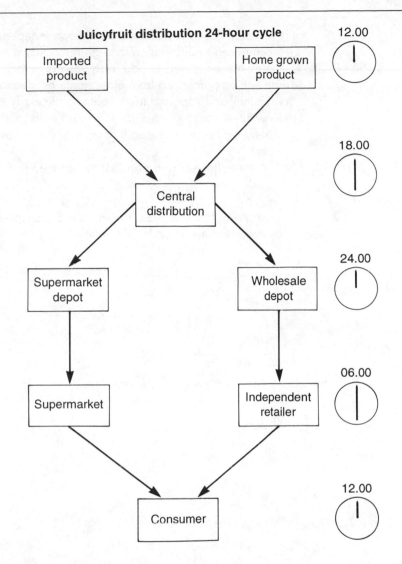

Juicyfruit distribution 24-hour cycle

(a) Explain the difference between an *imported product* and a *home grown product*. (2)

(b) Why is it important for Juicyfruit to distribute its products within 24 hours? (2)

(c) Why do Juicyfruit's own fleet of delivery vehicles play an important part in distributing its products? (3)

(d) Why would a supermarket chain be able to sell Juicyfruit's products at a lower price than an independent retailer? What contribution are transport costs likely to make to the price difference? (3)

(e) Describe the way that transport arrangements might differ in Juicyfruit's distribution?
   (i) for imported goods when compared with home-produced products, and

(ii) when products are distributed through independent retailers as compared to distribution through their own supermarket chain? (4)

(f) Juicyfruit have decided to add fresh flowers to their product range. These will be purchased from other home producers in the UK during the summer and imported from Spain, particularly in the winter months. How will the transport arrangements for flowers be likely to differ:

    (i) between home-produced flowers and those from abroad, and

    (ii) between flowers and bananas which they import from the Caribbean? (6)

2 The following graph shows the cost per mile of transporting bulky and heavy loads for various journeys up to 350 miles.

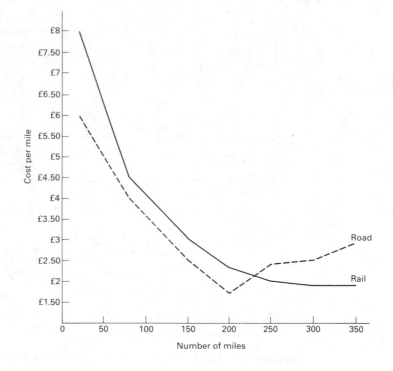

(a) (i) Which is the cheapest method of transport for a journey of 100 miles? (1)

    (ii) Which is the cheapest method for journeys exceeding 300 miles? (1)

    (iii) At what distance does it cost the same to transport goods by road as it does by rail? (1)

(b) Complete the table on page 233 which aims to show the difference in total cost between road and rail transport for various journeys. (3)

(c) Why does road transport have an advantage over rail transport for shorter journeys, but is at a disadvantage for journeys exceeding 230 miles? (4)

(d) Why does rail transport depend heavily on road transport? (4)

Miles	Road	Rail
125		
200		
300		

(e) Other than distance, what other factors will influence a business's choice between road and rail transport for delivering goods? (6)

3 Read this article about transport and its importance to the market process and answer the questions that follow:

REACHING THE MARKET ON TIME

The marketing process cannot work unless products can be delivered when needed in an efficient manner. The marketing function that makes physical distribution possible is transportation.

Transportation is the movement of goods from where they are produced or stored to where they are sold. For transport to be effective it must be capable of delivering goods at the right times and at reasonable costs.

Transit time is the total time that it takes from pickup to delivery of the freight. Transit time is affected by *double handling* which occurs when moving goods from one form of transport to another. Wherever possible a consignor will try to avoid this happening, but with some forms of transport it is unavoidable.

(a) What is meant by 'transit time'? (1)
(b) Why would transit time be more important for some goods than others? (2)
(c) Why is the marketing process so dependent upon transportation? (3)
(d) Why is 'double handling' unavoidable with some forms of transport? (4)
(e) One of the activities that firms carry out to support the physical distribution of goods is packaging. What factors would a firm take into account when designing its packaging that will help physical distribution? (4)
(f) What are the main factors likely to be considered by a business when choosing the method of transport to be used for the distribution of their goods? (6)

Extended Answer Assignments

1 Consider the pattern of transport communication in your town. Comment on its strengths and weaknesses from the point of view of both local traders and consumers.

2 Study any firm which you know sends its goods to a number of different markets. Comment on the various delivery methods the firm uses.

3 If a new factory were established in your locality producing household utensils for sale throughout the UK and overseas, what transport facilities would it be likely to use? Present evidence to support your research.

4 Carry out a minor research project to show how a change in some aspect of transport (e.g. road bypass, new bridge, Channel Tunnel, etc.) can create advantages for business but also perhaps disadvantages for other groups of people.

5 Complete a survey of all the businesses in a clearly defined area in your locality and identify the legal structure (legal identity) of each. Present the information collected in some appropriate diagrammatic form (with a key if necessary). To what extent are the firms investigated reliant upon the local transport network?

14 Business communication

14.1 The importance of business communication

What is communication?

Communication is a means of making contact. The contact may be between people, organisations or between places. It is the process by which the business passes knowledge, information and even items to others. In this respect communication may take written, oral, visual or physical form.

Physical communication through transport was examined in Chapter 13. Advertising, which is another important method of communication, was examined earlier in Chapter 9. The post and telecommunication services provide important communication services by which most external business communication is carried out, and some internal communications also. These latter aspects of communication are examined in detail in this chapter.

The need to communicate

Communication is one of the most important activities of any organisation. It is used within the firm as a means of controlling its operations, co-ordinating the activities of departments and employees and motivating personnel. Communication also provides important external links between the firm and its suppliers and customers.

| The transmitter | The message | The medium | The receiver |

There are four basic elements of all communication:

1 *The message* – the information or item that is to be communicated.
2 *The transmitter* – the sender, person or organisation that is the source of the message.
3 *The medium* – the method used, for example memo, letter, telephone, telex, fax, vehicle, etc.
4 *The receiver* – the person or organisation where the communication terminates.

For communication to be effective all the four elements above must be clear and precise. If any of them are not clear some confusion is likely to occur. For example, imagine that a person giving some instructions to others cannot express themselves clearly, or that those receiving the instructions are not very attentive. Obviously the chances of the instructions being followed are limited. The ability to communicate well is an important aspect of 'leadership' (*see* Chapter 3).

Apart from the importance of the need for businesses to transmit messages accurately, communication is also important to businesses because it not only helps them to operate efficiently, but can play an important part in creating a good public image.

Communication can be an expensive part of a firm's operations, so it is important that the most appropriate methods are chosen, and then used efficiently and economically.

14.2 Internal methods of communication

Purpose of internal communications

Informing

The different parts of the firm must be kept informed of the activities of other sections so that they can ensure that their work fits into the overall pattern.

Organising

The various sections of the firm must be organised and co-ordinated so that they carry out the part they must play in the control and operation of the organisation's activities.

Directing

Circumstances on occasions require parts of the organisation to be directed in the specific tasks and duties they are expected to carry out in order to achieve the firm's aims.

Motivating

The various levels of management use communication to motivate departments and employees in order to gain maximum benefit from their efforts.

Negotiating

Policies have to be formulated and decisions have to be taken and communicated between members of the organisation. This may well require the resolving of conflicts of interest. This may be achieved by informal discussions and interviews, although frequently it is achieved through formal business meetings.

Methods of internal communication

Written

- *Letters* are not generally used as a means of internal communication except in the case of letters such as those related to employment, for example appointments or promotion.
- *Memoranda* (memos) are the most frequent method of internal communication between members of the same firm. They tend to be brief and to the point, without formal opening or close.
- *Minutes* are summaries of discussions that have taken place at a meeting.
- *Reports* may be received from committees, be feedback from the salesforce or be in the form of information supplied by specialist employees, for example technical reports, financial reports, etc.
- *Notices* may be displayed to convey information to employees, for example jobs being advertised internally, safety regulations, social/welfare information.
- *Suggestion schemes* make it possible for employees to communicate ideas to the management for improvements in the firm's practices.
- *Manuals* and instruction booklets covering equipment use or detailing business procedures make employees aware of company requirements and safety measures.

Oral

- *Spoken* communications are the most commonly used of all means of passing information. Within the organisation this will most frequently be face-to-face contact, often in the form of instructions from superior to subordinate.
- *Telephone* and intercom usefully allow contact between sections of the organisation where face-to-face contact is not convenient.
- *Interviews* are a common means of selecting employees or considering a person for promotion, and for individual discussions.

How many methods of internal communication in this illustration can you describe?

- *Meetings* provide a convenient means of communication between several people where individual discussions are not convenient or practicable. Meetings are examined in greater detail in the next section of this chapter.

Visual

Pictures, diagrams, maps and plans, wallcharts, flowcharts, pictograms, pie charts and graphs are all ways in which visual communication is typically used within an organisation. They are used to make complicated ideas or information easier to understand. This is examined again later in this chapter, together with other applications of storage and retrieval of information.

14.3 Business meetings

Meetings are an important means of communication within organisations. They give the opportunity for exchange of ideas and collective efforts to solve problems and formulate policies. They also provide a convenient means of issuing instructions or information to many people at one time.

Principal officers

The principal officers of a meeting are the chairman, secretary and treasurer:

- *The chairman* is responsible for the correct conduct of the meeting.
- *The secretary* sends out notices of the meeting and a copy of the agenda, records minutes and ensures meeting decisions are carried out.
- *The treasurer* is responsible for financial matters. Sometimes the job of secretary and treasurer are combined.

Committees

- *Standing* – permanent committees elected to carry out specific regular duties such as discussion of finance, overseas policy, etc.
- *Ad hoc* (or sub) – committee elected to deal with a particular matter over a short period of time, for example the organisation of a social event or to investigate a specific short-term problem.

Types of meeting

- *General* – open to all members of the organisation, these are held monthly, quarterly or annually (annual general meeting – AGM), and used for committee members to communicate with all members of the organisation. The AGM also serves as a useful time for re-election of principal officers.
- *Extraordinary* – additional general meeting called to discuss some special business or unexpected event.
- *Committee* – only attended by committee members, these deal with a specific aspect of the organisation's function. Committees report back to a full general meeting.

Agenda

The agenda is a summary of the items of business to be discussed at a meeting. The agenda follows an accepted form of order in presentation as follows:

AGENDA

1 **Apologies** – received (usually in letter form) from those unable to be at the meeting.

2 **Minutes** – the minutes or notes made from the last meeting are read.

3 **Matters arising** (out of the minutes) – discussion and follow-up of matters or decisions taken at the last meeting.

4 **Correspondence** – discussion of important letters received since the last meeting.

5 **Reports** – may be made by people who have special information to give to the meeting, for example reporting back from the work of a committee.

6 **Special matters** – here will be discussed the purpose of the present meeting; decisions which have to be made; proposals to be discussed and voted on; action to be followed before the next meeting.

7 **Next meeting** – date, time and place of next meeting.

8 **Any other business (AOB)** – at this point members bring up matters or questions not included in the agenda.

Minutes

The minutes are a record of what was decided at a meeting and they may include a 'verbatim report', which is a word-for-word record of a report verbally presented.

Voting

There are four basic ways of recording votes at a meeting.

1 *Secret ballot* – votes are marked on a slip of paper by the voters and then put into a ballot box for later counting.
2 *Show of hands* – hands are raised and counted for or against a motion.
3 *Standing* – at large meetings voters may be asked to 'stand and be counted'.
4 *Proxy* – members unable to attend meetings may vote by post or give permission for someone else to vote on their behalf.

 14.4

External communications

Business correspondence

External communications are the ways in which a firm makes contact with other organisations and people with which it is involved, for example customers, sup-

CHANTREY ELECTRONICS LTD

a — 22 Albion Drive, Minworth, Sutton Coldfield, West Midlands B76 9Y
Telephone: 0628 294609   Telex: 24356 CHANLEC   Fax: 33615
Directors: P. Chantrey A. Jones A. Massmann K. Daley P. Beckwith

b — Your Ref:

Our Ref:

c — 23 March 199-

d — Florida Trading PLC
Florida House
Falkland Road
GLASTONBURY
Somerset
BA4 6BE

e — Dear Sirs

f — International Exhibition

g — Following your instructions at our last meeting we are pleased to confirm
that we have arranged for production of the display models you require for
the exhibition. These will be delivered to the exhibition centre on 7th
July and, so long as your representatives are present, we will assist with
the construction of your display.

We are enclosing herewith our artist's outlines of the proposed models,
together with detailed specifications. Kindly return one copy of these
with your confirmation that our plans meet with your approval.

h — Yours faithfully
CHANTREY ELECTRONICS PLC

i — *P Chantrey*

Mrs P Chantrey
Sales Director

j — enc

The parts of a letter		e	Salutation
a	Letterheading	f	Subject heading
b	Reference number	g	Body of letter
c	Date of letter	h	Complimentary close
d	Name and address of	i	Signature
	addressee	j	Enclosures

pliers and other sections of the organisation which are sited elsewhere. The effectiveness with which these communications are carried out can enhance or tarnish the firm's reputation, and help or hinder its efficiency.

The most basic way that a firm makes contact with others in through correspondence (letters). Although letters are slower than the telephone and other electronic means of communicating, they are relatively cheap. They are also in printed form which enables them to be stored in a simple filing system, and to be read without the aid of 'reading' or transmission devices.

Most business letters have a printed letterheading. This shows the name of the firm, the address, and other information that is important to people the firm corresponds with. The letterheading also reflects the individuality of the firm, perhaps in the form of a logo, trade mark or special form of lettering.

There is a basic format that most business letters tend to follow. Quite apart from the style or structure of the letter the wording is important. This needs to be clear and precise if the message it contains is to be conveyed accurately.

Postal communications

This type of communication is used in the form of letters, circulars and forms such as orders, invoices and other trading documents that were examined in Chapter 12. Postal services are dealt with later in this chapter.

Telecommunications

These methods provide a wider and more speedy means of communication and include the telephone, telex, facsimile transmission, intercity conference links, data transmission services and other electronic communication systems that are examined later in this chapter.

Advertising

This was the topic of Chapter 9 and is also a means of external communication. It is through advertising that the firm makes potential customers aware of the goods and services it wishes to sell.

Transport

Transport provides a physical means of contact, particularly with respect to the delivery of goods. This was the subject of more detailed examination in Chapter 13.

14.5 **Information technology**

Storage and retrieval of information

The use of modern technology for communication within organisations (both internally and externally) is increasingly evident today, particularly for the storage and retrieval of information. Word processors and computers are playing a major part in this important aspect of business. The following are typical business applications of this technology.

● *Company registers* – of shareholders are constantly changing as company shares are bought and sold. A company can speedily update these records.

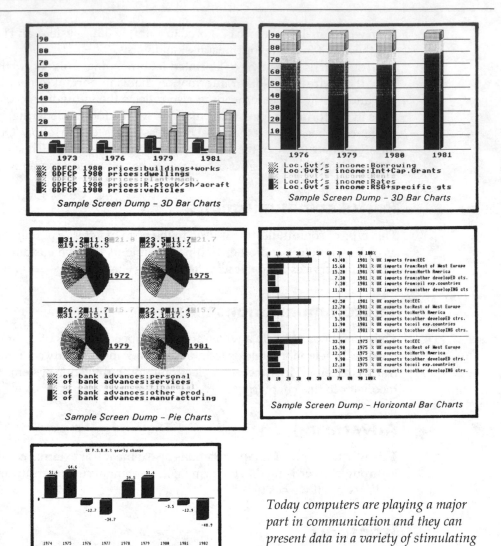

Sample Screen Dump – 3D Bar Charts

Sample Screen Dump – 3D Bar Charts

Sample Screen Dump – Pie Charts

Sample Screen Dump – Horizontal Bar Charts

Sample Screen Dump – 3D Histograms

Today computers are playing a major part in communication and they can present data in a variety of stimulating and meaningful screen displays.

- *Stock records* – automatic updating of records as stocks are removed or added to store. Warnings are automatically given when stock levels fall too low, and immediate stock valuation is available.
- *Payroll* (wages system) – maintenance of payroll and personal records for employees. Automatic calculation of wages, income tax, national insurance and issue of P60s, etc.
- *Word processing* – copies of letters, invoices and statements of account can be typed into a computer and stored on magnetic disc or tape for later retrieval for review on a visual display unit (VDU) or line printer. Word processors are playing a major part in this kind of computer application. Standard letters can be stored on 'memory' for future recall and updating for reproduction, thus allowing much of the repetitive typing to be reduced.
- *Accounts* – issue of invoices, statements of account and maintaining records of customers' accounts.

● *Display* – of data in graphic form is particularly effective with a VDU. Graphs and charts can be displayed in a variety of forms and colours to give a simple representation of complicated data, making it easier to understand. For example, a comparison of the performance of different members of a sales team becomes immediately clear when displayed in the form of a bar chart or graph.

Spreadsheets and databases

Spreadsheets and databases are two important ways of using computers for the storage and display of information.

Spreadsheets

A spreadsheet is a computer software package that allows the computer operator to enter and store data in columns and rows of figures, called *cells*, to be spread out on a VDU screen in 'grid' format. This data can be printed out as a whole or in part.

Spreadsheets are used particularly for financial planning, and the preparation of management reports. They are also used to carry out 'experimental' work. For example, a spreadsheet can be used to assess what would happen to a set of figures if a particular factor were changed.

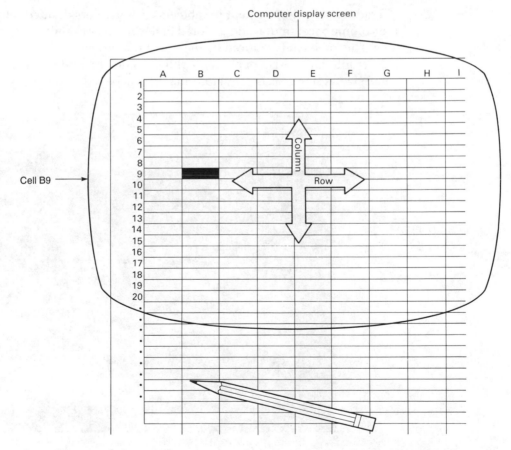

Spreadsheet worksheet.

Databases

A database is a form of electronic filing. It is an organised collection of data. The information is held in such a way that it can be recalled and updated as required.

It is simple to search and sort the information held in a database. For example, the data base can be interrogated to locate a particular item of information, or instructions can be given to sort the database records into a certain order.

Once the database has been searched, sorted and updated the record can all be printed or in part.

Filing

Filing is the most basic form of storage and retrieval system. Filing systems provide a means of storing within the organisation copies of the wide variety of communications in which it is involved.

The purpose of a filing system is to keep papers safe and tidy and easy to find (retrieve) again. Files contain:

- originals of letters and documents received;
- carbon copies of letters and replies sent out;
- copies of documents issued, for example orders, invoices, etc.

Traditionally, filing is kept in cabinets with drawers divided into sections, but the volume of communications stored in this manner is limited by the space available. This problem is reduced by the use of microfilming.

Microfilming consists of photographing documents and reducing them to a very small size. A single sheet of A4 information can be reduced to the size of a postage

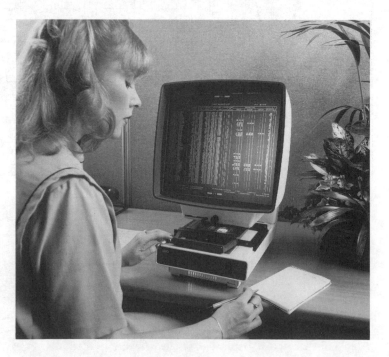

Microfiche reader.

stamp or even smaller, and 8 000 'pictures' can be stored on a single spool of film. The film can be stored in a variety of convenient ways – reels, strips, aperture cards or microfiche. The documents stored in this way can be viewed by using a 'reader' or 'scanner' which magnifies the image and displays it on a viewer or VDU.

Advantages of microfilming

- Saves space and weight.
- Convenient for posting.
- More durable than paper.

Disadvantages of microfilming

- Requires special viewer.
- Cannot update film: it must be replaced.

Postal communications

Businesses need to be able to communicate with each other in order to exchange the correspondence and documentation necessary for transactions to take place. The variety of postal services operated by the Post Office enable businesses to send and receive letters, parcels and payments. The existence of these services makes a considerable contribution to the effective operation of industry and commerce.

The Post Office is a public corporation and a detailed explanation of all postal services is contained in the *Post Office Guide*. The Post Office User's National Council exists to investigate complaints and enquiries related to the Post Office services.

Letter services

In the UK we say that we have a two-tier postal service. *First-class mail* is fast and costs more than *second-class mail*.

Today, in a move towards greater mechanisation of mail handling, the Post Office has identified standard sizes of envelopes (Post Office preferred – POP) which help the mechanised handling of mail movement. In addition, postcodes have been issued to help the Post Office to sort mail automatically.

- Every street has a separate postcode.
- The postcode is shown as letters and numbers at the end of an address.

Business reply service

The trader provides potential customers with specially printed envelopes displaying a licence number and the class of postage. The trader pays postage on letters received, thus encouraging custom.

Freepost

This service also allows people to write to traders in reply to advertisements without paying postage, as long as the envelope is addressed in a special way.

```
BUSINESS REPLY SERVICE
  Licence No. KE 5244
```

2

CNA Reinsurance of London Limited
Accident and Health Division
Fountain House
125–135 Fenchurch Street
LONDON EC3M 5DJ

Business reply service envelope.

- The address must include the word FREEPOST.
- Only second-class service is available.
- The trader is saved the expense of providing envelopes.

Registered post

This service provides compensation to the sender for a lost postal packet. The compensation paid for a loss is proportionate to the value of the packet and the registration fee paid on posting. The letter or packet to be posted in this way must have a large blue cross on it. A certificate of posting is issued as proof of posting, and a signature is obtained on delivery. All valuable items should be sent using this service.

Recorded delivery

The recorded delivery service is cheaper than registered post, but in the case of a loss only a nominal compensation is paid. The service provides proof of posting and delivery and is suitable for important documents (e.g. a final demand for payment of a debt) but is not suitable for posting valuables.

Selectapost

The Post Office will arrange for an addressee's mail to be subdivided (e.g. into departments) prior to delivery so long as some indication of the division required is shown in the address.

Poste restante

Packets may be sent to a post office in a particular town 'to be called for'. The Post Office keeps the packet for up to two weeks and only releases it upon proof of identity. The service is particularly useful to sales representatives who are unsure where they will be residing during their sales tour.

Certificate of posting

- The Post Office gives a receipt to confirm a package has been handed over the counter.
- No charge is made for this receipt.
- Useful in establishing date of posting when there is a possibility of dispute.

How to use *Recorded*

1. On the front of this certificate of posting enter in ink the name and full address, including postcode, as written on the letter or packet.

2. Enter your details in the section for sender's name and address.

3. Peel off and affix top portion of label (which says '*Recorded*') to the top left-hand corner on the front of the letter (or close to the address on a packet).

4. Peel off and affix middle portion of label (which includes barcodes and sender's details) to the reverse of the letter or packet. To enable accurate tracing barcodes should be attached to a single flat surface, and not bent or crumpled.

5. Affix postage stamps to the letter or packet for the correct postage and *Recorded* fee.

6. Hand this certificate together with your letter or packet to an officer of the Post Office.

7. This certificate will be datestamped and initialled as your receipt. Please keep it safely and produce it in the event of a claim or to make an enquiry.

Additional Services
Advice of Delivery can be used in conjunction with *Recorded*. For more information ask at any post office or telephone your local Royal Mail Customer Service Centre.

Recorded

Recorded gives you proof that your mail has been posted and that it has reached its destination. Compensation for loss, damage or delay is limited to the maximum amount available for First and Second class mail. If you need a guarantee of delivery next day you should use *Special Delivery*, or *Registered* if sending money or valuable items up to £500 in value. For money or valuables above £500 and up to £2200 value you should use *Registered Plus*.

Recorded Features
● We give you a certificate of posting as proof that your letter has been posted.
● Signature collected on delivery.
● It can be used in conjunction with First or Second class post.
● Barcoded so that the day after delivery is due you can telephone Royal Mail to confirm delivery (see below for phone number).

How to Confirm Delivery
Should it be necessary to confirm delivery of your *Recorded* item telephone *LocalCall* 0645 272100 and quote the 13 digit reference number on this receipt.

Terms & Conditions
Full terms and conditions can be obtained on request at any post office, or from your local Royal Mail Customer Service Centre (look under 'Royal Mail' in your local telephone book).

Parcels and special services

Parcel post

Used for packages too large for letter post, and up to size and weight limits imposed by the Post Office. A 'postage forward' (postal charges to be paid by receiver) service is available using special labels and a licence allowing use of the service.

Swiftair

This service is available for all letters to Europe and for airmail letters to countries outside Europe. Items are handed over a post office counter and an additional fee is paid. The packet receives accelerated treatment within this country, and within the country of destination.

Express post

Letters and parcels up to a certain size and weight are accepted for delivery by special messenger. The word EXPRESS must be written clearly in the top left-hand corner of the package. Charges are based on distance as well as weight and, therefore, the service is only generally used for relatively short distances.

Special delivery

Available as part of the first-class service only, special delivery is carried out by messenger after the packet has arrived at the destination Post Office. It is suitable for use as a complementary service to the delivery of letters, parcels, recorded delivery and registered post. Packets must be marked 'special delivery'.

Compensation fee (CF) parcels

The Post Office will pay compensation for any parcel lost or damaged in the post if CF has been paid on posting. Amount of compensation is related to fee paid and a nominal maximum amount. Not suitable for very valuable items.

Cash on Delivery (COD)

For a small charge the Post Office will collect a specified amount (not exceeding £100) before parting with a package and pass it to the person who sent the parcel. The money collected is known as a *trade charge*. All letters and packets sent COD must be registered.

Datapost

● Provides door-to-door overnight delivery service.

- Packets are collected and can be returned at times pre-arranged with the Post Office.
- Particularly suitable for exchange of data such as computer material.
- International service also available.

Red Star

The Red Star service is operated by British Rail and not the Post Office, but it is sometimes used by businesses as an alternative to the Post Office parcels services.

Red Star is a strictly timetabled express service. Packages are handed in at railway stations and a number of different transit services are available: same day, overnight, station to station or delivered to the door – each with its own tariff.

Railway letters

Under an agreement with the Post Office some railway companies will accept first-class letters at certain railway stations for transmission to another station on their own lines. The parcel may be collected at the railway station, or transferred to the post.

Franking machines

- Machines are bought or hired from firms licensed by the Post Office.
- Hirer pays for units of postage value.
- Machine is used to stamp letters and parcels with postage paid amount.
- A slogan can be printed at the same time as postage paid to advertise company's products.

A postal franking by machine with a slogan.

14.7 Telecommunications

Telecommunications and technological change

Although the postal services described in the previous sections are varied and effective, they have one major limitation. Even the speediest of the postal services cannot compare with the instant delivery of messages possible through most telecommunications services.

The essence of speed has become an increasingly important aspect of business communication. Stockbrokers and other organisations in the financial markets need to know minute by minute changes in market prices; companies want to be able to contact their representatives in their cars at any time; contracts, plans, specifications and other important documents need to be transmitted around the world in seconds; access to a wide range of information from databanks must be at finger-tip control. All of these facilities, and many more, are available through an ever increasing number of telecommunications services which have not been slow to exploit new advances in technology.

British Telecom is one of the major suppliers of telecommunications in the UK, although there are a considerable number of other companies such as Mercury Telecommunications Ltd competing with British Telecom. Until 1984 British Telecom was a public corporation. In that year the corporation was privatised (sold to private enterprise), but it still holds a monopolistic position for the supply of many telecommunication services. All of the following services, apart from Teletext, are operated by British Telecom, but you should remember that there are other firms competing in the telecommunications market.

Telephone

Telephone services

Advice of duration and charge (ADC)

Call connected and timed by operator. Caller is advised cost of call by operator when call is terminated.

Alarm call

Subscriber arranges for exchange to ring a specified telephone number at a particular time.

Transferred charge call (reversed charge call)

Operator connected call where the receiver of the call accepts the charge.

Personal call (person-to-person)

Telephone operator connects caller with a particular person. Charge does not begin until the requested person is obtained.

Telephone credit card

Allows holder to make operator connected calls and charge costs to their normal telephone bill.

Radiophone

Telephone contact to and from moving vehicles, e.g. Excel.

Freefone

Operator connected calls on a transferred charge basis. Used by businesses that wish to allow their customers or agents to make telephone calls to them without payment, thus encouraging custom.

Call card

Call cards can be bought in the Post Office and some newsagents and used in special public call boxes. They are a useful alternative to coins.

Telephone directories

Issued free to subscribers together with dialling code booklets. Subscribers are listed alphabetically. Those who choose not to be listed are known as 'ex-directory'.

● *Classified Trades Directories* (Yellow Pages)
  Lists local businesses alphabetically by trade.

Correspondence facilities

Electronic mail

Electronic mail refers to a variety of facilities which allow businesses to exchange printed communications rapidly using telecommunication links.

British Telecom in particular has several services within this area of the communication market, e.g. ITT Dialacom, Telex and Telemessage, and these are marketed by Telecom Gold. Facsimile transmission is also another aspect of electronic correspondence.

In recent years, following the privatisation of British Telecom, an increasing number of firms have entered into the electronic correspondence field to challenge the supremacy held by British Telecom for so long.

Telemessage

Messages are accepted by telephone or Telex at Royal Mail sorting centres for delivery with the next day's first-class post.

Facsimile transmission services (FAX)

This service provides facilities for transmission of black and white documents, letters, photos, etc. Customers can use machines:

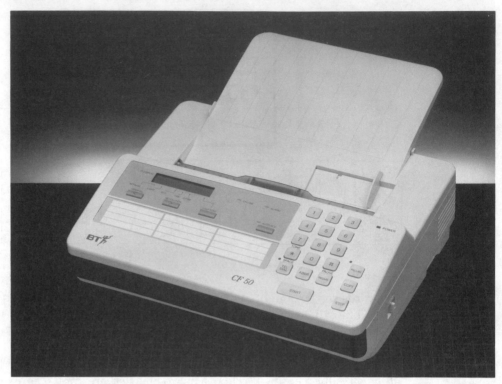

British Telecom CF50 fax machine.

- on their own sites;
- through British Telecom local centres;
- in association with services offered by organisations other than British Telecom.

The prepared A4 size document is fed into a machine and a copy of it is immediately transmitted to another machine sited elsewhere at home or abroad. The facilities can be used as an electronic mailing service, reducing the need to use conventional postal services.

Telex

The main disadvantage of the use of the telephone in business is that the communications are not in printed form, and there are times when it is essential that a message is delivered immediately and also in printed form.

Subscribers to the Telex service rent a machine called a teleprinter and have their Telex call number listed in the *Telex Directory*. Subscribers can call up directly other subscribers at home and overseas.

Messages, which can be in code, are typed into the teleprinter and transmitted immediately to the receiving machine. The receiving terminal can be left unattended and will record messages twenty-four hours a day.

Charges for Telex calls are based on:

- distance between Telex subscribers;
- length of message.

Teletex

Typed messages or letters can be prepared in the normal fashion on a special electronic typewriter terminal. The prepared text can be automatically transmitted in seconds, over ordinary telephone lines, to a receiving terminal where it is printed out or displayed on a screen in exactly the same format as the original.

(Do not confuse with Telex or Teletext.)

Conference facilities

Confravision

Attending conferences and meetings between executives is time-consuming and expensive. Those attending have to:

● travel many miles to get to the meeting place;
● face the hazards and delays likely to occur;
● arrange overnight accommodation.

The Confravision service allows people to hold face-to-face discussions, but without the inconvenience of everyone travelling to the same meeting place. The Confravision service provides studios in cities throughout the UK, which link up by sound and vision, so that discussions can take place as if all those attending the meeting were present in the same room.

Teleconferencing

Teleconferencing is a service which allows several people to be connected by telephone at the same time, allowing an audio conference to take place.

Confravision.

Data links

Datel

A telecommunications system which allows a computer in a firm to communicate with computers on sites in other parts of the country, and in many overseas countries.

Prestel

Prestel is a two-way computerised information service. The service can be used by anyone who has a specially adapted television set and a telephone. The telephone connection is used to obtain up-to-the-minute news and information from an extensive databank for display on the television screen. The Prestel service can respond to questions presented to it. For example, the databank can be asked about road or weather conditions, availability of air or theatre tickets, and bookings can be placed and accepted through the system.

Teletext

The CEEFAX and ORACLE services are provided by the broadcasting authorities whereby people with suitable televisions can call on a wide variety of information and news items from a central databank. These are sometimes referred to as viewdata systems because the information is viewed, but they do not respond to inputs in the ways that the Prestel system does.

Internal telecommunications

- *Intercom* – used for verbal communication between offices, departments or boss and secretary. Message relayed through small loud-speaker.
- *Telephone answering machine* – apparatus connected to telephone to record message when telephone is unattended.

Ceefax.

Combined telephone answering machine.

Office switchboard system.

- *Private manual branch exchange* (PMBX) – switchboard requiring telephone operator to connect all calls incoming, outgoing and between extension.
- *Private automatic branch exchange* (PABX) – switchboard providing automatic transfer of internal calls and connection to outside line by dialling a special number (9).
- *Paging* – lightweight receiver carried on person which 'bleeps' when signal sent out to tell holder to telephone some central point.

Make a note of it

1 Why is communication important to a firm?

2 Name the four basic elements of communication.

3 What is the purpose of the internal communications of a firm?

4 List the main methods of internal communication available.

5 Give an example of the way in which graphs and charts may be used as a means of communication.

6 Name the two principal officers of a meeting.

7 What is the function of the chairman of a meeting?

8 Describe the purpose of three types of meeting.

9 What do the letters AGM stand for?

10 List in correct order six items shown on an agenda.

11 What do the letters AOB stand for?

12 Explain the difference between the minutes and a 'verbatim' report.

13 Describe four methods of voting at meetings.

14 What is the purpose of the external communications of a firm?

15 List the four main forms of external communication.

16 Name the two forms of modern technology that are now making a major contribution to the storage and retrieval of information.

17 Briefly describe four applications of modern technology as a means of handling information.

18 What do the letters VDU stand for?

19 List the three categories of papers likely to be found in files.

20 What are the advantages of storing filing on microfilm?

21 Why are postal services important to businesses?

22 Where are full details of all postal services to be found?

23 'The Post Office is a public corporation.' What does this mean?

24 What is the function of the Post Office User's National Council?

25 Why do we say we have a two-tier postal service in the UK?

26 What are POP envelopes?

27 What is the correct name for the letters and numbers at the end of an address?

28 Compare the business reply service with Freepost.

29 Describe the registered post and recorded delivery services giving appropriate examples when each would be used in preference to the other.

30 Name the postal service where mail is subdivided prior to delivery. Give an example of how use of this service would help the firm that is receiving the letters.

31 Briefly describe the poste restante service and give an example of how it might be employed by a company engaged in sales.

32 What is the purpose of a certificate of posting?

33 Who would pay the postal charges for a package that is sent 'postage forward'?

34 The Swiftair and Red Star services both provide 'special' handling of packets. Explain what is special about these two services.

35 What is the basis of the charge to send a package by express post?

36 Briefly describe the special delivery service.

37 What do the letters CF stand for?

38 What do the letters COD stand for? Why is this service of particular use to a mail order company?

39 Briefly describe the Datapost service and give one example of how it might be used by a firm.

40 What is a franking machine? How can the use of such a machine help to increase efficiency in dealing with outgoing mail?

41 What is the main advantage that telecommunication has over postal communication?

42 Give three examples of circumstances in which businesses particularly need telecommunications facilities.

43 In 1984 British Telecom was privatised. What does this mean?

44 What is an ADC telephone call?

45 Who pays the cost of a transferred charge call?

46 Give an example of a situation where a business might decide to make a personal call.

47 What is the purpose of a telephone credit card? Give one example of how a firm might use this service.

48 Who pays the cost of freefone telephone calls? How might a company use this facility?

49 What kind of information is to be found in Classified Trades Directories?

50 With reference to telephone services, what do the letters STD and IDD stand for?

51 What is telemessage?

52 Briefly describe a facsimile transmission service.

53 What is Teletex?

54 Give a detailed description of the Telex service.

55 What is Confravision and how can this save time and expense for businesses?

56 Briefly explain Datel.

57 Although Prestel and Teletex have some similarities, Prestel has a far wider application.' Explain this statement.

58 What is an intercom?

59 With a telephone answering machine you can be in when you are out. How could this machine be particularly useful to a small business person?

60 What is paging?

Structured Questions

1 The following questions are all related to the Post Office business reply service and you should consult *The Post Office Guide* for relevant information.

   (a) Refer to *The Post Office Guide* and find out the following information related to the Business Reply Service:
- How much in addition to the first or second class postage is payable by the addressee for each item received? (1)
- The additional fee charged is subject to various discounts depending on the number of items received by the addressee per year. What would be the percentage discount for 100 000 items received during one year? (1)

   (b) How does the business reply service encourage potential customers to write to advertisers? (2)

   (c) Briefly explain the purpose of the 'licence' necessary for a business to operate the business reply service. (2)

   (d) Summarise the regulations for the use of pre-paid stationery for this service. (4)

   (e) Compare the business reply service and Freepost including examples of circumstances where a business might decide that one is preferable to another. (10)

2 Look at the advertisement on the next page and answer the questions below.

   (a) What is a credit reference agency? (2)

   (b) What sort of information will a credit reference agency hold on a databank? (2)

   (c) Jenny Fox applied for a loan from a finance company. She was refused the loan because her name is included in a credit agency 'black list'.
- What is a 'black list'? (2)
- Assuming that the information held on computer file is incorrect, what action can Jenny take? (3)

   (d) Where do credit reference agencies obtain the information contained in their computerised references? (3)

   (e) How might a business legally use a credit reference agency to its advantage? (4)

   (f) Examples of 'wise' use of personal computer data include the police and doctors. Briefly describe three other 'wise' examples and one 'unwise' example. (4)

3 Consider the information on page 260 and answer the questions below.

   (a) What do the letters MD stand for? (1)

   (b) What is the function of an MD? (2)

   (c) In what ways can Dorothy's firm's problem be seen to be one of communication? (3)

Who's checking on the computers when the computers are checking on you?

Where would you expect to find the biggest list of people's names in the country? Perhaps your first thought would be the telephone directory.

If so, you would be wrong. Certainly there are over 23 million telephone subscribers in the UK and the gas and electricity boards and some government departments have similar sized information or data banks.

But even these do not match, for example, the 40 million separate records kept by the nation's leading credit reference agencies. And the Department of Health and Social Security has records on virtually everybody in the country.

The increasing use of computer technology allows such information to be compiled quickly and referred to almost instantaneously from anywhere in the country.

So why should this concern you? Well, as someone who will have to face the challenge of leaving school and establishing a career, you may well find that you, yourself, are soon placed upon such a list – if you are not on one already!

In most cases, these lists, and the information they contain, are used wisely as part of everyday life. For instance assisting police in their enquiries, government departments in deciding upon benefit entitlements, and many Doctors in providing health care.

These activities are sensible enough, assisting rather than hindering the normal processes of society. However, there can be problems for if the information on the lists is incorrect, or if your details are mixed up with someone else's then things may go wrong. You may find your claim for benefit payment or credit being turned down, the mortgage for a house you want to buy refused, or even the police arresting you, all because of a simple mistake in the records.

Happily, this doesn't happen too often. But when it does, you will want to know how to identify – and to correct – that mistake.

The Data Protection Act is now here to help, giving us all new rights. Rights which enable us to inspect the information held about us on computer records, and to correct it if it is wrong. As importantly, the Act also allows us to claim compensation if we are damaged by any misuse of this information.

The Act is supervised by the Data Protection Registrar. He can follow up any complaints about the misuse of computer records, no matter how large or small the organisation concerned.

For more information on the Data Protection Act, please contact:-

Information Services (BTA), Office of the Data Protection Registrar, Springfield House, Water Lane, Wilmslow, Cheshire SK9 5AX. Telephone: 0625 535777.

THE DATA PROTECTION REGISTRAR

A question of communication

Dorothy Whitehead is the Managing Director (MD) of a medium-sized company in the North East. Her firm manufactures a range of cardboard boxes. In the years since the firm was established in 1980, Dorothy's company has steadily increased its sales until about six months ago. Then Dorothy noticed a distinct fall in orders received, even though the firm's prices still compared favourably with those of competitors.

One of the regular customers who had ceased to place orders was AJ Products of Redditch. Dorothy arranged to visit Mr Jones the MD of AJ Products, in an attempt to find out why his company had not placed an order with her firm for some time.

'Your sales staff could do with a bit of a shake up', said Mr Jones, 'Whenever my people 'phone your firm the person they want to speak to is never there, and it seems that the people in the office never know where they are or when they are likely to return. We have requested that someone 'phones us back, but this doesn't happen. And another thing, the people you have answering the 'phone are not particularly helpful, in fact some of them could be said to be downright rude. Quite frankly, until your staff learn to be a bit more helpful and efficient I can't see any immediate prospect of further trade between our companies'.

(d) Imagine that you are Dorothy's personal assistant. Compose a brief memo to all senior staff requesting that they attend a meeting next Wednesday at 5.00 pm to discuss the problem. Include an indication of what the meeting will be about. (4)

(e) Dorothy has asked you to open the meeting by giving a brief summary of the reasons why the firm has been losing orders.
Write out notes for this introduction to the meeting. (4)

(f) Assuming that you were given sole charge of improving the company's image, explain the steps you would take in an attempt to solve the current problem. (6)

4 An extract from *The Post Office Guide* is shown on page 261.

(a) Briefly describe the purpose of the electronic post service in your own words. (2)

(b) Why is the use of postcodes an important feature of the electronic post service? (2)

(c) Why do the Post Office stress that 'the service is completely secure'? (4)

(d) Briefly describe circumstances when a business would use each of the two service options available. (4)

(e) Compare the electronic post service with two competing telecommunication services. (8)

> **Electronic Post**
> Electronic Post is the Post Office's laser printing service for business mailings, combining sophisticated technology with traditional delivery methods. All the customer needs to do is supply the Post Office with a computer tape containing a fully postcoded address list and details of the text to be mailed. The information on the tape is sorted and transmitted electronically to one of 6 regionally located Electronic Post Centres where it is printed in postcode order, enveloped and inserted with enclosures where appropriate, and placed in the mail stream for normal 1st Class delivery.
> The service has the facility to incorporate the customer's own logos, letterheads, signatures and graphics. Textual personalisations can be inserted in every line and 24 different type faces are available to provide maximum variety.
> Two service options are offered by Electronic Post; the Standard Service is available for mailings that can be organised in advance, ie the customer and the Post Office negotiate a drop date and time table the mailing accordingly. The Priority Service is designed to cope with those more time critical mailings – the customer submits his tape at a pretimed point during the day (the exact time will be determined by the size and geographical coverage of the mailing), the items are then processed and put into the 1st Class mail stream that night. Electronic Post is suitable for a wide variety of mailings; eg bills, dunning notices, statements, information updates, minutes of meetings, subscription reminders, advertisements, stop notices, etc. The service is completely secure, all mailings are processed in lockable rooms accessible to authorised personnel only and are identified by an individual code number visible through the envelope window to ensure that undelivered letters can be forwarded to the sender.

5 Look at the article on the next page and then answer the questions below.

(a) How does a 'laptop' differ from a portable computer? (2)

(b) In what way can a laptop computer reduce time wastage for a busy executive? (2)

(c) State four items that a business person would be likely to produce using a laptop computer and while travelling. (2)

(d) What sort of information would a business executive be likely to want to receive from their base while travelling? (4)

(e) Why has the development and wider use of portable telephones made the application of laptop computers more practicable? (4)

(f) Why is the use of a laptop computer limited by its power, memory store and storage capacity? (6)

Extended answer assignments

1 Considering the speed of telecommunications why do postal services continue to play an important part in business operation? Support your study with data obtained through local research, e.g. a firm you are familiar with.

2 Take one large and one small business in your area. Compare the communication methods they use and comment on any differences found.

Computing on the move

CAR   PLANE   TRAIN

Laptop computers provide tremendous benefits for those who need computing power while on the move. And when used in conjunction with the telephone network, laptops become the business traveller's lifeline for essential and complicated messages to and from base.

The computer industry differentiates between what it calls a portable and a laptop. Portables are full-sized mains-driven desktop micros that can be carried, e.g. to a car boot and then, set up at home.

Laptops are light, slim machines that can literally sit on your lap while you are in a car, train or aircraft seat. They are often battery-powered, and to minimise power loss the screens are usually liquid crystal displays (LCDs) – the same technology used in calculator screens. Depending on the machine's power, memory size and storage capacity, laptops can be used for all the jobs that are normally done on desktop micros, i.e. wordprocessing, communicating with electronic mail services, data storage, production of spreadsheets, keeping diaries, calculating figures, etc.

Both types are useful because they enable constructive use to be made of time often wasted while travelling or in hotel rooms. Memos, telexes, letters and reports can be written on the move and either printed on an office or portable printer, or sent to another computer over the telephone. Up-to-date price lists and quotations can be printed on demand for customers.

3 Choose any firm in your area. Explain why telecommunications is an important aspect of the firm's operations.

4 Investigate any firm in your community and describe the forms of internal communication it employs.

15 Banking

Central banks

Most major countries today have a single central bank which plays a major role in controlling the monetary system. Our central bank, the Bank of England (the Bank), is the heart of the British banking system, exerting a considerable influence on other parts of the banking sector.

The functions of the central bank

It is the government's bank

This is the major function of the Bank. In this respect it manages the government's banking accounts, for example for the Exchequer and other government departments.

The Bank advises the government on formulation of monetary policy and assists the government in carrying out that policy.

The Bank also handles the arrangements for government borrowing:

The Bank of England is at the centre of the British banking system.

263

- short-term – principally through the sale of Treasury bills;
- long-term – management of government stocks which form the bulk of the national debt.

Management of the exchange equalisation account is also carried out by the Bank and it is through this that the Bank can influence the value of sterling by selling or buying pounds to affect the foreign exchange market prices.

It controls the note issue

The Bank has the sole responsibility for the issue of banknotes in England and Wales.

It is the bankers' bank

Each of the clearing banks has an account with the Bank, and during the process of cheque clearing (see later) debits and credits are made to these accounts as a means of interbank settlement.

The clearing banks keep about a half of their liquid reserves (short call money) deposited at the Bank and use these for settling debts among themselves (e.g. in cheque clearing activities).

The commercial banks rely on the Bank if they run short of money or require loans.

It has international responsibilities

The Bank provides services for other central banks and some of the world's major financial organisations such as the International Monetary Fund (IMF).

It is the 'lender of last resort'

If the commercial banks run short of cash they recall deposits they have in the money market. This leaves the discount houses short of funds. The Bank of England 'lends as a last resort' to the discount houses, but at a higher rate of interest than that obtainable elsewhere in the City.

15.2 Central banks and monetary control

The Bank of England (like other central banks) is responsible for carrying out the monetary policy of the government. This particularly involves the Bank in exercising control of the money supply and the lending activities of the banks. It does this in a number of ways.

Open market operations

The Bank seeks to keep interest rates within an unpublished band through its bill dealing with the discount houses. By buying and selling bills from and to discount houses the Bank influences the amount of funds available to the banking system as a whole.

Basically, this action influences short-term interest rates, but leaves the influence of long-term rates to market forces.

Minimum lending rate (MLR)

The use of MLR has currently been suspended by the Bank, although it can be reintroduced at some future date, maybe temporarily. When in operation, MLR is the minimum rate of interest at which the Bank will normally lend to the discount houses. All other interest rates tend to follow MLR movement when used in this way.

Cash at the Bank

The Bank requires all institutions in the monetary sector with eligible liabilities of £10 million or more to keep 1/2 per cent of their eligible liabilities in non-interest earning balances at the Bank of England. Eligible liabilities are the liabilities of the banks *less:*

(a) funds lent by one institution in the monetary sector to any other;
(b) money at call (can be withdrawn on demand) placed with money brokers and jobbers in the Stock Exchange, and secured on gilt-edged stocks, Treasury bills, local authority bills and eligible bank bills (e.g. bill of exchange).

Money at call

Each bank whose bills are recognised as eligible is required to maintain:

(a) 6 per cent of its eligible liabilities with members of the London Discount Market Association (LDMA) and/or with money brokers and gilt-edged jobbers;
(b) the proportion held with members of the LDMA must not fall below 4 per cent on any one day.

Special deposits

Banks and deposit-taking institutions with eligible liabilities of £10 million or more can be called on to deposit a percentage (decided by the Bank) of their liabilities with the Bank, which earns interest at a rate close to Treasury bill rate. This process can be used as a means of withdrawing cash from the money market.

Lender of last resort

(See also the earlier section on the functions of the Bank.) If the commercial banks run short of cash they recall their loans made to the discount market. Consequently, the members of the discount market are forced to borrow funds from the Bank which charges a rate of interest higher than that charged anywhere else in the City.

15.3 Special financial institutions

Merchant Banks

These are not banks in the commonly understood sense but private firms that offer highly specialised services almost exclusively for business customers. The main activities of merchant banks can be divided into accepting house activities, issuing house activities and capital market activities.

Acceptance house activities

The traditional activity of merchant banks is 'accepting' (i.e. lending their name to) a bill of exchange issued by less well-known traders, so that it becomes more acceptable because of the bank's good reputation in the financial world. By endorsing the bill, the accepting house guarantees payment of the bill should the drawer default. (See Chapter 11 for application of bills of exchange in finance of international trade.)

Issuing house activities

Merchant banks play a major role in assisting in raising company finance by sponsoring first issues of company shares on behalf of their clients, or acting as intermediaries between companies seeking capital and those willing to provide it. It should be noted that not all issuing houses are merchant banks (see Chapter 17 for notes on share issue).

Capital market activities

In addition to raising capital for companies by their issuing house activities, merchant banks are also involved in a wide range of other capital market operations some of which are as follows:

- they operate some current account services for customers;
- they accept larger (e.g. over £25 000) deposits, generally for one year or more;
- they offer consultancy services to businesses wishing to become limited liability companies;
- they advise on company problems such as capital reorganisations, dividend policy, mergers and takeover bids;
- they provide finance for hire-purchase, local government and industry;
- they operate unit trusts (see also Chapter 17);
- they assist in the investment of trustee funds for large institutions;
- they act as agents to companies establishing branches overseas;
- they deal in the precious metals market.

Discount houses

The London Discount Market Association (LDMA) consists of twelve companies basically concerned with borrowing and investing money on a short-term basis. The majority of the dealing is carried out by telephone and personal contact.

The main functions of the discount houses can be summarised as follows:

- accepting very short-term deposits from businesses, particularly banks, in return for a low rate of interest;
- using funds raised in this way to purchase a variety of assets, for example Treasury bills, bills of exchange and gilt-edged securities;
- providing immediate finance for companies by discounting reliable bills of exchange, that is buying them for less than their face value and holding them

until they mature to obtain the full value, or reselling them and charging a higher rate of discount to achieve a profit.

Foreign banks

There are now about 400 foreign banks (particularly from European countries) in London existing to give service and credit to companies from their own countries operating in Britain. A number of these banks have expanded their activities and they now make substantial sterling loans to British borrowers.

Finance houses

The Finance Houses Association (FHA) consists of forty-three member companies who control 80 per cent of the instalment credit business in the UK.

15.4   The clearing banks

'Clearing' banks are so-called because they handle the exchange and settlement of cheques through the clearing house system which is dealt with later in this chapter.

The clearing banks consist of:

- the Northern Ireland clearing banks
- the Scottish clearing banks
- the London clearing banks:
  - (a) Barclays
  - (b) Lloyds
  - (c) Midland } sometimes referred to as the 'big four'
  - (d) National Westminster Bank
  - (e) Coutts & Co. (owned by National Westminster)
  - (f) Co-operative Bank
  - (g) Trustee Savings Bank
  - (h) National Girobank.

The functions of the clearing banks can be summarised as follows:

- acceptance of deposits of money;
- provision of a system of payments mechanism;
- supply of finance;
- provision of a wide range of services.

Can you identify the logo that belongs to each of the 'big four' banks?

15.5 Bank accounts

There are three basic types of bank account: budget account, deposit account and current account.

The budget account

This type of account helps to even out the payment of annual household expenses. Upon payment of an agreed weekly or monthly amount the bank gives the account holder permission to draw cheques, standing orders or direct debits up to a given credit limit. The limit is calculated proportionate to the regular in-payment. While the account is in credit, the money earns interest, and interest is charged when the account is overdrawn. There is also a charge for each cheque or other withdrawal.

The bank budget account is particularly useful for someone who finds it difficult to organise and stick to their own personal budget plan.

The deposit account

The bank deposit account is used by individuals and businesses for the safekeeping of funds not needed for immediate use. Credit slips are used to pay money, cheques, postal orders, etc. into the account.

No cheque book is issued with this account and, therefore, transfer of sums of money from the deposit account is normally in the form of cash. The bank can request seven days' notice of withdrawal of money from the account, although this rule is usually waived, especially for relatively small amounts.

Depositors are paid interest on money left in the account, and the bank then lends the money to borrowers who are charged a higher rate of interest. A statement of account is issued periodically to the account holder. The account cannot be overdrawn (see later).

The current account (cheque account)

This type of account is used by individuals and businesses for the safekeeping of funds needed for current use, in other words funds which are required to be immediately available.

The current account can be opened with a small deposit, a specimen signature, and a reference from someone acceptable to the bank.

Credit slips are used to pay deposits into the account and cheques are used to draw cash or transfer funds to others. Funds can also be withdrawn from the account twenty-four hours of the day through a cash dispenser.

Interest is not always paid on this type of account although some banks have experimented with paying interest on the maintenance of a minimum balance. Bank charges may be incurred if a minimum balance is not maintained.

A statement of account is issued to the account holder periodically or on request, and a current balance figure can also be obtained twenty-four hours a day through a cash dispenser.

With the permission of the bank the current account may be 'overdrawn', that is the account holder will be allowed to draw on more money than is in the account. This is examined in more detail later.

A 'joint' account may be shared by two or more persons. In the case of a joint account or a business account, the account holders can make a variety of arrangements for signing cheques, for example signed by any one, or any two of a number of authorised signatories.

15.6 The cheque system

Cheques

A cheque is a written instruction to the bank (the *drawee*) to pay money to the account holder (the *drawer*) or to another person (the *payee*). Most cheques are *order* cheques, which means they must be signed (*endorsed*) on the reverse by the named payee if they wish to pass it on to someone else.

Although today we recognise cheques as special slips of printed paper, these are only issued by banks for both the convenience of their account system, as well as to help account holders. However, there is no reason why the instruction to the bank cannot take the form of a letter, or even a less formal message. There have been occasions when, for a variety of reasons, these instructions have been written on such widely diverse items as a door, a paving slab, various items of clothing and even a fish.

The bank will ensure that the cheque:
- *has been written out correctly*
- *has not been altered*
- *has a valid date*
- *has a signature which compares with the specimen held.*

Things written on a cheque

- The date from which the value of the cheque is payable (a post-dated cheque is one dated for sometime in the future).
- Name of payee (person cheque is to pay).
- Amount to be paid in words.
- Amount to be paid in figures.
- Signature of drawer (person from whose account funds are to be withdrawn).

Open cheque (uncrossed)

The open cheque does not have two parallel lines drawn across it. It is 'uncrossed'. The payee of an open cheque can:

- pay the cheque into his own account;
- pass it to someone else by endorsing it;
- exchange it for cash at the bank on which it is drawn.

The open cheque can be paid out to whoever presents it at the bank, and, therefore, it is not very safe. Banks prefer their customers to use crossed cheques and open cheques are used far less frequently than crossed cheques.

Crossed cheque

A crossed cheque has two parallel lines drawn vertically across it. This type of cheque must be paid into a bank account and cannot be exchanged for cash except

1   This crossing ensures that the cheque can only be paid into the account of the payee, although they can pay it into their account through any branch they wish.
2   This means the same as the above crossing except that the cheque can only be paid in at the branch stated in the crossing.
3   When written as a cheque crossing this warns anyone other than the payee accepting the cheque that they do so with some degree of risk. The risk they face is that if the cheque has been stolen or fraudulently used, then the person accepting it is liable to refund the rightful owner with the amount shown on the cheque.

by the drawer at his own bank, or at another bank with the use of a cheque card. These rules help to eliminate fraud in the use of cheques.

If you look at the cheque shown you will see that it has a 'general' crossing; there is nothing written between the lines of the crossing. This means that the cheque must pass through a bank account and cannot be exchanged for cash. However, a cheque with this sort of crossing can still be endorsed and passed to someone else, and such a cheque is still open to fraudulent use, although less so than the open cheque.

There is a variety of wordings that can be written between the lines of a cheque crossing to give more specific instructions on how the cheque may be used, and to make it safer. The three most frequently used 'special' cheque crossings are shown on page 270.

Dishonoured cheques

Cheques which are not passed for payment by the drawer's bank are said to have 'bounced' or been dishonoured. When a cheque is refused for payment the drawer's bank will write 'refer to drawer' or R/D on the cheque and return it to the payee who must find out from the drawer why the cheque has not been honoured.

Reasons why a cheque might 'bounce'

- Cheque contains an error or is unsigned.
- Cheque is 'stale' (more than six months old).
- Signature differs from specimen held at bank.
- Drawer does not have sufficient funds in account.
- Cheque has been altered.
- Cheque is post-dated.
- Cheque has been 'stopped' by the drawer (drawer has instructed bank not to make payment).

Bank statement of account

The bank statement of account is issued to the account holder periodically or on request. The account holder can also obtain a figure to show the current balance in the account from the bank cash dispenser which will provide information and cash twenty-four hours of the day. The statement sums up all the transactions which have taken place since the last statement was issued and shows the current balance held in the account.

Amounts which reduce the balance (e.g. cheques issued) in the account are shown in the payments column, and amounts which increase the balance in the account are shown in the receipts column. As each payment or receipt is recorded a new balance figure is shown in a third column.

Cheque clearing

The reader's attention is directed again to the point made earlier that a cheque is an instruction to their bank by the drawer of the cheque. Consequently, when a payee deposits a cheque into their account it does not mean the transfer of funds

Midland Bank plc

MISS A. N. OTHER

COVENT GARDEN BRANCH
16 KING STREET LONDON WC2E 8JF

Statement of Account

1988	Sheet 42	Account No. 51149903	DEBIT	CREDIT	BALANCE Credit C Debit D
AUG 5	BALANCE BROUGHT FORWARD				62.08 C
AUG 8	AUTOBK COVENT GDN2		10.00		52.08 C
AUG 9	100142		35.00		17.08 C
AUG10	100146		10.30		
AUG10	100147		8.15		
AUG10	AUTOBK NATW 601533		10.00		11.37 D
AUG15	100148		10.00		21.37 D
AUG16	100144		5.00		26.37 D
AUG19	100149		10.00		
AUG19	PITMAN PUBLISHING			506.33	469.96 C
AUG22	AUTOBK NOTT HLL GT		15.00		
AUG22	SUNDRIES			65.00	519.96 C
AUG23	100473		41.00		
AUG23	AUTOBK NATW 503021		60.00		418.96 C
AUG24	100150		80.00		
AUG24	100474		160.00		
AUG24	AUTOBK NATW 503021		10.00		168.96 C
AUG30	AUTOBK COVENT GDN2		10.00		158.96 C
AUG31	100475		38.40		
AUG31	AUTOBK COVENT GDN		20.00		
AUG31	AUTOBK NATW 503021		45.00		55.56 C
SEP 2	AUTOBK NATW 503021		10.00		45.56 C
SEP 6	AUTOBK NATW 503021		10.00		35.56 C
SEP 6	BALANCE CARRIED FORWARD				35.56 C

Please refer to the Customer Information printed overleaf, and then file away safely.

A bank statement.

has taken place. The instruction is to the drawer's bank, and transfer cannot be carried out until the drawer's bank has received the instruction. In the meantime the payee cannot draw on the amount stated on the cheque. The process by which cheques are passed for payment is known as the *clearing system*.

A cheque can only be 'cleared' for payment at the bank on which it is drawn. If the drawer and payee use the same branch bank then, so long as the drawer has sufficient funds, a simple paper transfer is carried out within the branch bank. If the drawer and payee use the same bank but different branches the system of clearing the cheque for payment is still relatively simply carried out through the headquarters of the bank.

If the drawer and payee have accounts with different banks the cheques are cleared through the *Bankers' Clearing House* where representatives of all the clearing banks meet daily to exchange cheques they have received belonging to other banks.

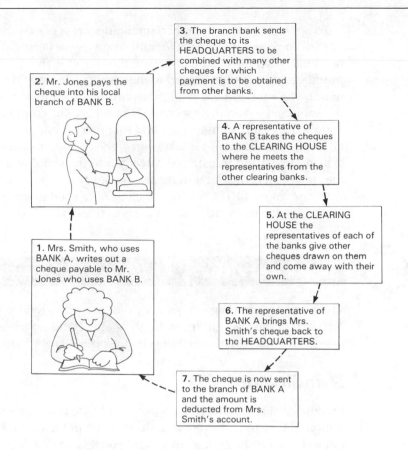

The lifecycle of a cheque.

At the Clearing House the representative from the headquarters of each clearing bank meets the representatives of the other banks and gives them cheques drawn on their banks and accepts cheques drawn on his bank. During this process an account is kept of the value of the cheques changing hands. The difference between the value of the cheques received and handed over shows how much each of the banks owes the other. This information is used daily to credit or debit the balances of the clearing banks which are kept at the Bank of England.

The cheque passes through a complete cycle, from the time the drawer writes out the cheque until the drawer's bank has released the payment to the payee, in just three days.

15.7 **EFTPOS**

A payment system called EFTPOS is one of the latest developments of the banking system. This title stands for 'Electronic Funds Transfer at Point of Sale'. EFTPOS is a method of paying for goods or services in shops, garages, etc., using electronics instead of paper.

To operate the system the account holder has a plastic card (such as a credit card or cash card) and a means of identification (e.g. a Personal Identification Number or PIN). When the customer gets to the shop till and is required to pay for their purchases they give their card to the cashier who runs it through a computer terminal. The amount to be paid is displayed at the top of a small key-pad on which the shopper keys in their secret PIN number. The computer checks that the card and the PIN number match up, and that there is enough money in the account. If all is in order, the money is taken out of the customer's bank account (if a cash card is being used) and transferred directly into the shop's account. With credit cards the statement comes later in the usual way.

In due course EFTPOS will be increasingly used in the many places where payments need to be made by consumers to traders.

15.8   Bank services

There are a wide range of services that are provided by the commercial banks, National Girobank, and increasingly by the building societies. These assist businesses and individual consumers by making it easier to make payments.

Standing order

Imagine that a company has purchased an item of equipment on hire purchase. This could mean that every month someone in the firm has to remember to write out a cheque and covering letter, and address an envelope and post it to the hire-purchase company.

This is not only time-consuming and inconvenient, but there is the danger that the payment could be overlooked, perhaps damaging the firm's reputation for paying debts promptly. The bank standing order service solves this problem, for individuals or organisations, by making regular payments of a set sum from one bank account to another on behalf of the customer.

This service is available to current account holders and it saves the bank customer the need to remember, and to post off, payments. The service is only useful if the amount to be transferred does not change.

Direct debit

This is a variation of the standing order service. Instead of instructing the bank to make regular payments on their behalf, customers fill in and sign a form which gives permission for a payee to withdraw regular amounts from their account. The amount may be varied by the payee and notified to the account holder at some later time. This service is suitable for repayments of forms of credit where the repayment amount may vary due to changes in interest rates.

The standing order and the direct debit have dual roles in respect of business application. They not only make it easy for the business to make regular payments, but they also enable businesses to receive regular payments from their customers.

STANDING ORDER MANDATE

TO _Lloyds_ Bank PLC

ADDRESS _16, Waterend Rd, Kendal, Cumbria_

	BANK	BRANCH TITLE (Not address)	SORTING CODE NUMBER
Please pay	Midland	Bridge Rd	40 — 15 — 20
	BENEFICIARY'S NAME		ACCOUNT NUMBER
for the credit of	Sally Carstairs		1 0 0 9 2 3 4 1
	AMOUNT IN FIGURES	AMOUNT IN WORDS	
†the sum of	£		

	DATE AND AMOUNT OF FIRST PAYMENT			DUE DATE AND FREQUENCY
commencing	*NOW	£ 100	and thereafter every	month
	DATE AND AMOUNT OF LAST PAYMENT			
*until	—	£ —	*until you receive further notice from me/~~us in writing~~	
quoting the reference	—		and debit my/~~our~~ account accordingly.	

*Delete if not applicable
†if the amount of the periodic payments vary they should be incorporated in a schedule overleaf

THIS INSTRUCTION CANCELS ANY PREVIOUS ORDER IN FAVOUR OF THE BENEFICIARY NAMED ABOVE, UNDER THIS REFERENCE.

SPECIAL INSTRUCTIONS _____

ACCOUNT TO BE DEBITED	ACCOUNT NUMBER
current account	7 1 2 4 6 0 8 1

SIGNATURE(S) _J. C. Carstairs_   DATE _6. 4. 19X8_

NOTE: The Bank will not undertake to (i) make any reference to Value Added Tax or other indeterminate element
  (ii) advise payer's address to beneficiary
  (iii) advise beneficiary of inability to pay
  (iv) request beneficiary's banker to advise beneficiary of receipt

Standing order form.

Bank giro

The bank giro is a method of transfer (credit transfer) of funds directly into the account of someone else, who may hold his account at another branch or even a different bank to the person making the payment. The person making the payment does not have to hold a bank account as in-payment can be made with cash or cheque. There are two basic methods of credit transfer that are generally used, the single transfer and the multiple transfer.

Single transfer

A bank giro form similar to that on page 276 is filled in to make a single payment directly to a stated bank account. The major suppliers of domestic facilities, such as gas, electricity and water, help their customers to use the system by printing bank giro credit forms at the bottom of their bills.

Single transfer bank giro form.

Multiple transfer

Using this method the drawer only writes out a single cheque to pay several bills or a number of different people.

A list or schedule is passed to the bank showing details of a number of different accounts to be credited by direct transfer. The account holder writes out a single cheque in favour of the bank itself and the bank credits each payee, saving the account holder the necessity of writing out many cheques.

The system can be used to pay the bills of several traders but it is particularly useful in paying the wages of many employees.

Bank cards

It is sometimes said that we have become a largely 'cashless' society. This not only refers to the cheque and giro systems of money transfer already examined, but also to the function of some of the bank cards that are now being used, often reducing the need for cash transactions. Three of the main bank cards are now examined, but it should be remembered that there are card systems apart from those issued by the banks (e.g. retailers' charge cards, telephone credit card and others discussed in other chapters) which also contribute to the conception of a 'cashless' society.

Cheque card

Cheque cards are issued by banks to reliable, well-established customers. The card is used to guarantee payment of a cheque up to a maximum amount which is stated on the card. The card shows an identification number and a specimen signature, and payment of a cheque cannot be stopped if a cheque card has been used to guarantee it.

Credit card

Credit cards are a financial service run by the commercial banks. The card shows the identification number and specimen signature of the rightful owner who can use it for purchasing without using cash or cheque.

The card-holder signs for goods or services and presents the card to the trader. The bank pays the trader and the customer later pays the money to the bank. The system is used by account holders for shopping, travel, garages, restaurants, etc.

- A monthly statement is sent to the account holder.
- No interest is charged if the account is paid immediately.
- Interest is charged on balances left outstanding.

Cash dispenser card

The bank customer is issued with a card and a secret personal identity number (PIN) known only to them and the bank. The cash dispenser card also has its own separate identity code incorporated into it.

A cash dispensing machine is set into the wall outside the bank and is connected to the bank computer. The card-holder feeds his card into the machine and 'keys in' the PIN.

If the card data and the keyed in PIN match up with the record the bank computer holds, the dispenser issues the money requested up to a daily individual limit. The customer's account is immediately automatically debited with the amount withdrawn.

The machine operates twenty-four hours a day and it will also provide information such as current account balance.

Electronic funds transfer

One of the most recent money transfer systems to be developed is the movement towards a national electronic payments system. This refers to a system known as EFT (Electronic Funds Transfer) and EPOS (Electronic Point of Sale). These are computer-controlled payment systems.

While a checkout till operator in a shop is totalling up the customer's purchases using a computer (EPOS) the customer inserts a bank card into a machine linked to their bank, building society, or credit card company. Their PIN (personal identification number), is keyed in and verified by the terminal computer. The computer will authorise the payment immediately (EFT) and debit the customer's account if sufficient funds are available; the transaction may be rejected if there are not enough funds available.

Miscellaneous bank services

Night safe

This facility is provided by banks to enable customers to deposit money when the bank is closed. Cash for depositing is placed in a special cash wallet together with a credit or paying-in slip. The wallet is dropped into the bank through a trap in the wall, and the amount enclosed is credited to the customer's account on the morning of the next bank working day. This service is particularly used by traders wishing to make deposits at the end of a day's trading.

Safe deposit box

This is a secure box kept in the bank's vault for the customers for the safe-keeping of valuables, important documents, etc.

Traveller's cheques

These are special cheques charged against a bank and, therefore, guaranteed by the bank. This makes them acceptable throughout the world and useful to the business person or the individual when travelling. They can be purchased at the local bank for use abroad to obtain foreign currency. The cheques are 'safe' because if they are lost or stolen abroad they can immediately be cancelled and the bank will replace them. A further safeguard requires those encashing the cheques to sign in front of those cashing them, having first produced proof of identity (e.g. passport).

Bill of exchange

A method of payment whereby the seller draws up a document and the buyer signs it (the opposite of the normal cheque transaction) agreeing to pay at some future date. The bill of exchange can be kept until payment is made, sold to someone else at a discount *(discounted)*, or used as collateral against a loan *(negotiated)*. These bills are particularly evident in international trade where exporters use them to guarantee payment for goods prior to despatch.

Bank draft

This is a cheque drawn on a bank instead of a person's account. A bank draft is guaranteed by the bank (which makes it as good as cash) because the customer pays the value of the draft in advance.

Banks also render a wide variety of services too numerous to deal with fully here, these include:

- investment advice;
- wills and trustee advice;
- sale of foreign currency;
- taxation guidance.

15.9 Borrowing from a bank

There are three main methods of borrowing from a bank: overdraft, loan and bridging loan. Banks often require some form of security (called 'collateral') to safeguard against possible non-repayment of the amount loaned. Collateral might take the form of property deeds, stocks and shares, or other items of value that can be sold by the bank in the event of default by the borrower.

The bank manager takes the following information into account before agreeing to allow a customer to borrow from the bank:

- income of the individual or organisation;
- debts and commitments of the borrower;
- assets owned by the borrower;
- past banking record of the borrower.

Note: Interest is the 'price' of borrowing money or the 'reward' for leaving money in the bank.

Overdraft

With permission of the bank the current account holder may write out cheques for more money than there is in the account. When this happens the account is said to be overdrawn or 'in the red'. The actual amount the account is overdrawn by is known as the *overdraft*.

Irrespective of what overdraft facility is granted, the customer is only charged interest (calculated daily) on the actual amount overdrawn. Any deposits made to the account while it is overdrawn have the effect of reducing the overdraft, while any cheques paid out increase it.

The overdraft tends to be used for temporary or short-term borrowing when the borrower is not sure exactly how much is needed, or for how long it is needed.

Loan

In the case of a bank loan, the total amount requested is transferred to the customer's account and, therefore, the customer is required to pay interest on the total amount borrowed, even if all the money is not used immediately.

The loan is repaid in regular fixed amounts, including interest, over a specific period of time agreed between the bank and the customer.

The bank loan tends to be used for a particular purpose when the amount required and length of repayment time is known, because the annual rate of interest on a loan is likely to be less than that of an overdraft.

Bridging loan

A bridging loan is provided by a bank as a temporary measure for a very short period (a few days or weeks) until other expected funds become available.

Make a note of it

1 Name the institutions which make up the British banking sector.

2 What do we mean when we say that the Bank of England is a central bank?

3 State one way in which the Bank of England influences the value of sterling.

4 Briefly describe the functions of the Bank of England and say how they differ from the functions of the commercial banks.

5 What is the purpose of the Bank of England's open market operations?

6 What do the letters MLR stand for? What is the purpose of MLR?

7 Briefly describe what is meant by 'money at call'.

8 What are 'special deposits'?

9 In what way does the Bank of England act as 'lender of last resort'?

10 Why are merchant banks sometimes referred to as acceptance houses?

11 In what way does a merchant bank help in raising capital for businesses?

12 List six other services which are provided by merchant banks for businesses.

13 What is the London discount market?

14 What are the main functions of discount houses?

15 Name the form of business that controls the majority of the UK instalment credit business.

16 In what way does National Girobank differ from other banks?

17 Why are commercial banks often referred to as 'clearing' banks'?

18 Name the London clearing banks and identify the 'big four'.

19 What are the four main functions of the clearing banks?

20 Briefly explain the difference between the two types of National Savings Bank accounts. What happens to money whilst it is invested in these types of account?

21 Compare a bank budget account with a personal budget.

22 Give a brief description of the deposit account.

23 How does the function of a current account differ from that of a deposit account?

24 What is a cheque? List the five things written on a cheque by the drawer.

25 Who is the drawer, the payee and the drawee of a cheque?

26 How is a cheque endorsed? What is the purpose of doing this?

27 In what way will a bank examine a cheque before passing it for payment?

28 Explain the difference between an open cheque and a crossed cheque.

29 Use simple diagrams to help you to explain the special ways a cheque may be crossed to make it safer.

30 What is a dishonoured cheque? Why might a cheque be dishonoured?

31 What is the function of a bank statement of account?

32 Explain clearly how the bankers' clearing system works.

33 What is EFTPOS and how does the system benefit both the trader and the shopper?

34 Compare the standing order and direct debit services.

35 Give a description of the bank giro service.

36 Briefly say why it is sometimes said that we have become a largely 'cashless' society.

37 Clearly explain the difference between a cheque card and a credit card.

38 What is the purpose of a cash dispenser card? What safeguards are there to prevent dishonest use of this service?

39 Explain the difference between a bank loan and a bank overdraft.

The cash dispenser system. Different departments of the bank are involved in the issue of a cash card. One department sends out the card which shows a number that can be 'read' by a cash dispenser. Another part of the bank issues a personal identification number (PIN) to the account holder. Both of these are filed in the bank computer. The account holder puts the cash card into the cash dispenser and keys in their PIN. Both numbers are relayed to the bank computer, and if they pair up correctly the machine will issue cash up to the permitted daily amount, so long as enough funds are available. The customer's account is debited immediately. Should some unauthorised person try to use the card, after the person has made a few unsuccessful attempts at obtaining money by guessing the PIN, the machine will confiscate the card.

40 What factors does a bank manager take into account before agreeing to allow a customer to borrow from the bank?

41 How does a bridging loan differ from other forms of bank loan?

42 Why is the bank night safe service of particular use to retail traders?

43 What is the purpose of traveller's cheques? What makes them readily acceptable as well as 'safe'?

44 Why are bills of exchange particularly evident in international trade? Explain the difference between discounting and negotiating a bill of exchange.

45 Why would a bank draft be more acceptable than a cheque for making a large payment?

Structured Questions

1 This question is related to the bank cash dispenser system information on page 282.

   (a) Why is the machine referred to here called a 'cash dispenser'?   (1)
   (b) What do the letters PIN stand for?   (1)
   (c) Explain the words 'permitted daily amount' included in this explanation.   (2)
   (d) The first question the bank will ask a customer who reports their cash dispenser card as stolen is usually, 'Has the PIN been revealed?' Why do you think this question is asked?   (3)
   (e) Why do you think that different parts of the bank are involved in the issue of a cash card and PIN?   (3)
   (f) In what way does the cash dispenser system make it difficult for someone to fraudulently obtain cash?   (4)
   (g) State two checks that the bank computer carries out before issuing cash.   (6)

2 Refer to the life assurance schedule on the following page.

   (a) What is the premium payable under the policy shown?   (1)
   (b) What is the maximum time the premium is payable for?   (1)
   (c) Calculate the amount that C Moody would receive from the family income part of the policy if D H Letchford died on 2.4.2002.
   (d) Explain why D H Letchford and C Moody may have taken out this policy.   (3)
   (e) The premiums for this policy could be paid by standing order or direct debit through a commercial bank. Explain how each of these facilities operate and say, with a reason, which you feel would be most appropriate in this case.   (5)
   (f) Compare an endowment policy to any National Savings scheme as a method of saving.   (8)

LIFE POLICY SCHEDULE

TYPE OF ASSURANCE

Certain "TYPES OF ASSURANCE" appearing in the schedule are defined below.

WHOLE LIFE

The benefit is payable on the death of the life assured.

ENDOWMENT

The benefit is payable on the termination date or previous death of the life assured.

TEMPORARY

The benefit is payable on the death of the life assured on or before the termination date.

FAMILY INCOME

The benefit is payable only if the life assured dies on or before the termination date and consists of annual instalments of a capital sum commencing on the date of death with subsequent instalments on each anniversary of that date. The last instalment shall fall due on the anniversary prior to the termination date and shall be proportionate to the remaining period.

THE ASSURED	POLICY NUMBER
DAVID H. LETCHFORD AND CHRISTINE A. MOODY	CR 2531812
	COMMENCING 16. 6.1978

THE LIFE ASSURED	DATE OF BIRTH
DAVID H. LETCHFORD	12. 4.1954
CHRISTINE A. MOODY	10. 3.1954

TYPE OF ASSURANCE	BENEFIT	TERMINATION DATE
MORTGAGE ENDOWMENT	£11,000 DECREASING AS IN SCALE BELOW WITH PROFITS ON £1,100 PLUS	16. 6.2003
FAMILY INCOME	£1,100 PER ANNUM WITHOUT PROFITS	16. 6.2003

PREMIUM (ceasing on death of the life assured)	FIRST PAYMENT DUE	FREQUENCY	LAST PAYMENT DUE
£8.51	16. 6.1978	MONTHLY	16. 5.2003

WHERE PAYABLE	SURRENDER VALUE
LIVERPOOL	AFTER FOUR YEARS' PREMIUMS PAID

ADDITIONAL INFORMATION

REFERENCES TO THE DEATH OF THE LIFE ASSURED SHALL MEAN THE FIRST OF THE LIVES ASSURED TO DIE.

THE POLICY SHALL BE SUBJECT TO THE SPECIAL OPTIONS ATTACHED HERETO.
IF DEATH OCCURS WITHIN 3 YEARS PRIOR TO THE TERMINATION DATE THREE ANNUAL INSTALMENTS OF FAMILY INCOME SHALL BE PAYABLE.

ADDITIONAL INFORMATION

THE MORTGAGE ENDOWMENT BENEFIT AS IN SCALE BELOW IS PAYABLE ON DEATH IN YEAR ENDING ON DATE SHOWN OR £1,100 PAYABLE ON SURVIVAL TO THE TERMINATION DATE, WITH PROFITS IN EITHER EVENT ON £1,100

16.6.79 £11,000	16.6.88 £9,911	16.6.97 £6,644
16.6.80 £10,934	16.6.89 £9,702	16.6.98 £6,006
16.6.81 £10,857	16.6.90 £9,460	16.6.99 £5,280
16.6.82 £10,769	16.6.91 £9,196	16.6.00 £4,466
16.6.83 £10,659	16.6.92 £8,888	16.6.01 £3,553
16.6.84 £10,549	16.6.93 £8,536	16.6.02 £2,508
16.6.85 £10,417	16.6.94 £8,151	16.6.03 £1,331
16.6.86 £10,274	16.6.95 £7,711	
16.6.87 £10,109	16.6.96 £7,205	

3 Look at the bill on page 285.

(a) With which bank do the Essex Water Company hold their account? (1)

(b) (i) Calculate the total standing charge on this bill. (1)

    (ii) Why are standing charges levied? (2)

(c) If Mr Leicester paid this bill by cheque through the post, on the cheque who would be:

    (i) the payee;

    (ii) the drawer;

    (iii) the drawee. (3)

(d) In the interest of security such a cheque should be crossed. What could Mr Leicester write between the lines of the crossing to make the cheque safer? (1)

(e) How is this particular bill going to be paid? (2)

(f) State two advantages of using this method of payment from the point of view of:

    (i) Mr Leicester;

    (ii) The Essex Water Company. (4)

(g) Describe two ways in which this bill could be paid with the aid of National Girobank. (6)

ESSEX WATER COMPANY

Principal Office: Hall Street,
Chelmsford, Essex CM2 0HH

Revenue Office: P.O. Box 700,
Chelmsford, Essex CM2 0DP

If you have a query about this
bill please telephone

CHELMSFORD
(0245) 491011

For all other queries please telephone
Chelmsford (0245) 491234

WATER SERVICES BILL

Customer Reference Number	Owner No.	Supply size in millimetres Water Sewerage	Year Commencing
433 852 00301 6		15	1ST APR 1988

MR W LEICESTER
42 GREEN LANE
CHELMSFORD
CM23 9HQ

433   S T A T E M E N T
852   - - - - - - - - - -
00301 FOR INFORMATION ONLY

RE:

Rateable Value £	Yearly Rate p in £	Rate Based Charge £	Standing Charge £	Amount £	Total £
WATER SUPPLY CHARGES FOR ESSEX WATER COMPANY					
302	12.000	36.24	14.00	50.24	50.24
SEWERAGE-ENVIRONMENTAL CHARGE FOR ANGLIAN W.A.					
302	28.490	86.04	23.40	109.44	109.44

YOU MAY SETTLE THIS ACCOUNT BY A SINGLE PAYMENT OF   **XXXXXXXX** REACHING THE COMPANY

ANNUAL AMOUNT DUE
£   159.68

PAYMENT WILL BE AUTOMATICALLY DEDUCTED
FROM YOUR ACCOUNT - SEE DETAILS BELOW

ALTERNATIVE INSTALMENTS AND VARIOUS WAYS TO PAY ARE EXPLAINED ON THE BACK OF THIS BILL

National Girobank Trans cash
Bootle Merseyside GIR 0AA

**PAYMENT
SLIP**

Bank Giro Credit

135 205	Customer reference number	Credit account number	Amount due	By transfer from Girobank a/c No.
	433 852 00301 6	357 0959	£	

Standard fee payable at PO counter

Cashier's Stamp

ITEMS

FEE

Signature ....   Date ....

57-09-59

National Westminster
H.O. Collection Account
Essex Water Company

Total Cash

Cheques etc.

£

Name of Customer

MR

Year Commencing

1ST APR 88

Please do not write or mark below this line

IN ACCORDANCE WITH YOUR SIGNED MANDATE YOUR VISA CARD
ACCOUNT WILL BE DEBITED FOR £79.84 ON 28/04/88 AND
FOR £79.84 ON 28/10/88

V7003570959 91   X

Buying on credit

Most people need to buy on credit at some time in their life, particularly when purchasing consumer durables which become increasingly important once we set up a home of our own.

There are times when we need to purchase something essential, such as a cooker, which is beyond our immediate means. But advertisements frequently tell us that 'credit facilities are available'.

If you want to purchase a modern cooker, you may well have to pay £400. Often you will be required to pay a deposit calculated as a percentage of the cash price. The balance would be required to be repaid in regular instalments over a period of time.

If you are under 18 years of age you will be unable to undertake a formal purchase on credit due to a law that prevents this. However, your parents could act as guarantor on a credit purchase made by you.

Source: CSO, *Financial Statistics*, August 1984 and August 1985.

4 Consider the data above and answer the questions which follow.

   (a) What does the term 'credit' mean?   (1)

   (b) How does a parent acting as 'guarantor' make it possible for someone under 18 years of age to enter into a credit agreement?   (2)

   (c) What is meant by the 'cash price' in relation to a credit purchase?   (2)

   (d) Why do 'consumer durables' become increasingly important once we set up a home of our own?   (3)

   (e) Explain how the bank standing order service assists someone making repayments against a credit agreement.   (3)

   (f) Complete the following table of data related to the purchase of a cooker on credit:

Cash price	£400	
Minus 10% deposit	?	
Plus interest	£120	
Balance	?	
12 payments of	?	(3)

(g) How does a credit sale agreement differ from a hire purchase agreement? (6)

Extended Answer Assignments

1 What evidence is there that we are now largely a cashless society?

2 Make a comparison between a commercial bank and National Girobank as a means of money transfer from the point of view of a large business organisation.

3 Choose any large firm selling consumer durables and describe the various methods of payment it allows customers to use. State which methods you would personally prefer, giving reasons for your choice.

4 A business has a project that is expected to earn a 10 per cent rate of return each year. How will interest rates influence the decision of the business on whether to proceed or not? To what extent will this be likely to be related to the government's monetary policy?

5 Explain the differences between central banks, state banks, commercial banks and building societies. Refer to the *Yellow Pages* for your area and count the number of each in your area. Comment on your findings.

6 How do interest rates affect the demand for money? Does it matter?

16 Business finance

16.1

Balance sheet

The primary aim of a business is to make a profit for its owners or shareholders. How successful the business is in achieving this aim depends upon how efficiently the capital or assets (things owned) are employed. It is possible to get an idea of how 'healthy' a firm is by examining the financial facts and figures which show how efficiently the assets are being used. A balance sheet provides a basis for understanding the financial position of a firm.

Balance Sheet **Daly Designs plc** as at 31 December 19—

Liabilities	£	Assets	£
Capital owned	100 000	*Fixed assets*	
Long-term liabilities		Land & Buildings	80 000
Mortgage	44 000	Equipment/Fittings	20 000
		Vehicles	10 000
Current liabilities		*Current assets*	
Tax to be paid	2 400	Stock*	32 000
Bank overdraft	5 600	Debtors	12 000
Creditors	8 000	Bank balance	5 400
		Cash float	600
	£160 000		£160 000
		*at cost price	

A firm's balance sheet shows where the capital used in a business has come from, and what it has been spent on. It shows the financial position of the company at any particular moment in time. It is basically two lists, one showing all sorts of property the company owns *(assets)* and one which shows who the company is responsible to for various sums of money *(liabilities)*. The assets are placed in order of 'liquidity', the most liquid (most easily or quickly turned into cash) being at the bottom. From the lists we can classify the capital used by the firm in various ways.

16.2

Cash flow

The flow of money in and out of a business is called *cash flow*. It is the difference between the receipts from sales and the amount spent on expenses such as raw

It is important that money going out of the business does not exceed the money it receives.

materials, wages, interest paid on loans, dividends paid to shareholders, etc. A trading surplus adds to the reserves whereas a deficit reduces reserves.

From the diagram it will be obvious that if income from sales is equal to expenditure the firm will not have a cash flow problem. Where expenses exceed income the business may have to obtain additional capital in order to continue operating and avoid bankruptcy. A cash flow statement is a report of the income and expenditure of a business over a particular period, usually one year. The items are listed in the same manner as they might appear on a balance sheet.

The explanation above is a relatively simple way of looking at cash flow. In reality it is more complex. We can understand this complexity if we look at a simple 'cash flow' forecast. By this we are referring to a statement or estimate of cash receipts and payments over a given period.

The Florida Trading Company produces ornamental pots. Of whatever it sells, 50 per cent of its income goes in expenses. Most customers take at least four weeks to pay for the goods supplied. Today, in the fourteenth week of this year's trading, Florida has received an order of £5000 worth of pots. Should it accept the order? At first sight the answer to this might seem to be obviously 'yes'. But look at the simple cash flow forecast and then see what you think.

Cash flow forecast **Florida Trading Company Ltd**					
Week	*11*	*12*	*13*	*14*	*15*
Cash at bank	£5000	£3500	£3000	£1500	?
Order received	£5000	£5000	£5000	£5000	?
Cost of production	£2500	£2500	£2500	£2500	?
Cash receipt	£1000	£2000	£1000	Nil	?

From the cash flow forecast you can see that at the start of week 11 of this year's trading Florida had £5000 at the bank. It then received an order worth £5000 which will cost £2500 to produce. In that same week one of its customers paid Florida £1000. On this basis Florida started week 12 with a cash balance of £3500 (£5000 minus £2500 plus £1000 = £3500). Now follow this process through to weeks 14 and 15 – you will see that Florida has a cash flow problem. This is sometimes called a 'liquidity problem'.

The difficulty described here does not mean that Florida should not accept the new order, but it does mean that they have to decide how they will finance the cost of production if they do accept it. Should they borrow from the bank – which will take some of their profit? Should they pressurise some of their customers to pay outstanding debts – which may cause them to lose customers?

To achieve even cash flow is far from simple. It is important to recognise that payment for goods or services supplied will often not be received until some future date. This means that the business must budget with this possibility in mind. If the company budgeting is unsound the firm will have to request extended credit from its own suppliers, seek financial support from a bank or some other financial institution, or obtain capital from another source. These considerations have to be taken into account before Florida Trading accepts their most recently received order.

One way of solving a cashflow problem is by using a 'factor'. A firm that is owed money can 'sell' its debts to a type of business called a 'factor'. The factor collects all the payments due and pays the firm the amount owed, less the charges for the factoring service. A greater percentage of the payments due may even be paid by the factor before they have been collected. The charges for the factoring service can be very high but can solve a cash flow problem and can also save a business the cost of employing its own staff for debt collection.

16.3   Capital

Source of capital

Capital is money, or the assets bought with money, used to run the business. There are three main sources of capital used in a business.

1 *Share capital* (equity) – money subscribed to the company by shareholders in return for a share of the company's profits ('dividend'). Share capital is not repayable.
2 *Loan capital* (loan, debt or debenture) – usually a long-term loan which must be repaid at some time.
3 *Reserves* (retained earnings, undistributed profits, reinvestment) – percentage of gross profits ploughed back into business.

Categories of capital

Capital can be usefully divided into groups and used in calculations as a means of analysis, and further interpretation of the balance sheet.

Fixed capital/assets

Durable (long-term) assets of a business which are used over a long period of time and are tied up in permanent use. Examples: land, buildings, machinery, furniture, vehicles, etc.

Circulating capital/current assets (working capital)

Capital which is continually changing in quantity, total value or nature. Examples: stocks, cash, bank balance, and the amount of money owed to a firm by its customers (debtors).

Employed capital

This is obtained by adding together the fixed and current assets of the firm. In other words, it is the total of all the assets being used by the business.

Current liabilities

Debts which will have to be repaid in the near future. Examples: bank overdraft, debts owed to suppliers (creditors), taxes payable to the government, etc. 'Acid test' is an accounting term that refers to the ratio of the total cash, trade and marketable securities of a business to its current liabilities, i.e. a measure of a firm's liquidity and its ability to meet its short-term debts.

Capital owned

Net value of the assets owned by a business. In other words, it is employed capital minus current liabilities.

Liquid capital

That part of the current assets which are cash or are easily changeable into cash without delay, for example bank balance, cash in tills and debts owed by others (debtors). It is important because it is used to pay creditors immediately and, therefore, should always be above the current liabilities figure.

Net working capital

Current assets minus the current liabilities. Net working capital is particularly important because it takes into account the possibility of all the creditors to the business calling for payment. Therefore, it is important for a business to have sufficient working capital to exist as far as possible without borrowing from a bank.

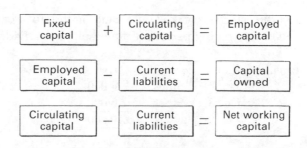

Daly Designs plc

	£		£		£		£		£
1 Fixed capital	80 000	+	?	+	10 000			=	110 000
2 Circulating capital	?	+	12 000	+	?		+ 600	=	?
3 Employed capital	110 000	+	?					=	?
4 Current liabilities	?		?		?			=	16 000
5 Capital owned	?	–	?					=	144 000
6 Liquid capital	12 000	+	?	+	?			=	18 000
7 New working capital	?	–	16 000					=	?

Refer to the balance sheet on p.288 and complete the above analysis of the trading figures of Daly Designs plc.

16.4 Turnover

This refers to the gross income or sales of an organisation over the previous year. Turnover can indicate how 'active' the firm has been in a given period. Generally speaking, the greater the turnover the more business the firm is doing, although this is not always the case.

Net turnover

This is calculated by taking the total sales of the business minus the value of goods returned or credit notes issued.

Rate of turnover/rate of stock turn

Rate of turnover is the number of times the average stock of a business has been sold in the year. There are two methods of calculating the rate of stock turnover depending whether the stock is looked at in terms of cost price or selling price:

$$(1)\ \text{Rate of turnover} = \frac{\text{Cost of stock sold}}{\text{Average stock at cost price}}$$

$$(2)\ \text{Rate of turnover} = \frac{\text{Net turnover}}{\text{Average stock at selling price}}$$

Average stock is worked out by taking the stock value at the beginning and at the end of the trading period, adding them, and dividing by two.

Example

		£
Jan 1	Stock	4 000
Dec 31	Stock	6 000 +
		£10 000

$$\text{Average stock } \frac{\text{£10 000}}{2} = \text{£5000}$$

Application
Daly Designs plc has a net turnover of £50 000 and average stock at cost price is £5 000

$$\frac{50\ 000}{5\ 000} = 10 = \text{Rate of stock turnover}$$

Importance of rate of turnover

Rate of turnover is important because it indicates how 'busy' the firm is. The figure can be used to make comparisons with the previous years of trading or with the rate of other firms engaged in the same type of business.

Comparisons of rates of turnover

- A low rate of turnover is associated with sellers of highly valued goods or consumer durables.

  Example

	Normal rate of turnover
Jewellers	3
Electrical shops	6
Furniture shops	6
Confectioners	12

- A high rate of turnover is associated with businesses selling perishable goods.

  Example

	Normal rate of turnover
Butchers	78
Dairies	67
Greengrocers	53
Bakers	42

- An increasing rate of turnover indicates that the firm is doing more business in real terms, assuming all other things remain unchanged. It is selling more products, so profits should also be increasing.

16.5 Profit

Profit is the reward the business person receives for taking the risk involved in business and for being able to combine all the factors required to produce and sell goods or services.

The profitability of a business can be looked at from the point of view of gross profit or net profit.

Gross profit

The gross profit of a firm is the net sales minus the cost of the goods sold. Gross profit can be expressed as a percentage of the cost or selling price.

Example

	£
Selling price	1.00
Cost price	0.75
Gross profit	0.25

$$\text{Mark-up (on cost price)} = \frac{25}{75} \times 100 = 33\tfrac{1}{3}\%$$

$$\text{Profit margin (on selling price)} = \frac{25}{100} \times 100 = 25\%$$

Gross profit takes no account of the overheads the business has to pay, for example wages, advertising, heating, etc.

As a percentage figure gross profit can be used for comparison with previous trading periods, and with the gross profit of other firms. The method for calculating the gross profit percentage is as follows:

$$\text{Gross profit percentage} = \frac{\text{Gross profit}}{\text{Turnover}} \times 100$$

Example

	£
Turnover	80 000
Cost of goods	60 000
Gross profit	£20 000

As a percentage $\dfrac{20\ 000}{80\ 000} \times 100 = 25\%$

Falling gross profit

Most businesses require a gross profit of between 20 per cent and 40 per cent to ensure they are covering their overheads (expenses) easily. Over the years, gross profit percentage should stay relatively stable. If it starts to drop there is cause for concern. If it drops too much the business may fail to cover its overheads, and start to make an overall loss. There are a number of reasons for a falling gross profit percentage:

- staff stealing stock or takings;
- stock being damaged or allowed to perish;
- rising cost of stock not being passed on to customers;
- too many staff employed (overmanning);
- rising expenses, for example wages, heating, lighting, etc.

Net profits

This is the residue of gross profit after allowing for expenses incurred in carrying on the business such as wages, rent, rates, advertising and bills of all kinds.

Net profit = Gross profit − Expenses

If expressed as a percentage, net profit can be used to make comparisons.

Method

Net profit percentage = $\dfrac{\text{Net profit}}{\text{Turnover}} \times 100$

16.6 Financial projections

Deciding a price

One of the tricky questions the entrepreneur has to answer is

- What should the selling price be?

Initially this looks a simple question to answer. It might be suggested that all the costs involved are added up, i.e. the entrepreneur adds on a bit extra as profit and makes sure that the eventual selling price remains competitive with other firms. Unfortunately the answer to the question is a lot more complex than it appears at first sight. For example, not all costs have the same characteristics. *Fixed costs* (e.g. rent and local taxes) are relatively constant figures up to the point where the business has to be expanded. On the other hand, the cost of the products sold by the business is dependent on the volume of sales and, therefore, these costs are *variable*.

For this reason it is not practicable to add up these two costs until a decision has been made about how much the firm plans to sell.

Example

A firm sells only one product and has only two relatively fixed costs, i.e. rent and local taxes. The variable costs are £20 per article.

Rent and local taxes	£10 000
Cost of producing 1000 units	20 000
Total costs	£30 000

The cost per article is £30 000 divided by 1000, which is £30 per article.

So long as the firm sells at a price above £30 per article it will always be profitable. But what happens if all the 1000 items are not sold? If a selling price of £35 were decided and all 1000 items are sold, a profit of £5000 will be achieved (£35 × 1000 = £35 000 *less* £30 000 costs, profit = £5000). But if only 500 items were sold, the revenue drops to £17 500, which means that the business makes a £12 500 loss. This loss could be even greater if the 500 unsold items were perishable and could not be stored for later sale. Conversely, the greater the number of articles produced the lower will be the cost per article, because the fixed costs are spread over a greater number of articles.

Breaking even

You can see from the above that there is a need to keep several factors in focus at the same time, e.g. costs, sales, volume, selling price and profit margin. The manner of doing this lies in a sales volume/price equation applied over a given period of time. This equation is shown in graphical form below.

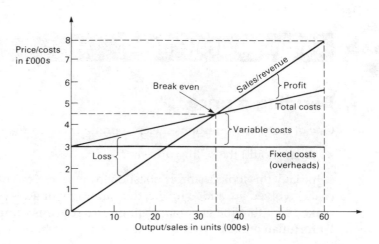

In the graph the vertical axis shows the value of sales and costs in £000s and the horizontal axis shows units of sales volume in thousands. In this case the volume is 60 000 units.

The lower horizontal line represents the fixed costs. These do not change as the volume of sales increases. The graph shows an example of fixed costs of £3000. The next horizontal line shows the firm's profit objective (what it is aiming to achieve). In this case it is £2000. To obtain this profit sales of 60 000 units for a total of £8000 will have to be reached.

The top angled line represents the variable costs. These costs vary directly with output and include items such as raw materials; every extra unit produced adds to variable costs.

The lower angled line shows how much sales revenue is needed to cover fixed costs and variable costs (to *break even*). In this hypothetical case it is necessary to sell 33 000 units to break even.

From this illustration it can be seen that 'break even' is the point where income from sales equals costs. In other words, it is the point which sales must exceed in order for a profit to be achieved. Conversely, if sales do not reach break-even point the business will make a loss.

16.7 Return on capital invested

This figure is the most important to the business person because it shows how much profit has been made as a percentage of the capital originally put into the business. The return on investment must be sufficient to make it worthwhile for the owners of the business to face the risks of business. If the return on the investment is not sufficient the owner(s) may be tempted to place their money in other less risky forms of investment.

$$\text{Return on capital invested} = \frac{\text{Net profit}}{\text{Capital at start of year}} \times 100$$

Make a note of it

1 What is the main aim of a business?

2 What is the purpose of a balance sheet? What kind of information is contained in a balance sheet?

3 Explain the main difference between assets and liabilities.

4 What steps must a firm take in order to avoid creating a cash flow problem?

5 What is business capital and from what is it obtained?

6 Briefly describe each of the categories that capital can be divided into. Why is it useful to categorise capital in this way?

7 Why is it important that liquid capital should not fall below current liabilities?

8 A firm has fixed capital of £60 000, circulating capital of £6000 and £7000 current liabilities. What is its capital owned and its net working capital?

9 Define turnover. Explain the difference between gross turnover and net turnover.

10 What is 'rate of turnover' and why is this important to a firm?

11 The following figures relate to Akela Ltd:

Jan 1	Stock	£ 6 000
Dec 31	Stock	£ 9 000
Net turnover		£60 000

Calculate the rate of stock turnover and estimate whether the rate would be good for a butcher's shop. Give reasons for your answers.

12 Explain the relevance of 'high', 'low', and 'increasing' rates of turnover to the business person.

13 Define profit and explain the difference between gross profit and net profit.

14 Give three examples of 'overheads'.

15 State at least four reasons that might account for a falling gross profit.

16 What do you understand by the term 'breaking even'?

17 Why is the 'return on capital invested' probably the most important figure to the owners of a business?

Structured Questions

1 Sources of capital funds (£m) for industrial and commercial companies 1989–1994

	1989	1990	1991	1992	1993	1994
Retained profit	24 328	18 618	20 569	18 236	26 771	33 019
Bank borrowing	3 981	6 340	5 847	6 568	1 552	7 967
Ordinary shares	879	900	1 660	1 033	1 872	1 127
Debentures and preference shares	−22	523	738	245	608	249
Other	3 167	2 590	3 069	3 175	3 733	1 350
Total	32 333	28 971	32 621	29 257	34 536	43 712

(a) How much capital was raised by the sale of ordinary shares in 1994? (1)

(b) Calculate the percentage of the total capital (to the nearest 5%) that the most popular source represented in 1994. (2)

(c) What explanations can you suggest for the low investment through bank borrowing in 1993? (2)

(d) State three factors that a bank would take into account before granting a business a loan. (3)

(e) If you own a large number of shares in a company which needed £1/4 million to finance expansion, would you prefer the capital to come from (i) retained profits, (ii) the issue of new shares or (iii) through a bank loan? Give reasons for your choice. (4)

(f) What role is played by (i) merchant banks and (ii) the Stock Exchange in the raising of new capital for industry? (8)

2 Refer to the data about wealth creation and answer the questions:

Wealth: its creation and distribution by a company

This illustration shows how a food-manufacturing Company creates wealth through added-value. The figures are based on the performance of 30 such companies which account for 40% of the food industry's sales.

The Company is seen to have bought raw material and services costing £229.6 million. A significant part of these costs would have been energy; rates on its factories and offices; tax and fuel duties for all its vehicles; and the cost of administering and collecting its employees' income tax for the Government.

The Company's finished products were sold, to wholesalers and retailers, for £308.8 million. The difference between costs of £229.6 million and the sales total of £308.8 million was the Added Value of £79.2 million, created by the Company's work.

However the Added Value was not the profit. The £79.2 million created had to pay wages, pensions and social costs, interest on borrowed money, and had to provide for the upkeep and replacement of all the equipment.

The Net Profit of £14.2 million was the amount left. Some of this went in tax, some to shareholders, but the largest single portion was re-invested in the development of the business.

RAW MATERIAL, SERVICES, RATES, TAXES ON VEHICLES AND FUEL, ETC. **£229.6M**

ADDED VALUE **£79.2M**

TOTAL SALES £308.8M

Corporation tax **£2.6m**

Dividend to shareholders **£4.9m**

Re-invested in the business **£6.7m**

Salaries **£39.2m**
Pensions **£6.2m**
National Insurance **£3.8m**
Welfare, including redundancy contributions **£1.5m**
Interest paid on borrowed money **£10.7m**
Replacement of worn-out out equipment **£3.6m**
Net Profit **£14.2m**

299

(a) How much money has the firm put back into the business this year? (1)

(b) If the firm spent £229.6m on raw materials, etc., and achieved sales of £308.8m., why is it not possible to say that the firm made £79.2m profit? (2)

(c) Part of the added value was used to pay 'social costs'. Give two examples of social costs included in the data. (2)

(d) Define the term 'overheads' and give two examples of overheads this firm has to meet. (2)

(e) How does net profit differ from gross profit and how much gross profit did this company make? (3)

(f) Explain the words corporation tax and dividend used in the data. (4)

(g) In what ways does the data shown demonstrate that this firm is generating wealth as well as profit for its owners. (6)

3 Read the following data and the extract below from the quotation that Akela Ltd has received for the purchase or lease of a 16 workstation computer system with a file server.

IT: RENT OR LEASE?

Many companies fail to recognise the true cost of buying their own information technology equipment, or how much it costs to maintain it.

It is a fact that companies also frequently fail to include depreciation allowances in their costings. Consequently, it is not unusual to find that when the time comes to renew equipment some firms find themselves hard pushed to finance replacement. Sometimes the answer can lie in leasing.

Leasing refers to annual renting of equipment as opposed to outright purchase. It is usual for such arrangements to be linked to specific time contracts, e.g. three-year or five-year lease. Often the difference in cost between purchase

and lease over, say, a five year period is minimal, but leasing can be attractive as a means of solving a cash flow problem.

Purchase price
£30 066
　+£793 annual maintenance

Lease (per year)
£11 590 3 year contract
£7 562 5 year contract

(a) What do the letters IT stand for? (1)

(b) Briefly explain the difference between leasing and purchase. (2)

(c) How can leasing help to solve a cash flow problem? (2)

(d) What is 'depreciation' and why is it important that a firm includes allowances for this in their costings? (3)

(e) Assuming Akela Ltd purchased outright, what would be its total cost, including maintenance:
(i) over a three year period?
(ii) over a five year period?

Clearly show all workings and give one advantage of outright
purchase over a leasing arrangement. (3)

(f) What would be the cost in total for Akela to lease the equipment:
(i) for a three year contract?
(ii) for a five year contract?
Show your calculations and say why there would be no
maintenance costs involved. (3)

(g) Using data supplied in the quotation to Akela Ltd, write a report to the
Finance Director summarising the alternative courses of action that
could be taken regarding purchase or leasing, and making your own
recommendation. Give reasons for your choice. (6)

4 Refer to the balance sheet for Daly Designs plc on page 288 and answer
these questions.

(a) What type of business organisation is Daly Designs? (1)

(b) Which date of each year would Daly Designs consider to be the start
of their financial year? (1)

(c) What is the purpose of a balance sheet? (2)

(d) Other than the shareholders of the company, state two groups of
people who would be particularly interested in reading the accounts
of Daly Designs. (2)

(e) Give two examples of current liabilities that could be owed by Daly
Designs and say why it is important that these should not grow too high. (3)

(f) Who are likely to be Daly Designs' 'debtors' and how has their debt
likely to have been created? (3)

(g) Name four items that could be included in the fixed assets figure of
'equipment and fittings'. (4)

(h) Write down one example of each of the following and distinguish
between each of them:
(i) fixed assets and current assets;
(ii) liabilities and assets. (4)

5 Refer to the illustration on page 294. The following questions are all related
to the circular flow diagram shown.

(a) What is the purpose of an invoice? (1)

(b) Define the term 'fixed assets'. (1)

(c) One of the examples of current assets shown listed in the diagram is
stock. Give two reasons why it is important that a firm does not hold
too much stock? (2)

(d) How is the gross profit figure obtained? (2)

(e) What are 'dividends' in relation to business finance? (2)

(f) Explain the meaning of the term 'reinvestment' used in the diagram. (2)

(g) Distinguish between the following forms of capital – loan capital,
share capital and reserves. (3)

(h) Explain the differences between gross profit and net profit. What are the implications for a firm if its expenses exceed its gross profit? (3)

(i) Name four expenses that are likely to be involved in the difference between gross profit and net profit. (4)

Extended Answer Assignments

1 Make a comparison between the final accounts of two firms of similar size and comment upon the differences between them.

2 Ivor is the director of a small but successful landscape gardening business in a town about 20 miles from where you live. He wanted to raise £100 000 to expand his business and set up a new site in your locality.
   (a) Examine the ways in which he might raise the £100 000 he needs.
   (b) Present a report recommending a local site for consideration by Ivor.

3 Discuss why it is important for a company to maintain proper financial records both from the point of view of its owners as well as for taxation purposes. Obtain examples of documents used by companies in this way and present them as a collection to support your discussion paper.

4 Why is cash flow forecasting important to all types of business? Use simple data to illustrate your answer using a small manufacturing company as an example.

5 Explain the various ways that a business might raise capital (a) for short-term and (b) for long-term use. Why does a firm need to make the distinction between sources of capital?

6 'Break-even charts do not give a precise picture of when a business will begin to make a profit, but they do provide a useful guide.' Explain this statement including a simple but clearly labelled break-even chart to illustrate your answer.

7 Write to a major public company in your region and ask for a copy of its most recent annual report and accounts. From the accounts explain in your own words the following:
   (a) How the net profit (or loss) figure is arrived at.
   (b) What percentage of the company's profit is paid to the shareholders and what percentage is retained.
   (c) Give your personal view of the prospects you see for the business and its shareholders in the year ahead.
   (d) Describe how a limited company may increase its capital employed:
       (i) temporarily;
       (ii) permanently.

8 What is meant by a company's capital? How is it that a business might only have £1000 in petty cash and at the bank, and yet have capital of £50 000? Use specimen figures to illustrate your answer.

9 A large public company needs further capital for expansion. Describe three different ways in which it might try to raise this money, including your views on what factors will be likely to influence the method chosen.

10 The following is the balance sheet of a retailer:

	£		£
Owner's savings	850	Fixed assets	8225
Mortgage	8000	Current assets	625
	8850		8850

(a) What is meant by each of the following:
  (i) mortgage?
  (ii) fixed assets?
  (iii) current assets?
(b) Why distinguish between these different aspects of a balance sheet?

11 (a) Ask a local retail trader to allow you to produce a specimen balance sheet which shows the value of his 'fixed' and his 'working' capital.
(b) Explain what is meant by 'fixed' and 'working' capital, using data from your balance sheet to clarify your explanation.

The Stock Exchange

17.1　Functions and control

When a company invites the public to invest in it the managers then put the money invested to permanent use. They will buy the buildings, machinery, stock and other assets that the business needs to operate. The money cannot be returned to the investor because it has been used. The only way that the shareholders can get their money back is by selling their shares to someone else. The Stock Exchange provides a market place where they can do this.

The Stock Exchange is a market place for the buyers and sellers of all kinds of existing securities. It is a 'free' market, that is one where the prices of securities are allowed to fluctuate in response to supply and demand. The market price of shares is particularly influenced by the past performance and profitability of a company. General market trends can provide an indicator or barometer of the future outlook for industry and the economy as a whole.

The fact that the Stock Exchange enables people to dispose quickly of any listed shares they hold is particularly useful for individuals but also for institutional investors (those who collect and invest the savings of many others) such as insurance companies, pension and union funds and investment and unit trusts. These organisations need to obtain a good return on the capital invested for their members, but at the same time the securities must be easily turned into cash.

The Stock Exchange is often referred to as if there were only one exchange, the London exchange. However, there are in fact a number of other Stock Exchange trading floors in important provincial centres. They all work closely together following the same rules and standards. The stock market business is worldwide, and there are exchanges situated in many other countries.

The Stock Exchange is controlled by The Stock Exchange Council which is elected by the members of the Stock Exchange. The Council has the following functions:

- it controls the admission of new Members;
- it disciplines Members who are guilty of misconduct;
- it formulates the Stock Exchange rules;
- it settles disputes between Members;
- it provides settlement and information services to Members.

17.2　New shares

Although new issues of shares are made outside the Stock Exchange on the part of the capital market known as the 'new issue market', application is usually made for the shares of public companies to be listed (quoted) on the Exchange. This encourages investors to buy a new issue because they know that the shares can easily be resold. New shares are sold by one of the following methods.

Offer for sale

Issuing houses acting as agents on behalf of the company will sell the shares direct to the general public. This may be done by publishing a prospectus giving details of the company and its aims. If all the shares offered are not taken up by the general public, the issuing house will guarantee to buy all shares that are left and then dispose of them as best they can. This ensures that the company raises the full amount of capital it requires.

Placing

All the shares are 'placed' in blocks with large buyers such as institutional investors, for example pension or union funds.

Rights issue

These are shares offered only to existing shareholders of the company at lower than current market prices and in proportion to their shareholding. This method is used to raise additional capital for a firm.

17.3 | Membership

Only member firms of the Stock Exchange are allowed to take part in dealing on the Exchange floor and outsiders must carry out their buying and selling through them. The member firms are called broker/dealers (brokers) and some of these specialise as what are known as market makers. These member firms include many organisations from outside the Stock Exchange such as banks and other financial organisations from the UK and overseas.

Broker/dealers (brokers)

These are Stock Exchange member firms which buy or sell shares as agents for public investors, or as principals for their own account with other Member firms or outside investors, or they can act in a dual capacity as both agent and principal. Some broker/dealers specialise as market makers.

Market makers

Market makers can operate on the Stock Exchange floor, off-floor, or both on- and off-floor. They make a market in shares by being prepared to buy or sell shares at all times to and from broker/dealers. They may deal direct with the broker/dealers on the Exchange floor, or indirect through the Stock Exchange Automated

Quotation System (SEAQ – described later). They are required to maintain a two-way price on SEAQ, whereas broker/dealers are not permitted to operate in this way.

Bargains are often carried out by private negotiation and sealed by verbal agreement. These agreements are honoured thus upholding the principle of the Stock Exchange motto 'Dictum meum pactum' – My word is my bond.

Market makers tend to specialise in a particular range of securities. For example, there are specialists in shares related to shipping, aircraft, oils, property, mining and industry.

The Stock Exchange operates a computer system (SEAQ) which details competing market makers' quotes to broker/dealers by VDUs. A market maker will quote a double (two-way) price verbally and also on SEAQ, for example, 420 to 428 – indicating that he is willing to buy a certain share at 420p and sell at 428p. A broker/dealer interested in buying or selling the shares in question can compare the quotes of all the market makers via SEAQ and choose the 'best' deal for themselves or their clients.

Clerks

The staff of broker/dealers consists of two groups: those who are engaged in work outside the Stock Exchange, and those who are involved with work inside the Exchange. The latter group can be subdivided into 'authorised' and 'unauthorised' clerks.

- *Authorised clerks* have the authority to act on behalf of their principals and to enter into transactions on their behalf.
- *Unauthorised clerks* are permitted to enter the House but do not have the authority to enter into transactions.

17.4   Share transfer procedure

The broker

It is through the broker that the outside investor contacts the central market to buy or sell shares. The broker may decide to carry out the deal with the client on their own account, or they may deal with a market maker.

Stock Exchange dealing room (by permission of the Stock Photobank).

Contract note

The contract note is a document which provides evidence that the broker has carried out his client's instructions. It tells the client:

- the number of shares bought or sold;
- the unit price;
- the commission to be paid by the client;
- government taxes – contract stamp, VAT and transfer duty;
- total payment due to the broker;
- settlement date.

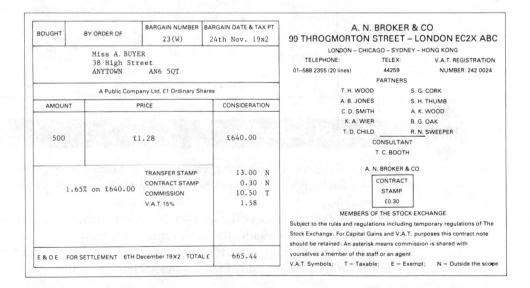

Settlement date

The contract note shows a date on which the transaction is due for settlement and on that date the outstanding amount should be paid to the broker by the client.

If the buyer wishes to postpone payment until a later date, an additional fee called 'contango' has to be paid.

If the seller has contracted to sell some stock and finds it inconvenient to deliver at the settlement, a fee called 'backwardation' has to be paid to 'borrow' the stock from another dealer.

Share certificate

The broker sends the registrar of the company whose shares have been sold details of the new owner of the company's shares. The registrar records the details of the new owner and sends them a share certificate through the broker. The new owner of the shares will eventually receive dividends direct from the company whose shares are now held.

 ## 17.5 Types of security

'Security' is the collective name given to the wide range of investments with which the Stock Exchange is concerned. Securities fall into two categories, 'fixed interest' and 'equities'.

With fixed interest stocks the investor knows in advance the amount of interest he is due to receive. Usually, the rate of interest is truly 'fixed' and is stated prior to investment; in a few cases the stock may receive a 'variable rate' of interest, for example in the case of index-linked stocks. Here the actual interest received can vary, but the amount payable is governed by a set formula, linked to some well-known index.

Equities are so called because they represent an equal share of the capital of the business, and an equal division of the profits. Nothing is 'fixed' in respect of equities – if the company does well, so does the shareholder, if the company does badly, the shareholder may receive no return on his investment.

Government stocks or bonds (gilt-edged securities)

Often referred to as 'gilts' these securities are used to raise money to finance government projects. They represent a very safe form of investment because they are backed by government resources. They are issued for a fixed period of time and receive a fixed rate of interest. If the rate of inflation exceeds the rate of interest the value of the stock is eroded.

Local authority bonds

These are issued by local authorities and the money invested represents a loan to the authority. They are initially placed with institutions, but can be bought by the public through the Stock Exchange. They are a secure form of investment paying a fixed rate of interest and having a fixed date for repayment.

Debentures

Debentures are in effect a loan to a company and are often referred to as 'stocks'. They receive a fixed rate of interest which must be paid even if the company does not make a profit. Debenture holders have no involvement in the management of the company.

Debentures may be secured against specific assets or by a general charge on all the assets of the company, and are backed by an agreement similar to a mortgage. They may be bought and sold on the Stock Exchange and are redeemable at a fixed date or before.

Preference shares

Ordinary preference shares

Preference shareholders have a priority call on the profits of the company after debenture holders. Preference shares pay a fixed rate of dividend, but only if sufficient profits are available to make a payment. Usually preference shares carry no voting rights.

Cumulative preference shares

If cumulative preference shareholders do not receive their full dividend in one year, the balance is carried forward and must be met from profits earned in subsequent years, and until these have been paid no payment can be made to ordinary shareholders.

Participating preference shares

Because of the relatively safe nature of preference shares, and the fact that they pay a fixed rate of dividend, the preference shareholder does not reap any additional reward when the company does well and makes good profits.

Sometimes companies will create participating preference shares in which preference shareholders can take dividends at a fixed rate and, if there is still any profit left after payment of other dividends, the participating preference shareholder may receive a further dividend additional to the fixed rate already paid.

Ordinary shares (equities)

Ordinary shares or 'equities' represent a share in the ownership of a company. Each share is entitled to an equal proportion (dividend) of the company's profits. The amount of dividend to be paid is decided by the directors of the company and

Annotations around the table:

Highest price of share this year, i.e. £8.18

Lowest price of share this year, i.e. £7.11

Current share price (halfway between buy and sell price) i.e. £8.10

Change in share price since previous day, i.e. −1p

Yield. Each £100 invested in the company at the current market price will give a £7.50 return

Table columns (repeated three across the page): High | Low | Stock | Price | + or − | Cvr | Yld

Section headings within the table: **INVESTMENT TRUSTS**, **OIL & GAS**, **PAPERS & PUBLISHERS**, **SHIPPING**

Share prices.

(a) (i) Which three shares have the highest price shown?

    (ii) Which three shares have the highest yield?

(b) Why is the yield figure important when deciding whether to buy a particular share?

(c) Why do you think there is such a wide variation in share prices?

is dependent upon the profitability of the firm and, therefore, ordinary shares are somewhat speculative.

In return for accepting the speculative risk involved, the ordinary shareholder usually stands to receive a relatively high return on the investment. The shareholder may gain not only through his share of the company's profits, but also from an improvement in the current market price of the shares. In addition, the ordinary shareholder has some power (through voting rights) in the running of the company.

Ordinary shareholders are generally the last in line for distribution of profits, and, therefore, they are the most risky form of shareholding. However, they can give the highest rate of return when the company is successful.

The money paid for a share when it is first issued is used by the company and cannot be returned to the investor. However, ownership of ordinary shares can be bought or sold second-hand on the Stock Exchange. Ordinary shares with the highest status as investment are known as 'blue chips'.

Unit trusts

A method of minimising the risk of holding ordinary shares is for the investor to spread his investment between a variety of different holdings. Unit trusts also work on this basis.

Trust managers offer 'units' of the funds for sale direct to the public. The expert knowledge of the trust managers is used to invest the funds wisely in a wide range of company and government stocks to enable a profitable investment to be made with the risk of loss minimised.

17.6 Speculation

There is an important distinction between an investor and a speculator. An investor buys shares in order to receive a share of the company's profits (a dividend). A speculator on the other hand hopes to make a quick profit by anticipating changes in share prices. There are three types of speculator and they are known by the colourful names of 'bulls', 'bears' and 'stags'.

- *Bulls* – buy or hold shares anticipating a price rise and make a profit by selling at a higher price. In a 'bullish' market prices are generally rising.
- *Bears* – sell shares anticipating a fall in market prices, perhaps buying them back later at a lower price, for example, if they need to fulfil a contract to supply the shares. In a 'bearish' market prices are generally falling.
- *Stags* – buy new issues of shares expecting to resell them at a profit when second-hand dealing starts on the Stock Exchange.

It should be noted that when referring to bulls, bears and stags, we are talking about the way someone is behaving, and not three different people. An individual may be a bull at one time or bear at another. The terms may be used to describe someone even if he is not a member of the Stock Exchange.

AUTHORISED UNIT TRUSTS

	Init Chrge	Canc Price	Bid Price	Offer Price	+ or -	Yield Gr's

AIB Unit Trust Managers Limited (1000)F
51 Belmont Rd, Uxbridge, Middx UB8 1RZ — 0895 259783

	Init	Canc	Bid	Offer	+or-	Yield
AIB Grofund American	5	167.0	168.5	177.4	+0.60	0.00
AIB Grofund Equity	5	242.0	244.6	258.8	+1.20	1.69
AIB Grofund Euro	5	203.6	205.4	216.2	+1.50	0.00
AIB Grofund Expt Balanced	3	116.1	117.5	121.8	−1.80	1.03
AIB Grofund Gilt	3	79.23	79.25	81.70	+0.66	4.23
AIB Grofund Japan	5	186.3	188.0	197.9	+1.00	0.00

AXA Equity & Law Unit Tst Mngrs (1200)H
Equity & Law Hse, Corpn St, Coventry — 0203 553231

	Init	Canc	Bid	Offer	+or-	Yield
General Inc	5	477.7	479.2xd	509.8	−0.8	2.25
General Acc	5	534.6	536.2xd	570.5	−0.8	2.25
UK Growth Acc	6	358.5	363.1	386.3	−0.7	2.43
UK Growth Inc	6	251.1	254.2	270.5	−0.4	2.43
Higher Inc Acc	6	660.5	669.6	712.4	−1.0	3.38
Higher Inc Inc	6	395.0	400.5	426.1	−0.6	3.38
Gilts/Fxd Int Acc	5½	189.4	189.4xd	200.0	+0.8	5.78
Gilts/Fxd Int Inc	5½	94.62	94.62xd	99.94	+0.43	5.78
Nth America	6	255.2	261.3	278.0	+1.3	0.00
Far East	6	364.3	364.3	387.6	+1.6	0.00
Europe	6	275.1	277.3xd	295.1	+1.1	0.53
Brit Excell	6	71.93	71.93	76.53	−0.28	2.59
Brit Fndmtls Acc	6	99.93	101.3xd	107.8	.....	4.16
Brit Fndmtls Inc	6	74.91	75.98xd	80.84	+0.07	4.16
Global Opps	6	85.22	86.87	92.42	+0.32	0.00
Balanced Acc	6	54.10	54.77xd	58.27	−0.03	2.35
Balanced Inc	6	53.62	54.28xd	57.75	−0.03	2.35

Abbey Unit Tst Mngrs (1000)H
80 Holdenhurst Rd, Bournemouth — 0345 717373

	Init	Canc	Bid	Offer	+or-	Yield
Extra Income	6	46.45	46.70	49.68	+0.17	7.31
Gilts & Fixed Int	6	135.5	135.5xd	143.8	+1.0	5.89
High Inc Equity	6	170.8	173.5	184.6	+0.7	3.94
Managed Income	6	46.15	46.51	49.48	+0.12	4.65
Worldwide Bond	6	273.8	273.8xd	290.3	+1.1	3.62
American Growth	6	310.3	310.3	331.9	+1.4	.35
Asian Pacific	6	348.2	348.2	372.4	−1.8	
Assets & Earnings	6	275.3	280.3	298.2	+1.5	1.59
Capital Reserve Acc	0	131.3	131.3	131.3	.....	5.15
Comdty & Energy	6	128.5	131.6xd	140.0	+1.0	.39
1992 Enterprise	6	96.72	96.72	103.4	+0.3	1.50
Euro Capital Acc	6	142.3	142.3	152.1	+0.6	.66
Euro Capital Inc	6	133.7	133.7	143.0	+0.5	.68
General	6	232.9	236.8xd	251.9	+1.1	2.16
Japan	6	134.6	134.6	144.0	+1.0	
Mastertrust	6	148.3	148.3	158.6	+0.5	.83
UK Growth Acc	6	233.7	233.7	249.9	−8.2	1.53
UK Growth Dist	6	142.9	142.9	152.8	−5.0	1.58
US Emerging Cos	6	144.1	146.8	156.2	+0.4	—
Income & Growth	6	397.3	403.3	429.0	+1.5	3.06
Ethical	6	74.95	76.79	81.69	+0.23	1.96
International	6	118.3	120.0	127.7	+0.3	.09
Dividend & Growth	6	63.02	64.00	68.09	+0.26	3.73
Global Gwth & Sec	6	65.06	65.06	69.30	+0.11	1.99

Capel–Cure Myers UT Mngt Ltd – Contd.
Exempt Fund

	Init	Canc	Bid	Offer	+or-	Yield
High Yield	2	1362.00	1371.00	1414.00	+2.00	3.91
(Accum Units)	2	1638.00	1649.00	1701.00	+2.00	3.91

Capital House Unit Tst Mgrs (1200)F
Capital House, Festival Square, Edinburgh.
031–228 4477 — Dealing 0800 833561

	Init	Canc	Bid	Offer	+or-	Yield
American Gwth Tst	6	37.73	38.07	40.71	+0.17	0.21
American Gwth Tst Acc	6	37.95	38.29	40.95	+0.17	0.21
Cash Acc	0	61.88	61.88	61.88	+0.01	4.94
Do Income	0	50.61	50.61	50.61	.....	4.94
European Gwth	6	40.32	40.32	43.00	+0.09	0.35
Income & Gwth Acc	6	30.91	31.17xd	33.33	−0.72	4.02
Do Income	6	28.54	28.77xd	30.77	−0.67	4.02
Intnl Gwth	6	32.39	32.39	34.64	+0.11	0.53
Japan Gwth	6	28.97	29.01	31.02	+0.28	—
Managed Tst Acc	6	51.83	51.83	55.43	+0.09	1.49
Do Income	6	50.31	50.31	53.80	+0.08	1.49
Oriental Opps Acc	6	147.9	147.9	158.1	−0.7	—
Do Income	6	143.9	143.9	153.9	−0.6	—
Property Shares	6	45.05	46.56	49.79	−0.21	1.63
Smaller Cos	6	33.15	33.15	35.45	−0.05	1.49
UK Growth Tst	6	26.53	26.71	28.56	−0.06	2.64

Royal Scottish Assurance

	Init	Canc	Bid	Offer	+or-	Yield
Roy Scot/Cap Hse Global Acc	6	78.20	78.58xd	84.04	−0.14	1.64
Do Income	6	73.14	73.50xd	78.60	−0.14	1.64
Roy Scot/Cap Hse UK Acc	6	73.20	73.58	78.69	−0.26	2.34
Do Income	6	67.96	68.31	73.05	−0.24	2.34

CH Unit Managers Ltd (Formerly Brown Shipley)

	Init	Canc	Bid	Offer	+or-	Yield
CH Mgd Euro Inc	6	26.45	26.45	28.28	+0.18	0.38
CH Mgd Europ Acc	6	27.43	27.43	29.33	+0.18	0.38
CH Financial	6	152.4	152.4xd	162.9	.....	1.71
CH Foundation	6	92.35	94.35xd	100.9	−1.1	2.18
CH German	6	51.05	51.05	54.59	+0.18	0.07
CH High Income	6	77.69	78.55xd	84.01	+0.99	5.24
CH Income	6	137.9	137.9	147.4	−0.5	3.40
CH Mgd Intl Growth	6	39.36	39.36	42.09	+0.18	0.15
CH Mngd Pfolio Inc	6	108.0	108.0	115.5	.....	1.60
CH Mngd Pfolio Acc	6	206.4	206.4	220.7	.....	1.60
CH Monthly Income	6	85.26	85.26xd	91.18	−2.62	3.19
CH Mgd Nth American	6	107.6	107.6	115.0	+0.3	—
CH Orient	6	151.6	151.6	162.1	+0.8	—

Cazenove Unit Trust Mngmt Ltd (1600)F
3 Copthall Avenue, London EC2R 7BH — 071–606 0708

	Init	Canc	Bid	Offer	+or-	Yield
Cazenove Portfolio	5	83.19	83.19	88.86	−0.30	2.18
American Portfolio	5	90.69	90.69	96.65	−0.07	1.01
European Portfolio	5	98.68	98.68	105.24	+0.39	0.93
Japanese Portfolio ♥	5	74.24	74.24	78.90	+0.52	0.00
Pacific Portfolio ♥	5	142.30	143.28	154.07	−0.72	0.76
UK Income & Growth	5	76.16	76.16	81.57	−0.23	3.65
Utility & Bond	¼	56.47	56.47	57.17	−0.20	6.31

Century Unit Trusts Ltd (1400)F
5 Old Bailey, London EC4M 7BA — 071–332 5000

	Init	Canc	Bid	Offer	+or-	Yield
UK General Tst	5½	65.16	65.87	70.07	+0.02	2.86

Chartered Asset Mngmt Ltd (1700)F
151 Farringdon Rd, London EC1R 3AD — 071–837 7667

	Init	Canc	Bid	Offer	+or-	Yield
Intl Growth	5	147.01	147.01	159.32	.....	0.00
UK Growth	5	113.04	113.04	122.04	.....	0.00
UK Income	5	117.45	117.45	127.28	.....	3.69

FINANCIAL TIMES THURSDAY MARCH 17 1994

Unit trust prices from the Financial Times.

17.7 ▶ Return on shares

A dividend is a payment from a company's profits to its shareholders. It is the 'reward' paid to the investor. The dividend is usually calculated as a percentage of the nominal or par value of the share, for example as a percentage of the issue price or the price the share was originally sold for (normally 25p or £1). If the dividend is declared to be 9p, then investors will receive 9p for each share they hold e.g. in the case of shares with a par value of £1 = 9%.

However, the owner of the shares may well have bought them at a price above (or below) their par value. In this case the investor is interested in the 'real' return of his investment, taking into account the current market price. This is called the yield.

The yield on a share is calculated as follows:

$$\frac{\text{Dividend}}{\text{Market value}} = \text{yield}$$

The 'market value' refers to the price paid for a share on the Stock Exchange. If a shareholder had paid £2 for a share with a par value of £1 and a dividend of 9p is declared, the yield would be 4.5%

$$\frac{9p}{£2} = 4.5\% \text{ yield}$$

17.8 Factors affecting share prices

Obviously, if speculators could accurately predict share price movement they could guarantee that they would make a fortune several times in one week. However, investment in shares remains speculative because there are numerous factors that influence a rise or fall in share prices.

Some of these factors can be summarised as follows:

- supply and demand for the shares;
- recent performance of the company: good or poor profits;
- political changes affecting the company, for example change of government;
- changes in interest rates or taxation;
- popularity or otherwise of the company's products;
- changes in market trends;
- takeover or merger being considered;
- general national prosperity;
- industrial disputes, or settlements.

17.9 Importance of the Stock Exchange

Many large businesses need to appeal to the public for the vast sums of money they require to finance the purchase of new premises, new machinery, or to expand the business. People are not willing to invest money to finance this sort of development unless they can be sure that they can get the money back again. But, as we have observed earlier in this chapter, the business uses the money invested with it and it cannot be returned.

When an investor needs his money back, he does not need to go to the company with whom it was originally invested. Instead, the investor sells his shares to some other investor through the Stock Exchange. In other words, although the Stock Exchange does not directly raise new capital for business, it encourages people to invest in companies because it provides facilities for the sale of second-hand securities.

The government also needs to borrow money from the public to help finance the many industries and services it provides through central or local government. These require a continuous supply of new capital to fund new equipment and development research. Local and central government and the nationalised industries rely on the Stock Exchange to help raise the capital they need.

All stock exchanges have an international importance because they provide a market for the shares of foreign countries. For example, more than half of the value of the shares quoted on the London Stock Exchange is made up of the shares of overseas countries.

Make a note of it

1 List the functions of the Stock Exchange.

2 What is the function of the Stock Exchange Council?

3 Why is it usual for public companies to apply for new issues of their shares to be 'quoted' on the Stock Exchange?

4 Briefly describe the main methods involved in selling new shares.

5 What is the function of a stockbroker? How do they ensure that they obtain the best price for their clients?

6 'All market makers are broker/dealers, but not all broker/dealers are market makers.' Explain this statement.

7 Briefly explain the difference between an 'authorised' and an 'unauthorised' clerk.

8 What are market makers?

9 Describe the process of share transfer.

10 Explain the difference between fixed interest securities and equities.

11 What are gilt-edged securities? Give one example.

12 Why is the return on debentures invariably poorer than the return on equities?

13 How do preference shares differ from ordinary shares?

14 'Ordinary shares are the most risky form of investment, but they can also be the most rewarding.' Discuss this statement.

15 In what way do unit trusts spread the risks involved in investment?

16 Clearly describe the activities of stock market speculators including use of the terms 'bulls', 'bears' and 'stags'.

17 What is meant by the 'par value' of a share?

18 Explain the difference between the dividend and the yield of a share.

19 How is share yield calculated?

20 List at least six factors that influence the market value of shares.

THE PERSONAL EQUITY PLAN SCHEME (PEPS)

The PEPS scheme aims to make it more attractive and simple for people, especially small savers and first-time share-buyers, to invest in UK equities. The scheme allows people to invest a monthly or yearly amount, within a maximum defined by the government (currently up to £200 a month, or £2400 a year), in shares entirely free of tax.

Provided investors keep their money invested in their plans for a short qualifying period of between 12 and 14 months, they will not pay capital gains tax when selling or income tax on reinvested dividends or interest.

The scheme has been designed to be as simple as possible for investors, and is particularly suited to the small investor.

Plans are administered by plan managers, who:

- arrange the buying and selling of equities;
- hold share certificates on behalf of investors;
- keep records;
- deal with tax authorities, including claiming tax relief on dividends.

Structured Questions

1 Read the data above and answer the following questions.

   (a) What do the letters PEPS stand for? (1)
   (b) What are 'equities'? (2)
   (c) Why are PEPS likely to appeal to the small investor? (3)
   (d) Explain the difference between an investor and a speculator. (4)
   (e) In what way does this scheme try to ensure that it encourages genuine investors rather than speculators? (4)
   (f) How does the return and the risk of equity investment differ from that of a building society or bank account? (6)

2 The following questions are all related to the illustration shown on page 306.

   (a) State two ways that an individual could reap a reward through owning shares. (2)
   (b) Name two different forms of *organisations* that might want to buy or sell shares through the market shown in the illustration. (2)
   (c) In what way does the flow diagram show that the Stock Exchange is a 'market'? (4)
   (d) Clearly explain the difference in function between a broker/dealer and a market maker. (6)
   (e) 'A stock exchange performs an important function, not only for individuals but also for businesses and the economy in general.' Discuss this statement. (6)

3 (a) Why is a stock exchange an important feature of a *laissez-faire* economy? (2)

(b) Explain how both public limited companies and 'institutional investors', such as pension funds, benefit from the existence of stock exchanges. (3)

(c) What do we mean when we say the stock market is 'bearish'? (3)

(d) 'When we talk about "bulls", "bears" and "stags", we are not talking about three individual types of person but about the way people are behaving.' Explain this statement, including a description of the function of these specialisms in the Stock Exchange. (6)

(e) Discuss the view that speculation is not in the best interest of the investor. (6)

4 Refer to the illustration of the record of a share transaction shown on page 307.

(a) Name the company that issued this document. (1)

(b) Who now owns the shares shown on the record illustrated? (1)

(c) When these shares were first issued they cost £1 per share. What was the original total purchase price for the same quantity of shares, and what gross total gain in value has been achieved since first issued? (2)

(d) Give three possible different reasons why these shares have risen in value. (3)

(e) How can the new owner of these shares be confident that they have obtained them at a fair price? (3)

(f) How is a new owner of shares 'registered' and what do they receive to prove their shareholding? (4)

(g) What would be likely to happen to the total value of these shares in the following circumstances. Give a reason for each of your answers.

(i) A Public Company Ltd has received a large overseas order for its products.

(ii) A Public Company Ltd has one major competitor, Tokyo Traders plc. This competitor has had a disaster and its plant has been destroyed by fire.

(iii) All of the employees at A Public Company Ltd belong to one union. The union has instructed its members to begin industrial action. (6)

5 These questions are all related to the illustration of an extract of share prices typically shown in a financial newspaper given on page 310.

(a) If you refer to the last entry in the data (P&O) you will see it records −4. A little higher in the display you will see the Clarkson entry shows +2. Explain these plus and minus figures. (1)

(b) What is meant by the 'yield' of a share and why is this particularly important? (2)

(c) List three shares in the data which show a high yield. What would be the advantage of buying these shares? (3)

(d) List three shares with a low yield. Why could there be some benefit in buying low yield shares such as these? (3)

(e) What is an investment trust? How does investing money in these differ
   from placing money in ordinary shares? (3)

(f) You want to buy 1000 shares in Globe (Investment Trusts), and you
   ask a broker to purchase them at a limit of 143p per share (that is, no
   higher than 143p, and lower if possible). By referring to the
   information on page 310 answer these questions:
   (i) What price would your broker buy at?
   (ii) What is the highest and lowest price Globe shares have been in
       the past year?
   (iii) How much in total would you be required to pay for the 1000
       shares?
   (iv) Your broker will charge commission. What is commission in this
       respect? (4)

(g) Suggest some factors which are likely to affect the general rise and
   fall in share prices. Why is your purchase in investment trusts less
   likely to be affected by these fluctuations? (4)

Extended Answer Assignments

1 Choose ten different shares and monitor the movement of their market price
   over a period of six months. Present your record in diagrammatic form and
   explain the reason for the changes you observe.

2 Choose three contrasting methods of saving and investment and record their
   profitability over a six-month period. Give reasons for any differences in the
   rate of return you identify.

3 Congratulations! You have inherited £60 000. Invest this money in three
   contrasting ways and record the progress of each £20 000 over a six-month
   period. Give reasons for any differences in the return achieved.

4 Discuss the view that although the Stock Exchange does not provide new
   capital for firms, it has an important role in encouraging people to invest in the
   first issues of shares.

5 Take any five companies of your choice that are listed on the Stock Exchange.
   Invest an imaginary £5000, approximately £1000 in each company. Record
   the weekly change in value of each of your holdings over a twelve-week
   period. At the end of twelve weeks compare the total current value of your five
   shares with the original amount invested.
      Write a report that summarises your results and offer reasons for the
   changes that have taken place.

6 Why is it possible for £1000 invested in government bonds to become worth,
   say, £1500 in five years, whereas the same amount invested in a portfolio of
   ordinary shares could realise a market value of twice the original investment in
   just one year? Use examples from the press to support your answer.

18 Insurance

18.1 Importance of insurance

All individuals and organisations face a wide variety of risks, but only some of them actually suffer a loss during the course of a year. To offset the possible effect of a loss, all those at risk can contribute a small sum of money (called a 'premium') to a fund operated by an insurance company. These many small sums contribute to form a large pool of money. Managed efficiently the fund will be sufficient to compensate ('indemnify') those who suffer a loss.

The result of co-operating with others in this way is that risks are 'spread' or 'shared' between the many people and organisations that have contributed to the insurance pool. Hence, insurance is sometimes said to be the 'pooling of risks'.

Insurance is vital to individuals, all forms of business and to the economy. If as individuals we had to face all the risks of life ourselves there are many things that we would not do, and we would hesitate at times even to leave our homes. Similarly, many businesses would not be formed if those doing so had to face all the risks of enterprise themselves. Insurance relieves business people from some of the risks they face, and they are, therefore, encouraged to take part in enterprises which result in increased economic activity.

Much of the money collected by insurance companies in premiums is invested in industry and councils, thus giving resources and encouragement to economic

The insurance pool.

activity as well as to technological developments.

British insurance is the country's largest single source of 'invisible earnings' (*see* Chapter 14). British insurance companies insure the industries, buildings, ships, etc. of other countries. In addition, insurance companies of other countries seek to be insured by British insurance companies, thus spreading the risk of cover they have offered in their own countries. This process is known as 'reinsurance', that is accepting an insurance risk and then transferring it (or part of it) elsewhere.

When Britain receives payment from other countries for insurance, the effect is of bringing foreign money into the country, thereby assisting our balance of payment figures.

18.2 Uninsurable risks

The success of insurance is based on statistical analysis. Underwriters have to judge correctly how much they should charge to cover a particular risk if they are to have sufficient money in the pool to pay out against claims, and also meet running costs. From statistical records of claims underwriters can calculate the probability of a loss occurring, and fix the appropriate premium. Generally, insurance companies are willing to consider giving cover on all types of risks where they can calculate the probability of loss involved. But it is not possible to insure against happenings that are inevitable. The following are typical examples of uninsurable risks:

- when the probability of loss is inevitable (an exception is life assurance);
- where there is insufficient past experience to assess the premium;
- if the proposer does not have an insurable interest;

Not all risks can be insured.

- against fair wear and tear such as rust and corrosion;
- that a business enterprise will be successful.

18.3 Principles of insurance

For insurance to work effectively and fairly all those involved are expected to honour *four* legal principles.

1 *Insurable interest*
   (a) Only the person who stands to suffer financial loss or liability can insure against a particular risk.
   (b) To have insurable interest the insured must own, or be responsible for, the article to be insured.
2 *Utmost good faith*
   (a) This insurance principle requires the parties to an insurance contract to be truthful.
      - The insured must disclose all relevant facts to the insurer.
      - The insurers must honour all the promises in their policy.
   (b) Intentional withholding of information invalidates the contract.
3 *Indemnity*
   (a) This is the insurance principle by which a policyholder is compensated for the loss incurred.
   (b) The insured should not profit if the event insured takes place.
   (c) If the insured overinsures an item, in the event of a loss he will only be compensated for the true value.
   (d) If a loss occurs where the item is underinsured, the policyholder will only receive a proportion of the loss.

   e.g. House value   £50 000
        Insured for   £40 000
        Damaged by fire   £10 000 (i.e. one-fifth)
        Compensation
        (one-fifth)   £8 000

   (e) *Contribution*. This aspect of indemnity applies when more than one insurer is liable for a loss. In this case, each contributes a proportionate amount to the compensation. For example, a camera lost on holiday could be the subject of both a house contents policy and also holiday insurance.
   (f) *Subrogation*. This word means 'to take the place of'. Having received compensation from the insurer the insured has no further rights over the item insured. The right of ownership (e.g. for scrap value) passes to the insurer after the insured has accepted claim compensation. The compensation has taken the place of the item insured.
4 *Proximate cause*

This insurance principle states that the insurer is *not* only liable for a loss caused directly by a risk insured against. An insurance claim would be valid not only for damage caused by fire, but also for repairs to doors damaged by firemen breaking in to tackle the blaze. This damaged is not caused by the fire, but it is directly related to it.

18.4 Types of insurance

There are four broad categories of insurance: fire, life, accident and marine. These categories can be remembered by memorising FLAM which is a combination of the initial letter of each word.

Fire

Fire insurance, as the name suggests, primarily covers fire risk. But many policies combine cover with other risks such as theft, storm, flood and lightning, etc.

This form of insurance can include cover for loss of earnings (e.g. by businesses) or rental of alternative property while a building damaged by fire is being repaired.

Fire policies exclude certain special conditions such as fire resulting from earthquake or riots. In addition, items of high value (e.g. paintings, jewellery, antiques, etc.) must be insured separately.

Life assurance

This type of cover is referred to as 'assurance' rather than insurance. In the case of insurance, cover is given against a risk that *may* happen. Life assurance covers an event that *will* happen – death. There are two main types of life assurance, whole life and endowment.

1 *Whole life* policies provide for a payment after the death of the insured with the idea of providing for the dependents of the deceased.
2 *Endowment* policies provide for the payment of a basic sum at a certain age or on death of the insured, whichever occurs first. This provides not only for dependents, but a useful sum of money for the insured if he survives the period. A variation of this type of policy is one 'with profits' which, for a higher premium, entitles the insured to a share in the company's profits.

Accident

This type of insurance covers a wide range of policies. The following are the main examples.

Motor

Any vehicle taken on public roads is required to have a certain minimum level (third party) of insurance to ensure that drivers can meet their liability for injury to others. The two commonest types of motor insurance are:

1 *Third party, fire and theft* – the motorist insures the liability for damage to other people and their property, plus the loss or damage to his own car through fire or theft.
2 *Comprehensive* – policies not only give the above third party cover but also provide compensation for accidental damage to the vehicle of the insured.

Personal accident and sickness

These are policies which can be taken out against death or disability in special circumstances, for example holidays, flights, etc.

Liability

This type of policy covers the risk of liability for the injury or death of someone else. There are two main forms:

1 *Employer's liability* – covers the employer's legal liability for the safety of each employee.
2 *Public liability* – covers the liability of individuals and businesses for members of the public visiting their premises.

Property

Covers a wide variety of items from goods in transit or in store to buildings or contents. Applies to both the business person and the private householder.

Credit

Covers against losses resulting from bad debts, for example the failure of customers to pay for goods obtained on credit.

What insurance risks can you see in this illustration? Which ones do you think an insurance policy would not cover?

Fidelity

Used particularly by businesses to protect against loss by fraud and stealing by employees.

Insurance for business

- Employer's liability
- Public liability
- Damage to premises
- Stock damage
- Consequential loss (earnings)
- Theft, burglary
- Motor fleet
- Bad debts
- Product liability

Business interruption (or consequential loss)

Loss from fire in business premises may not only result in physical damage. Business may have to be suspended for a time resulting in loss of earnings for both the owners of the firm and the employees. Insurance cover is available for such losses and the cover can include loss of wages, rent and the cost of temporary alternative accommodation.

Marine

Marine insurance in Britain mainly centres around Lloyd's of London, which plays a major role in this worldwide market. This insurance is applied to ships and their cargoes. There are four broad categories of marine insurance.

1 *Hull insurance* – covers damage to the vessel itself and all its machinery and fixtures.
2 *Cargo insurance* – covers the cargo the ship is carrying.
3 *Freight insurance* – it is customary for an insurance policy to be taken out to cover the possibility that for some reason the shipper does not pay the transport (freight) charges to the shipowner.
4 *Shipowner's liability* – the owner of a vessel has to insure himself against a wide variety of events, for example collision with other vessels or dock, injury to crew members or passengers, pollution of beaches, etc.

18.5 The insurance contract

Insurance is provided by insurance companies, friendly societies, Lloyd's underwriters and the government (national insurance). Non-government insurance may be taken out through agents working for a particular company or brokers selling insurance for a number of companies. Whichever approach is used a basic procedure is followed.

Proposal

This form is provided by the insurer to be completed by the person seeking insurance cover (the proposer). The form consists of a number of questions which the proposer must answer truthfully (in 'utmost good faith'). When completed and signed by the proposer it represents a proposition from the proposer to the insurer.

Premium

If the insurer is willing to provide cover on the terms of the proposal he will quote a premium, which is the amount the proposer must pay into the pool to effect cover.

Policy

Once the contract is completed the insurer issues a policy which states the details of the contract between the insured and the insurer. The following documents may also be issued in association with the insurance policy.

- *Certificate of insurance* – for employer's liability and motor insurance, the law requires evidence of cover to be provided by this certificate.
- *Cover note* – this is a temporary document provided whilst the certificate of insurance is being prepared.
- *Endorsement* – a notice of an amendment to a policy, usually by the insurer. The endorsement is attached to the policy and thereafter becomes part of the contract.
- *Renewal notice* – issued by the insurer prior to expiry date, invites the insured to renew the cover and advises the renewal premium and the date on which it is due.

Claim

If the risk insured against takes place the insured completes a claim form and submits this to the insurer for consideration. Loss adjusters are frequently engaged by insurers to ensure that claims are settled fairly from the point of view of both the insured and the insurer.

18.6 The insurance market

Insurance companies

Insurance companies have branches spread throughout the country to issue policies and deal with claims. 'Friendly' societies specialise in life and sickness assurance. Those wishing to take out insurance cover can approach insurance companies directly or through insurance agents or insurance brokers.

Insurance *agents* work for an insurance company or a friendly society selling only the policies of that company.

Insurance *brokers* work independently of insurance companies and, therefore, are able to give unbiased advice as to which is the best policy to buy.

Whether it is decided to buy insurance direct from the insurance company, their agents, or brokers, the cost of the insurance cover is the same because the agent or broker is paid by the company which actually provides the insurance policy.

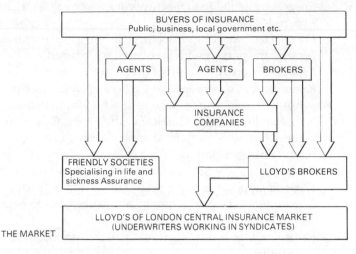

THE MARKET

The insurance market.

Lloyd's of London

Lloyd's of London is a corporation that provides market facilities for members engaged in selling insurance. There are two classes of membership of Lloyd's – Lloyd's brokers and underwriters.

Underwriters are the only people allowed to accept insurance at Lloyd's. Underwriters are backed by their own personal wealth and have unlimited liability to indemnify insurance claims made against them. Underwriters frequently form into groups called *syndicates* who work together to accept larger shares of risk than a single individual could manage.

Lloyd's brokers are the source of contact with Lloyd's insurance market. The function of Lloyd's brokers is to get the best deal they can for their clients, who may be insurance companies or large organisations such as businesses and local government.

The Lloyd's broker approaches underwriters who specialise in the risk to be covered. The premiums offered by several underwriters are compared, and the best offer is accepted. Sometimes the risk may be divided between several underwriters. Should a claim occur under the latter circumstances, each of the underwriters contributes to the compensation in proportion to the amount of the risk they have accepted.

18.7   Glossary of insurance terminology

Actuary: statistician who calculates premium based on degree of risk.
Adjuster: an independent professional who assesses loss.
Agent: employed by one insurer to sell insurance, on commission.
Assessor: a person who negotiates the amount to be paid out against a claim.
Broker: independent professional who sells insurance for a number of insurers.
Claim: a request by a policyholder for compensation under the policy.

Cover note: issued to give temporary cover against risks while a policy is being prepared.

Friendly societies: companies specialising in life assurance or sickness benefit schemes.

Insured: the person who is covered by insurance.

Insurer: the party who gives insurance cover.

Knock for knock: arrangement where each insurer pays for damage to its policyholder's vehicle irrespective of who was to blame.

No claim discount: a reduction in the renewal premium of motor insurance when there has been no claim during the previous year.

Policy: written evidence of the contract between the insurer and the policyholder.

Premium: the payment made by the policyholder for the insurance cover given.

Proposal: application by a person or company (proposer) requesting insurance.

Reinsurance: a system whereby an insurer sacrifices part of the premium to share part of the risk with another insurer.

Renewal notice: sent to insured to advise premium and renewal date for next year of cover.

Underwriter: the person who accepts risk and promises to pay compensation if a loss occurs.

Make a note of it

1 How does insurance spread risks?

2 Explain how insurance encourages business activity.

3 In what way does insurance contribute to the balance of payments?

4 What is reinsurance?

5 Why are some risks uninsurable? Give four examples.

6 In what way can insurance to be said to have a statistical basis?

7 Give a brief description of what happens to money contributed to an insurance pool.

8 Explain, giving an example, the meaning of insurable interest.

9 Name the insurance principle which requires the parties to an insurance contract to be truthful.

10 Insurance is said to be a contract of indemnity. What does this mean?

11 What do the terms contribution and subrogation mean in relation to insurance?

12 Give an example, and explain the insurance principle of proximate cause.

13 Name the four main types of insurance.

14 Explain the difference between insurance and assurance.

15 In relation to life assurance, explain the terms whole life, endowment, with profits.

16 Briefly explain the differences between third party, third party fire and theft and comprehensive motor insurance.

17 Why would a shop owner be likely to take out both employer's liability and public liability insurance?

18 Briefly describe the four broad categories of marine insurance.

19 Describe the process of putting an insurance contract into effect including mention of the documents and payment involved.

20 Why is the certificate of insurance particularly important to both employers and motor vehicle drivers?

21 Explain the purpose of a renewal notice.

22 What is the function of a loss adjuster?

23 Briefly describe the difference between an insurance agent and an insurance broker.

24 What is Lloyd's of London?

25 Describe the work of underwriters and Lloyd's brokers in the insurance market.

Structured Questions

1 Look at this article taken from the business section of a newspaper and answer the questions below.

Business News
The Danger of Being Underinsured

In a recent case two workmen of a firm were removing a large boiler from a cheese processing plant. The workmen secured a rope round one of the pillars supporting the factory. As a result the building collapsed causing £500 000 of damage, and the manufacturer had to close down the plant for several weeks.

The company presented a claim to its insurers for the repairs to the plant, and for the cost of the loss of business. But the insurers would only meet 80% of the value of the claim because the firm was underinsured. Although the firm took a variety of measures to find the shortfall, they could not make up the balance from their resources. And financial institutions were unwilling to loan money to a business that was in fact standing idle.

Within three months the firm was forced into bankruptcy, and what had been a thriving business employing 15 workers ceased to exist.

(a) What is the purpose of insurance? (2)

(b) What is meant by underinsurance? (2)

(c) Why is insurance unable to fulfil its main purpose in the example
     shown in this article?   (3)
(d) State at least three different categories of insurance that a business
     will generally need that a private individual will not require.   (3)
(e) Briefly describe how the insurance company will have decided that it
     can only meet 80 per cent of the cost of the claim of the dairy
     producer? Why not 85 per cent?   (4)
(f) What led to the failure of the firm? How could this have been
     avoided?   (6)

2 Refer to the diagram of the 'insurance pool' system on page 318.

(a) Explain what is meant by saying that insurance is based on 'the
     pooling of risks'.   (2)
(b) Not all of the money in an insurance pool comes from the
     policyholders' premiums. So where else does the money come from?   (2)
(c) The majority of the money in the insurance pool is used to pay
     compensation to policyholders. Where else does the money from the
     pool go?   (2)
(d) Explain each of the following words contained in the diagram:
     (i) policyholder; (ii) premium; (iii) compensation.   (3)
(e) Describe some of the administration costs an insurance company is
     likely to have.   (3)
(f) For an insurance pool to work effectively and fairly certain principles
     have to apply to all insurance contracts. Name four of these principles
     and explain fully what they mean for a person seeking insurance. Give
     an example in each case to show how these principles work.   (8)

3 These questions are all related to the diagram of the insurance market shown
on page 325.

(a) Briefly describe examples of the special insurance-related work that
     friendly societies do.   (2)
(b) How do insurance companies make a living?   (2)
(c) Explain the difference between the work of insurance agents and high
     street brokers. Which is a business likely to use?   (4)
(d) How does the function of a Lloyd's broker differ from that of a high
     street broker?   (4)
(e) Explain the function of 'underwriters' and 'syndicates' in the insurance
     market.   (8)

4 (a) In relation to insurance briefly describe the meaning of the following
         terms:
         (i)   indemnity   (2)
         (ii) utmost good faith   (2)
         (iii) insurable interest   (2)
         (iv) subrogation.   (2)

(b) State one type of insurance which you would particularly recommend for each of the following. Give a different example in each case and explain the reason for your choice.
   (i) A factory engaged in manufacturing a highly inflammable product. (3)
   (ii) A firm employing six sales representatives each of whom drives a company car. (3)
   (iii) A shop employing people handling large amounts of cash. (3)
   (iv) A partner in a firm of solicitors. (3)

5 The questions below are all related to the flow diagram shown below.

   (a) What is the difference between the insurer and the insured? (1)
   (b) At what stage in the process of taking out insurance does the 'proposer' become the 'insured'? (1)
   (c) Why is a business less likely to consult an insurance agent than an insurance broker? (2)
   (d) What advantage could there be in a firm taking out insurance through a broker rather than going straight to an insurance company? (2)
   (e) State two factors that the insurance company will take into account when calculating the premium it will charge the firm taking out insurance. (2)
   (f) Explain each of the following terms used in the flow diagram:
      (i) proposal; (ii) premium; (iii) policy. (3)
   (g) Give three examples of advice that an insurance company might give to a firm interested in taking out insurance cover. (3)

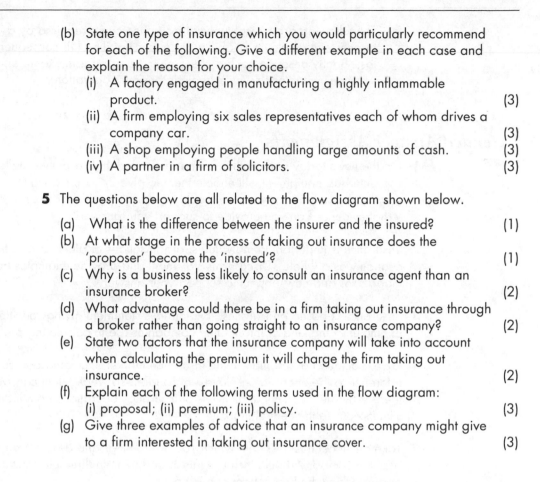

1. The business considers the many risks that it faces.

2. The firm decides what type of policies will cover the risks and the amount of cover required.

3. The business can seek advice from an insurance company or an insurance broker.

STEPS IN TAKING OUT BUSINESS INSURANCE

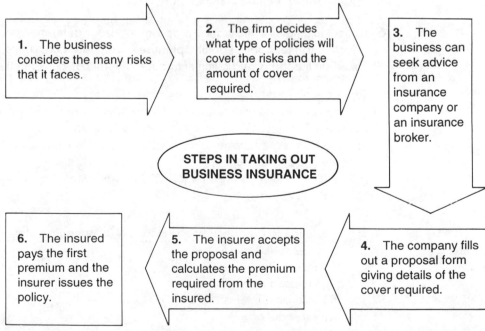

6. The insured pays the first premium and the insurer issues the policy.

5. The insurer accepts the proposal and calculates the premium required from the insured.

4. The company fills out a proposal form giving details of the cover required.

(h) The following are typical types of insurance cover required by a business: (i) employer's liability; (ii) public liability; (iii) consequential loss. Briefly describe each of these giving appropriate examples of situations when each would apply in business operations. (6)

Extended Answer Assignments

1 On the news today the weather forecasters stated that recently installed computerised equipment will enable them to give 24 hours advance notice of weather conditions. In what way could this help to reduce insurance claims? What evidence can you provide to support your answer?

2 'Insurance is important to individuals, organisations of all kinds and the economy as a whole'. Discuss this statement and provide examples from magazines and newspapers to support your answer.

3 'Insurance is based on statistics.' Explain this statement giving specific examples of the kind of information companies use in calculating premiums.

4 Give a detailed description of the insurance market, including particular reference to the operation of Lloyd's of London. To what extent can we say that there is business activity at all levels of insurance operations from individual transactions to the central market?

5 Take any local business with which you are familiar and describe any four risks the company should insure against, and explain three circumstances against which the firm cannot obtain cover.

6 Collect examples of insurance proposal forms for different types of risk, e.g. private car, life, public liability, premises. Compare contrasting questions asked on the forms and comment on the differences between the forms.

The standard of living

What is the standard of living?

The term *standard of living* refers to the quality of life that the people of a country have – for example, the type of houses they live in, the quality of food they eat and the clothes they wear. Obviously, this is dependent upon the work people do and the wages they receive. Even the methods that workers use to travel are seen as contributory to the standard of living, as are methods of communication used and entertainment that they have ready access to. The level of education the population receives is also seen as important.

The standard of living is often reflected in the average lifespan of the people of the country. It is likely that people who live where there is a high standard of living will generally live longer than those who have a poor standard of living.

Look at the following table containing data relating to the average life expectancy of people in a number of well known countries. What reasons can you give to explain the differences that exist between countries and between the sexes?

Country	Male	Female
Afghanistan	43	42
Barbados	73	77
Great Britain	72	78
Grenada	69	74
Jamaica	75	78
Libya	64	69
Madagascar	50	53
Nigeria	47	49

It is generally the case that countries with a poor standard of living are located in the tropics whilst countries which have higher living standards are found in the colder areas. This does not infer that the standard of living is a result of temperature or climate; rather it is very much to do with the stage of development that the country has reached, and the resources it has available. And, of course, the way that these resources are developed affects the standard of living.

Cost of living

As you can imagine measuring the standard of living is a formidable task because there are so many factors involved, and some of these are difficult to quantify. Some of the main methods of measuring national prosperity will be examined shortly, but the *cost of living* gives some indication of the quality of life of people, and how it is changing from one year to another.

The 'cost of living' refers to how much can be bought with a person's net income (after deduction of income tax). Measuring the cost of living is important because it is continually changing and, therefore, it shows whether 'real' income is changing – in other words, are people better or worse off taking into consideration rising costs and income increases? Measurement of the cost of living is achieved by constructing a *price index*. There is more than one type of price index, but the most popular and more generally well known index is the Retail Price Index (RPI).

The RPI is made up from the prices of goods and services purchased by consumers. It is often used in the UK and other parts of the world as a basis for negotiation of wage increases. The objective of this is to ensure that workers' wages maintain a constant value in 'real' terms.

A *cost of living index* is constructed by taking the total value of a collection of items purchased by consumers in a particular year, which is referred to as the *base year*. We say that the index figure for that year, say 1990, is 100. The same items are subsequently valued periodically (usually annually) and general price movements can be plotted for a group similar to the one shown here.

Depending upon whether each new plotted position is above or below the base line it is possible not only to know if prices have generally risen or fallen, but also to establish an approximation of the percentage of change. The change can then be equated with wage rises in order to establish if workers end up better off in real terms.

Cost of living index.

Useful though it is, a cost of living index gives only a limited indication of the state of the economy of a country. Statistics included in the national accounts are a more revealing indication of the state of the economy.

19.2 National income

Economic growth refers to an increase in the output of all things we consume, use, invest in or otherwise produce. Economic growth is important because it usually means that the country is increasing its wealth, and probably improving its living standards. One way to assess economic growth is through measurement of the national income.

What is national income?

Imagine you were asked to calculate the total income of your family for the year, how would you go about doing so? You would probably add together the total yearly income of each member of the household, including any return received from savings or investments. But there are other ways of reaching the same figure. For example, it can also be obtained by adding together the total amount spent, and the total amount saved by each member of the family in the year. You should understand that both methods reach the same answer because both look at the same amount of money, but in a different way. The national income of a country can also be assessed in a similar way.

If you were asked to assess your income you would refer to wages and other returns which add to your wealth. You would not count money you invested in the building society last year, but you would include the interest you received this

Circular flow of income.

year. Income is a *flow*, and not a stock of money or equipment. National income is concerned with new additions to the wealth of the country.

There are three approaches that can be used to measure the national income, and all the methods should reach the same answer because in a way they are all measuring the same thing.

1 *Income method* – the aggregate value of all forms of income, including personal incomes, profits of firms, rents, etc.
2 *Output method* – the total net output of every form of production taking care not to count any output twice. 'Net' in this case means including an allowance for capital consumption (depreciation – fall in value due to wear and tear) on all buildings and machinery.
3 *Expenditure method* – the total value of all expenditure by consumers, firms and the government.

Measurement of all of the foregoing three ways of looking at national income are made annually by the British government and are published in the Blue Book on national income and expenditure.

National income accounting problems

Quite apart from the obvious difficulty of data collection there are a variety of problems associated with the foregoing methods of national income measurement. The following are some of these problems.

Money terms

It is not possible to add together things such as tons of fish, bottles of wine and thousands of tractors. To evaluate items such as these we have to express them in money terms. But the value of money is constantly changing, and this can result in inflation causing it incorrectly to appear that national income is increasing. What is important is the *real* increase in national income and to establish this requires allowances to be made for the changing value of money. The government Blue Book on national income and expenditure contains tables of consumers' expenditure taking into account changes in the value of money.

Double-counting

Double-counting can occur when output is considered. If timber is included in output measurement, should furniture made from timber also be included? The answer to this difficulty is that each firm should only count the value added to products by its activities. Theoretically this avoids counting output more than once, but in effect the result is still not a very precise measurement.

The 'black' economy

Babysitting, bartending, taxi driving and car repairs are typical examples of jobs that are sometimes being done 'on the side', that is without the Inland Revenue knowing about them because the income is not declared for tax purposes. The work is usually done for cash rather than cheque payment, and for a charge lower than for 'official' work. Activities such as these are sometimes called the 'hidden' economy, but most commonly they are referred to as part of the 'black' economy.

Probably every developed country has its own 'black' economy, and in some countries it is so substantial that it props up the official economy. It has been estimated that the 'black' economy adds almost a third to the gross national product.

The 'black' economy is to be condemned because tax evasion by some in this way increases the tax burden of others. However, more important here is the fact that the 'black' economy creates a problem for recording domestic statistics. The main source of information for the income method is the Inland Revenue, but we have seen that the 'black' economy shows that a large proportion of income is not recorded.

Uses of national income statistics

The final national income figure is only an estimate because of the foregoing and other accounting difficulties which result in discrepancies. However, in spite of all the difficulties of measuring national income the figure has several uses.

1 *Changes in living standards* – most governments use national income statistics to indicate changes in living standards.
2 *Comparisons with other countries* – it enables comparisons to be made between one country and another.
3 *Economic growth* – a comparison can be made between one year and another in respect of economic growth.
4 *Instrument of economic planning* – it provides the government with information which can be used to assess the effectiveness or otherwise of its past policies. This information can then be used in the planning of the economy, and implementation or redistribution of wealth.

National income and standard of living

While national income is of vital importance in determining our standard of living, a high national income does not necessarily mean a high standard of living exists generally.

To illustrate this point, let us imagine that there is a Middle East country called Hullabahoo, and that country had made dramatic economic growth because of the discovery of vast deposits of oil five years ago. If Sheik Shinpad, ruler of the state of Hullabahoo, receives the vast majority of the national income, the country may be earning more, but its people will see little improvement in their living standards. Therefore, the way that the wealth is distributed is just as important to the population as the national income.

Gross national product (GNP)

When we looked at the output method of measuring national income earlier we said that an allowance was made for 'capital consumption' or loss in value (depreciation) of buildings and machinery. In other words, in the case of national income measurement we only know the total production output after taking away that allowance. But in national accounting it is useful to be able to measure the total value of all things actually produced in a country, that is a figure which does not include a reduction for capital consumption.

In Britain, the principal measure of the total output of the country is called gross national product (GNP). The word 'gross' indicates that no deduction has been made for capital consumption.

The word 'national' in this instance does not imply that GNP is the total output produced within the borders of the UK. The GNP measure includes some output taking place and produced by resources owned by people from other countries. Clearly, this outflow cannot be counted as part of our national income. At the same time, some sources of output are situated in other countries but owned by UK citizens. Therefore, the GNP can be defined as the total output of all the resources owned by residents of this country, wherever the resources themselves are situated.

Measure of the total output actually produced within the borders of the UK is called the gross domestic product (GDP). In this respect GDP can be defined as the output of all resources located within the UK, wherever the owners of the resources happen to live. In a similar manner to GNP, the GDP becomes net domestic product when an allowance for depreciation is deducted from it. In many ways GDP is the more important measure.

National Income of Noland
Simple imaginary analysis by expenditure method

	£ billions
Consumer expenditure	168.2
Public authorities expenditure	60.1
Gross domestic fixed capital investment	43.5
Value of physical increase in stocks	2.1
Exports of goods and services	73.3
Total final expenditure	347.2
less imports of goods and services	− 67.1
less taxes	− 38.3
plus subsidies	+ 4.1
Gross domestic product	245.9
Net property income from abroad	+ 2.2
Gross national product	248.1
less capital consumption	− 36.9
National income	211.2

The national cake

The amount of wealth or gross national product the country is generating each year is sometimes referred to as the 'national cake'. The national wealth 'cake' is made up of contributions from various parts of the economy and commercial activities such as services, distributive trades and transport make the largest contribution, followed by a smaller contribution by industrial production and a yet smaller contribution by agriculture, forestry and fishing. This illustrates the importance of commercial activities to the economy.

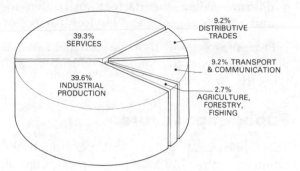

Where the national wealth comes from.

Wealth in this sense is more than a stock of money and possessions. Wealth is the total of what the economy produces each year in the form of goods such as clothing and food, or services such as those of doctors or teachers. We normally find it convenient to measure wealth in money terms, but this can create problems because not all wealth can be counted in money terms. For example, how do we put a precise value on the quality of education, medical care or environment? And yet sometimes the effect of things such as these can be greater and more important than the production of goods to which we normally attribute wealth.

The well-known saying 'you cannot have your cake and eat it' is undoubtedly true, and yet many people want to do just this. As a country we cannot have what we have not earned; we cannot eat more cake than we have. Consequently, the bigger slice of the cake one person or group takes, the less there is left to distribute to others. Clearly, we must make a bigger cake before we can distribute bigger slices from it. This is often the source of a continual wrangle between governments, employers and workers over demands for wage increases.

National expenditure

While the gross national product tells us what was produced in a country, national expenditure tells us who bought what was produced. In this respect we can say that national expenditure is the sum of:

1 *Private expenditure* – this includes every kind of consumption spending by the population, from food and clothing to cars and entertainment (but excluding the purchase of homes).

2 *Public expenditure* – central and local government spending on goods and services, for example salaries of teachers and soldiers, provision of pensions and family benefits, etc. (but excluding capital expenditure on durable assets such as buildings).

3 *Gross domestic capital formation (GDCF)* – this refers to the total investment by business firms, public enterprises and public authorities in new fixed capital such as new plant and equipment, buildings, ships and other durable means of production. The purchase of new dwelling houses is also included in GDCF.

4 *Overseas trading* – the effect of the net difference between the value of UK exports and imports of goods and services (balance of payments).

From the foregoing it can be seen that national expenditure is necessarily identical in value with the national product because it is merely another way of classifying the same information.

Public expenditure

This term refers to government spending. In the UK there are two types of government, central and local government. Central government governs the whole country, whereas local government is concerned with management of a smaller part of the country. Central government is the most important single spender in the UK, and local government is responsible for a considerably smaller proportion of public expenditure.

Central government expenditure

- *EC Budget* – Member States contribute to the EC Budget.
- *Defence* – maintenance of defence systems, army, navy and airforce.
- *National Health Service* – provision of hospitals, doctors, dentists, pharmacists, etc.
- *Social security and personal social services* – which includes benefits for the elderly, disabled and sick, unemployed, family (child benefit, etc.), widows and social security payments.
- *Higher education, science and arts* – grants to universities, subsidies for scientific research, subsidies for the arts.
- *Grants to local authorities* – mainly in the form of the rate support grant – particularly used to pay employees such as teachers, dustmen, social workers, clerks and other council employees.

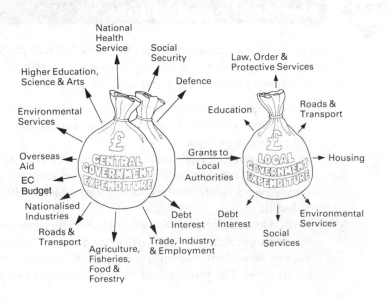

- *Trade, industry and employment* – operation of job centres, skill centres and the Training Agency, and grants to encourage firms to move into development areas.
- *Overseas aid* – money lent to poorer countries.
- *Agriculture, fisheries, food and forestry* – grants for research, land reclamation and subsidies to farmers, etc.
- *Roads* – money for trunk roads and motorways, and subsidies for various forms of state-run transport such as railways.
- *Debt interest* – when the government spends more than it obtains in revenue it has to borrow. The total amount owed is known as the national debt. The government has to pay interest on this debt.

Local government expenditure

- *Education* – the provision of nursery, primary, secondary and further education is the single most important item of local authority expenditure.
- *Law, order and protective services* – the police and fire services are the major items of this aspect of local government expenditure.
- *Roads and transport* – local authorities are responsible for minor local roads. They may also subsidise local bus and rail services.
- *Housing* – provision of council houses and sheltered accommodation.
- *Environmental services* – refuse collection, parks and cemeteries, etc.
- *Social services* – old people's welfare, and facilities for other people who need help, for example 'battered' wives and children or poor families. Also libraries, museums, sports facilities, magistrates, ambulances and probation services.
- *Debt interest* – like central government, local councils also borrow money and have to pay interest on it.

National debt

If you spend more than you earn you will end up in debt. There are two ways you can put the matter right. You can earn more or you can borrow to pay off the debt. In the latter case you are creating another debt, but delaying ultimate payment. The government faces a similar problem.

Each year the Chancellor of the Exchequer prepares the Budget in which he plans the next year's government revenue and expenditure. If expenditure equals revenue the budget is in *balance*. When income exceeds expenditure a *surplus* has been created, and a *deficit* results when expenditure exceeds income.

The public sector borrowing requirement (PSBR) indicates the extent to which the public sector borrows from other sectors of the economy and overseas to balance its deficit on the expenditure and revenue accounts. The public sector includes central government, local authorities and public corporations. PSBR is an important indicator of how the government's policies are affecting the economy.

The national debt is the total amount owed by central government to people both in Britain and abroad. The national debt has accumulated over many years and today the total is so huge it is no longer possible for it to be repaid, although it is still important to restrict growth of the debt as far as possible. Wherever there is a budget deficit, PSBR bridges the gap and results in an increase in the national debt. Most of the national debt is owed to British residents who hold government stocks or money invested in the various forms of national savings.

19.6 Growth and development

Growth refers to an all round expansion of the economy. It is concerned with the *quantitative* increases in the country's output. It is concerned with the *rate* of economic change, e.g. increases in tourism, increases in production, increased construction of roads, the building of more schools and hospitals, etc.

Growth can be measured by changes in GNP, which reflects general increases in total net output. *Negative growth* means that the country is doing less well than the previous year; *zero growth* indicates that there has been no change when compared with previous years. Obviously, all governments are keen to see their countries achieve growth because it generally results in an improved standard of living and greater economic and political stability.

Development is not the same as growth. It is a qualitative concept and is more concerned with the *pattern* of economic change. Development refers to the provision of facilities that enable growth to take place, e.g. availability of resources such as machinery and a workforce with appropriate education and skills. Often development will take place in just some sectors of the economy but provide thrust for other sectors. In order to have development, there must be growth. However, there may be growth but no development. Highly developed countries are better able to exploit their natural resources than underdeveloped countries, consequently more advanced economies have a better standard of living.

An underdeveloped country tends to have the following features:

- poor economic performance
- high rate of population growth
- low standard of living
- relatively short life expectancy
- high unemployment
- considerable dependency upon agricultural employment
- poor educational opportunities.

Many (but not all) European countries, the United States, Japan and Australia are examples of highly developed economies. By contrast, most underdeveloped countries are situated in Asia and Africa. The Caribbean countries are at the stage part way between the two extremes. They are sometimes referred to as *developing countries*. Many other countries are also in this category.

Economic growth

Whist economic growth is the desire of all governments it is affected by the following factors.

Investment

Capital accumulation and the use of this to create further wealth through the provision of capital or equipment is essential to economic growth. For this reason the government will be keen to encourage saving and investment and will also allocate a large share of its resources towards development.

Technical progress

Economic growth is promoted by exploitation of technical development so that increased productivity can be achieved with the same resources. For this to take place the workforce must have the skills to take full advantage of new technology. Consequently, there must be adequate investment in education as well as technology.

Balance of payments

A persistent adverse balance of payments will hinder growth and development. A continued unfavourable balance will 'bleed' the country of capital that it needs to direct towards development and growth. It will also have the effect of discouraging capital inflow from overseas investors who will be more interested in investing in more stable economies with healthy balance-of-payments positions.

Government expenditure

Government spending is so extensive that it has the power to stimulate particular sectors of the economy when carefully directed. Public expenditure should be used, at least in part, to stimulate those sectors of the economy that will assist future output.

Make a note of it

1 'The cost of living is just one aspect of the standard of living.' Explain this statement.

2 What is the retail price index?

3 How is the retail price index constructed?

4 Define national income.

5 What do we mean when we say that income is a 'flow' and not a 'stock' of wealth?

6 Describe the three methods of measuring national income.

7 What are the problems of measuring national income?

8 What useful purpose is there for measuring national income?

9 Define the term 'per capita' income.

10 'Rising national income does not necessarily imply a rising standard of living.' Discuss this statement.

11 List the factors that influence national income.

12 Define gross national product and say how this figure differs from national income.

13 The gross national product is sometimes referred to as the national 'cake'. What makes up the national cake? Why is it true to say that we cannot 'have our cake and eat it'?

14 What is 'national expenditure'?

15 What is the national debt and why does it exist? To whom is the debt owed?

16 In what way is growth different from development?

17 How does 'zero' growth differ from 'negative' growth?

18 Give simple definitions to show the difference between an underdeveloped country, a developing country, and a highly developed country.

19 Why are all governments keen to see economic growth?

20 Simply state the main factors that affect economic growth.

Structured Questions

1 (a) What is meant by the 'standard of living' of a country?   (2)
   (b) Why do some countries have a higher standard of living than others?   (3)
   (c) Describe four factors that influence the standard of living.   (4)
   (d) What is 'per capita income'? To what extent would you say that this
        can be seen as an indication of the standard of living of a country?   (5)
   (e) In what way could we measure the standard of living of any country?   (6)

2 (a) What is the purpose of a government's budget?   (2)
   (b) Explain the difference between a budget surplus and a budget deficit.   (2)
   (c) State three services that governments provide which private enterprise
        would be unwilling to supply at an economic price   (3)
   (d) List three methods governments use to influence business activities.   (3)
   (e) To what extent would you argue that governments interfere too much
        in business activities?   (4)
   (f) One type of business that all governments try to influence is importing
        and exporting.
        (i)   Why is this of such importance?
        (ii) How do governments try to influence this aspect of business?   (6)

3 The following questions are all related to national income.

   (a) One way to calculate national income is by aggregate expenditure. State another method. What problems are encountered using this method? (3)

   (b) Explain the difference between GNP and national income. Why is the distinction between them important? (4)

   (c) Outline four measures of national income and output of an economy. (4)

   (d) Give four reasons why national income is an imperfect measure of the well-being of our country? (4)

   (e) Briefly outline five ways that the real national income of our country may be increased. (5)

4 The following table shows a variety of comparative data related to a number of countries. Answer the questions that follow.

   (a) Which country has the highest GNP and which has the lowest? (1)

   (b) Why is the GNP measured in US Dollars for all countries in the table? (2)

   (c) State four differences between countries with a high GNP and those with a low GNP. (2)

   (d) GNP is used in the table as a measurement of a country's national income. An alternative measure could have been GDP.

      (i) What do the letters GNP and GDP stand for? (2)

      (ii) Why do you think GNP was used in this table? (3)

   (e) Compare the data for GNP and that for birth-rate and comment on any relationships you can identify. (4)

   (f) Explain why it is that there is such a large difference between GNP of countries in the table. (6)

	Country	GNP $US	Birthrate per 1000	% urban dwellers	Life expectancy	Calories per day	% in agriculture
Market (capitalist) economies	Sweden	14 881	11	83	75	2 849	6
	USA	11 363	16	76	74	3 580	4
	Japan	9 352	16	76	76	2 552	10
	UK	8 873	12	76	73	3 340	3
Centrally planned (socialist) economies	China	2 086	18	65	70	3 460	17
	Poland	1 876	21	62	70	2 880	44
High income (oil producing) countries	Kuwait	18 086	36	58	69	2 728	17
	Libya	7 289	50	41	56	2 690	21
Middle income (developing) countries	Costa Rica	1 860	31	43	70	2 329	38
	Bolivia	757	47	33	51	1 970	65
	Philippines	733	40	36	59	2 241	69
Low income (developing) countries	Uganda	222	46	17	54	2 146	68
	Bangladesh	145	40	11	47	2 113	71
	Ethiopia	97	49	13	40	1 826	76

Extended answer assignments

1 Find out the amounts your government spends on each of the main components of its expenditure. Present the data researched in some appropriate graphical form. Write a summary report which includes explanation of the ways your government raises the revenue it needs.

2 (a) Give a detailed description of *five* contrasting services provided by the government of your country.
  (b) In what ways would you say that there is a need for your government to improve the social services it provides? Give reasons for your answer.

3 Why is it difficult to use national income statistics to compare the standard of living in different countries? What other statistics might you consider using in order to make a realistic comparison?

4 Using real data, explain the way that your government attempts to redistribute incomes. Quote the source of your data.

5 A major priority of all governments is the provision of welfare for its citizens. To what extent would you say that this is dependent upon growth and development?

6 By examination of your household or a local firm, show that national income can be measured in terms of output, income or expenditure.

20 Taxation and inflation

20.1 ## Principles of taxation

Everyone pays tax in some form, either directly or indirectly. The government does not just take money from us without reason. The money taken is used to control and direct the economy as well as to fund government expenditure.

A tax is a compulsory money payment by individuals and businesses levied on income, property and the use of goods and services which has to be paid to the state. Government decisions about taxes and public spending are referred to as 'fiscal policy'.

The following four 'rules' of taxation were stated by Adam Smith over 200 years ago, but they are still sound guides that apply today.

1 *Equality* – taxes should be based on the ability to pay. Those with higher incomes should pay a higher proportion of their income in tax than those with low incomes. Thus, people bear an equal burden rather than all paying the same amount.
2 *Economic* – taxes should be collected as economically as possible because there is little to be gained if the cost of collection is more than the money received.
3 *Certainty* – the easier it is to understand a tax system the less incentive there is to evade paying the amount levied. The form and manner of payment, and the quantity to be paid should be clear and unambiguous to the contributor and everyone else. In other words, the tax system should be clear enough so that those liable know what is expected of them.
4 *Convenience* – a tax should be convenient to collect. The Pay As You Earn (PAYE) method of collecting income tax is convenient because it is collected by the employer before the employees receive their pay. PAYE is also a convenient system because it fits in with the normal activity of regular payment of wages.

20.2 ## Functions of taxation

There are five functions of taxation.

To raise revenue

The main function of taxation is to raise *revenue* to pay for things provided by the state which private enterprise would be unable or unwilling to provide at prices the majority of the population are generally able to pay. Police, medical care, education and roads are examples where provision is largely met through taxation.

To maintain economic stability

Governments use taxation to exercise overall control of the economy in a manner that attempts to level out the 'highs' and 'lows' in economic activity, to promote economic growth and to try to achieve full employment. A major factor involved here is the control of inflation.

To influence expenditure

Taxation can be used to influence the level of total expenditure. The higher the level of taxation the lower the level of real expenditure is likely to be and vice versa. This principle can be used to deflate or reflate the economy. Inflation is examined later in this chapter.

To redistribute income

Taxation can be used to effectively redistribute income and capital ownership in the community, by taxing some members of the community higher than others, e.g. redistribution in favour of poorer members of the community. Redistribution of income will, in the long term, influence the distribution of wealth.

To satisfy specific objectives

Taxation can be used to achieve specific objectives such as:

- to discourage habits like smoking, drinking and gambling;
- to encourage activities such as healthy eating and safe driving;
- to stimulate production, exporting and improvement of balance of payments;
- to encourage movement of industry into depressed areas;
- to promote mobility of labour.

20.3 Methods of taxation

Progressive, proportional and regressive taxes

These ways of looking at the different forms of taxes compare the amount of tax paid to the income of a person.

- *Progressive tax.* The proportion taken in tax rises as income rises; it takes a larger proportion of income from higher income groups. Income tax is a progressive tax.
- *Proportional tax.* A change in a person's income does not on average affect the proportion of their income that they pay in tax. National insurance is an example of a proportional tax.
- *Regressive tax.* The proportion of income taken in tax falls as income rises. Value added tax (VAT) is regressive because it is charged at a uniform rate irrespective of the purchaser's income.

Direct taxation

A direct tax is one which is paid directly to the tax authority by the person against whom the tax is levied. Income tax, corporation tax, capital gains tax, capital transfer tax and North Sea oil tax are examples of direct taxes.

Income tax

Income tax is both a direct tax and a progressive tax. It is a tax on personal earned income. Wage earners are allowed a certain amount in tax-free allowances and the rest of their income is taxed. The proportion of tax paid increases as taxable income increases.

Corporation tax

Corporation tax is a tax on the profits of companies. Similar to individuals and income tax, companies are allowed to deduct certain expenditure as tax-free allowances from their gross profit. The remaining net profit is liable for tax.

Capital gains tax

When individuals sell assets such as shares, land, property and works of art, any profit or gain above a certain 'threshold' is liable for capital gains tax. Certain personal assets such as a person's home are exempt from this tax.

Inheritance tax

Inheritance tax is a tax on gifts or gratuitous transfers of personal wealth from one person to another, whether they take place during a person's lifetime, or on their death. The rate of tax varies according to the sum transferred. There are various exemptions available to certain forms of enterprise such as farming and small businesses, and transfers to and from a husband or wife. There is also a 'threshold' below which transfers are tax free.

Indirect taxation

An indirect tax is paid by the taxpayer indirectly to the tax authority, i.e. levied on one person but is collected and ultimately paid by someone else such as a retailer, for example value added tax.

Value added tax (VAT)

VAT is the most important indirect tax in Britain, because it is the main general expenditure tax levied by central government. It is a tax imposed on the value added to goods and services at every stage of production.

When several traders are involved in the movement of goods from the producer to the consumer, each will charge VAT to the person to whom they sell. Each trader, however, only pays to Customs and Excise the amount of VAT they have charged their customers less the amount of tax paid to their suppliers. In this way we can see that each trader pays VAT on the difference between what he has sold the product for and what he paid for it. This difference is called 'value added'. Therefore, tax is paid on the value that has been added to the product, and this is how this tax gets its name.

The rate of VAT to be charged is announced by the Chancellor of the Exchequer in the Budget, and the rate is varied from time to time. Some goods and services are not liable for VAT because they are zero rated or exempt.

Where VAT is applicable, it is charged on the net value of the goods or services, in other words, the value of the invoice after taking into account trade or cash discounts (even if the buyer does not take advantage of them).

Example 1	£	*Example 2*	£
Gross invoice value	10 000	Gross invoice value	40 000
less 20% trade discount	2 000	*less* 25% quantity discount	10 000
	8 000		30 000
plus $17\frac{1}{2}$% VAT	1 400	*plus* $17\frac{1}{2}$ VAT	5 250
Invoice total	£9 400	Invoice total	35 250

Protective (customs) and excise duties

These taxes are collected by HM Customs and Excise Department and are charged in addition to VAT on a variety of important goods such as alcohol and tobacco products. Prior to Britain's entry to the then EEC, customs duties were taxes levied on imported goods, and excise duties were taxes placed on certain home-produced goods. Since Britain became a member of the EC the terminology has changed.

All revenue duties are now termed as excise, which is payable on both imported and home-produced goods. Protective duties refer to customs duties on non-EC goods, used to put into effect the common external tariff policy of EC member countries which was examined earlier in Chapter 11. The purpose of protective duties is to raise the final market price of cheaper foreign products to a level with which home producers can compete.

Other forms of taxation

National Insurance (NI)

NI is a form of direct taxation where contributions are made by both employers and employees. The money raised by this tax is used specifically for the National Insurance Fund, the National Health Service, and the Redundancy Fund.

Employers have to pay contributions for every person they employ, and in fact they pay over 50 per cent of NI contributions. Not surprisingly this tax has been called a 'tax on jobs', because every new person employed is an additional financial burden for the employer.

Motor vehicle duty

Sometimes referred to as 'road tax' or 'car tax'. The owners of motor vehicles must pay a tax for each vehicle used on public highways.

Local authority tax

About one-half of local authority income comes from central government, and this income is supplemented from local taxation. Unlike most other taxes, local taxes are not levied by the Inland Revenue but are raised by local authorities. In the UK the main local taxation is that paid by businesses and local residents.

The form that this taxation takes has varied in recent years. For many years a system called 'rates' existed and this was substituted by the 'poll tax', or to give it its correct name, the community charge, which was introduced into Scotland in 1989 and to England and Wales in 1990.

Unlike the rates which was a tax on property paid by some 18 million house-holders, the poll tax was to be paid by all 35 million adults with some exceptions. In other words, it was a tax on people as opposed to a tax on property. It was to be paid by all those entitled to vote – hence the term 'poll tax'.

Each local authority decided its own level of community charge, and every adult in the area was charged the same amount. Businesses, however, were treated differently. They still paid money to the local community under the rates system which was set by the government whereas in the past it had been set by the local authority.

The community charge was the subject of much controversy and eventually proved almost unworkable. Then, in April 1993, the government introduced the council tax which is based on the value of the home owned. This too has proved controversial because, people have argued, that the value of homes fluctuate. In addition, the full council tax bill for the resident assumes that there are two adults in a dwelling. If only one adult lives there, the bill is cut by 25 per cent, but many argue the discount should be 50 per cent. Consequently, some critics question whether the new tax will truly be easily collectable, workable and fair.

20.4 Economic effects of taxation

Effective taxation should achieve the functions stated earlier but at the same time meet the longstanding principles of taxation (equality, certainty, convenience, economic). No single tax can meet all of these requirements and raise all the revenue governments need, consequently governments use a variety of methods of taxation which tends to even out some of the inadequacies of some of the taxes. A key source of debate is whether direct or indirect taxation is more appropriate.

The main advantage of direct taxes is that the rate charged can easily be changed or varied for different circumstances. For example, the overall rate of income tax can be simply changed centrally by the government, and it is possible to have varied rates, i.e. it is generally charged at a progressively higher rate to the rich and, conversely, at a lower rate to the poor. The PAYE system ensures that income tax is not only relatively easily collected (employers do much of the work) but it also allows the taxpayer to make contributions in small regular payments.

The main disadvantage of direct taxes is that they are expensive to administer and collect; many civil servants are involved and complicated rules and paper-work persists. Direct taxation often results in disputes between taxpayers and tax officials over the amount of tax due. In addition, those who do not pay their income tax by the PAYE method can fall into the trap of not saving sufficient money to pay one or two large payments a year.

Indirect taxes have the advantage in that they are relatively easy and cheap to collect, the amount to be paid is generally clear and unambiguous, and it is difficult to evade paying them. In addition, indirect taxation collects money from foreigners (e.g. tourists) whereas they do not pay direct taxes.

The main disadvantage of indirect taxes is that they are regressive in that poorer people tend to pay a higher proportion of their income in tax than those on higher incomes. For example, payment of a purchase tax or VAT is at the same rate whether one is a high earner, a low earner, or even a non-earner.

20.5 Inflation

Earlier in this chapter we saw that one of the functions of taxation is to maintain economic stability. One of the main threats to this stability is inflation, and governments throughout the world are continually striving to offset the effects of it.

Inflation describes a situation when prices are persistently rising and the real value of money is declining, which means that the cost of living has increased. If people's incomes do not improve, then their income purchases less. Under such circumstances we say that real income has fallen, and this leads to a fall in the standard of living unless some factor changes.

Inflation in the UK is usually measured by the *Retail Price Index (RPI)*. This involves measuring the collective prices of a selection of goods and services which a typical household would purchase over a period of a month. Around 600 items are included in the RPI and each month researchers compare 130 000 prices of the 600 items in a variety of retail outlets to measure changes that have taken place.

If the average of all the prices is 1 per cent higher than the previous month, this indicates that inflation is approximately 12 per cent per year.

Rising costs push inflation up.

Types of inflation

Inflation is the result of many factors but two broad types of inflation can be distinguished: 'cost-push' inflation and 'demand-pull' inflation.

Cost-push inflation

This form of inflation is caused by rises in the cost of factors of production such as raw materials or labour, for example oil prices or wages. For instance, wage increases may not be matched by increased productivity. When such increased costs are passed on to the consumer in the form of increased prices this results in cost-push inflation. The resultant increase in the cost of living encourages workers to press for further wage increases causing a continuing inflationary spiral with rising wages chased by rising prices, or vice versa.

Demand-pull inflation

This type of inflation involves 'too much money chasing too few goods', that is an excessive supply of money relative to the goods and services available for purchase. Upward movement of wages can be an explanation of this, but 'too much money' usually refers to excessive credit expansion, for example easier bank loans and hire purchase, etc., which encourages people to spend money that they do not immediately have available.

The effects of inflation

Inflation has the effect of making us all worse off. If your country has more inflation than other countries this will mean that your prices will rise faster. Consequently,

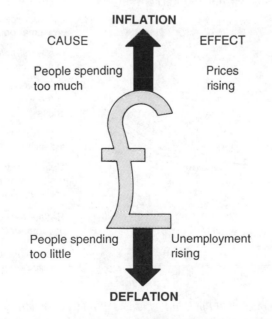

Consumer spending has an important effect on inflation.

your exporters will find it harder to sell their products. Consumers both in your country and abroad will be less inclined to buy the more expensive home-produced goods, preferring the less expensive foreign products. This will lead to reduced output at home and job losses, further adding to the rate of inflation. The following summarises the main effects of inflation:

- Prices are persistently rising, resulting in a decline in the standard of living, especially for those on fixed incomes.
- Saving is discouraged because people recognise that money saved will buy less in the future.
- Exports become more expensive because of increased production costs. Consequently, there is a tendency to import more goods since they are relatively cheaper than domestic production.
- People who owe money to others (*debtors*) gain from inflation, whereas those who are owed money (*creditors*) lose.

Controlling inflation

If a government believes that demand-pull is the cause of inflation it can put a number of measures into effect. The government can:

- reduce its own demand for goods and services;
- encourage increased productivity;
- try to reduce demand by consumers and producers;
- make credit more expensive and more difficult to obtain;
- take more in taxes than the government spends;
- introduce controls, e.g. of wages, prices, imports.

INFLATION – Government intervention

Summary

Inflation – persistent rise in the general level of prices of consumer goods and services.

Cost-push inflation – inflation caused by increases in costs to producers (e.g. higher wages or material costs).

Demand-pull inflation – inflation caused by more demand in the whole economy than can be supplied at existing prices.

Deflation – where the value of money is rising while prices are falling.

Deflationary measures – strategies used by the government in an attempt to reduce spending in the economy (usually through monetary or fiscal policies).

Reflationary measures – strategies used by the government to increase demand and encourage growth.

Hyperinflation – when prices are rising so fast that generally people prefer to spend their money rather than hold on to it.

The inflation line shows what the trend would be if inflation remained unchecked. The double line shows the possible effects of deflationary or reflationary measures.

Where cost-push inflation is thought to be the cause the remedies are more complex, and often open to political argument. For example, the prices of imported goods and raw materials are outside the control of the government. However, some control can be exercised over wage increases and the cost of home-produced goods through a firm prices and incomes policy, although the desirability of this is subject to political debate and there is no clear evidence that such a policy works.

Make a note of it

1 Describe the principles upon which taxation should be based.

2 Explain the five functions of taxation.

3 Explain the differences between the proportional, progressive and regressive forms of taxation.

4 Distinguish carefully between direct and indirect taxation. Include a description of at least two of each forms of taxation to illustrate your answer.

5 How does the tax VAT get its name? Calculate the missing figures in the following table

	(a)	(b)	(c)	(d)
Gross invoice value	240	1200	800	?
less 20% trade discount	?	?	?	100
Total goods	?	?	?	400
plus $17\frac{1}{2}$% VAT	?	?	?	?
	£?	£?	£?	£?

6 Explain the difference between protective duties and excise duties.

7 What is National Insurance and why is it sometimes referred to as a 'tax on jobs'?

8 To what extent does the current council tax meet the four principles stated by Adam Smith?

9 Define direct taxation and describe the forms it can take.

10 How does indirect taxation differ from direct taxation?

11 Describe the forms of indirect taxation commonly used.

12 Do you feel direct or indirect taxation the more appropriate? Give reasons for your answer.

13 What is inflation? How does 'cost-push' inflation differ from 'demand-pull' inflation?

14 What are the effects of inflation?

15 What steps might a government take in order to control inflation?

Structured Questions

1 Look at the notice of coding (Form P2) below and answer the following
questions.

```
┌─────────────────────────────────────────────────────────────────────┐
│ ☐                                                                     │
│        [CROWN LOGO]   Inland Revenue        Issued by                 │
│         INLAND        PAYE-Notice of Coding  H.M. Inspector of Taxes  │
│         REVENUE       Please keep this notice for future reference    │
│                       and let me know of any change    CODSALL        │
│                       in your address. Form P3(T) enclosed  QUEENS RD │
│                       (or previously sent) explains the entries.  CODSALL │
│                                                          SHROPSHIRE   │
│                                                              TF3 3CC  │
│          125                                                          │
│                                          ┌──────────────────────────┐ │
│        ┌────────────────────────────┐    │ Please use both lines of this reference if you │
│        │ MR K PEARSON               │    │ write or call - it will help to avoid delay. │
│        │ 21 HIGH STREET             │    │      125/D701              │ │
│        │ NEWTOWN                    │    ├──────────────────────────┤ │
│        │                            │    │ TN │ 11 │ 06 │ 60 │ A     │ │
│        │              ZT1 1AB       │    └──────────────────────────┘ │
│        └────────────────────────────┘    Date  10.05.91              │
└─────────────────────────────────────────────────────────────────────┘
```

This notice cancels any previous notice of coding for the year shown below. It shows the allowances which make up your code.
Your employer or paying officer will use this code to deduct or refund the right amount of tax under PAYE during the year shown
below.
Please check this notice. If you think it is wrong please return it to me and give your reasons. If we cannot agree you have the right
of appeal.
Please let me know at once about any change in your personal circumstances which may alter your allowances and coding.
By law you are required to tell me of any income that is not fully taxed, even if you are not sent a Tax Return.

See Note	Allowances	£	See Note	Less Deductions	£
17	PERSONAL ALLOWANCE	3295			
				Less total deductions	
	Total allowances	3295		Allowances set against pay etc. £	3295

Your code for the year to 5 April **1992** is **329L**   **Please see Part B overleaf**

P2 (T)

(a) What do the letters PAYE stand for? (1)
(b) What is the purpose of sending the notice of coding to the taxpayer? (1)
(c) What should the person receiving this notice do if they do not agree
with any of the information shown on it? (2)
(d) Briefly explain how the tax code is calculated. (3)
(e) Why is income tax said to be both a direct tax and a progressive tax? (3)
(f) To what extent do you feel that the PAYE system meets Adam Smith's
'rules' of taxation? (10)

2 Study the following newspaper extract and answer the questions below.

Two-tier system brings big gains for the highest-paid, but low earners lose out as their outgoings increase

'Champagne budget' slashes top rate and cuts basic payments to 25 per cent

Tax rates and allowances

Before the budget			After the budget		
Taxable income (£)	Rate (%)	Cumulative tax (£)	Taxable income (£)	Rate (%)	Cumulative tax (£)
0–17,900	27	4,833	0–19,300	25	4,825
17,901–20,400	40	5,833	Over 19,300	40	
20,401–25,400	45	8,083			
25,401–33,300	50	12,033			
33,301–41,200	55	16,378			
Over 41,200	60				

Personal allowances	Old	New
Allowances for people under 65		
Single person and wife's earnings	2,425	2,605
Married man	3,795	4,095
Age allowance for people aged 65–79		
Single person	2,960	3,180
Married man	4,675	5,035
Age allowance for people aged 80 and over		
Single person	3,070	3,310
Married man	4,845	5,205
Income limit for age allowance	9,800	10,600
Additional relief for single parent	1,370	1,490
Widow's bereavement	1,370	1,490

Source: *Guardian*, 16 March 1988.

(a) What was the highest rate of income tax:
   (i) before the Budget: (1)
   (ii) after the Budget? (1)
(b) Calculate the increase in the single person's allowance given in the Budget. (1)
(c) State two possible reasons why the government was able to reduce income tax rates. (2)
(d) Calculate the tax bill of a married man earning £12 095 a year. (3)
(e) Did the Budget make income tax more or less progressive? Explain your answer fully. (6)

(f) How might the changes affect:
  (i) workers
  (ii) unemployment
  (iii) overall spending in the economy? (6)

3 (a) What is the current basic rate of income tax in the UK? (1)
  (b) Express the higher rate of income tax in the UK in terms of pence in the £. (1)
  (c) What is the meaning of 'fiscal policy'? (2)
  (d) What indicates that a tax is 'regressive'? (2)
  (e) Briefly describe two methods of taxation that can be used generally to promote economic activity. (4)
  (f) Identify two social problems and two economic problems which exist in the UK today. (4)
  (g) Choose two social problems and two economic problems and show how each might be solved using taxation. (6)

4 (a) What is inflation? (1)
  (b) State two categories of people who would benefit during a period of high inflation. (2)
  (c) Give two ways in which the process of inflation may begin. (2)
  (d) Give three reasons why prices are more likely to rise as employment approaches the full level. (3)
  (e) What do the letters RPI stand for? How does the RPI indicate the level of inflation? (4)
  (f) Explain the difference between cost-push inflation and demand-pull inflation. (4)
  (g) Briefly describe policies a government could follow in an attempt to check:
  (i) cost-push inflation;
  (ii) demand-pull inflation. (4)

Extended Answer Assignments

1 Why does any government need to redistribute income? To what extent do you feel taxation achieves this aim? Give specific examples to illustrate your answer.

2 Using data quoted from any reliable source, describe the effect of inflation on your country and explain how the government is attempting to control it.

3 Describe four taxes levied on individuals by the government. How far do you consider them to be either progressive or regressive?

4 Explain the difference between direct and indirect taxation. How, if at all, do they affect the rate of inflation as measured by the Retail Price Index? Use official data to support your observations.

5 Use a collection of newspaper articles and headlines, together with our own explanations, to show the difference between demand-pull and cost-push inflation. What policies might a government adopt to reduce inflation?

6 Investigate the following question over a six-month period. To what extent is your family's personal rate of inflation the same as the official government rate?

7 Discuss the suggestion that the British taxation system is progressive. Provide evidence to support your views.

8 Should the government levy a 'health tax' on alcoholic drink to partly fund the National Health Service? Include a survey of local views.

9 Identify a varied selection of 30 goods and monitor price changes over a three-month period. Make a personal record of the rate of inflation. Write a detailed report of your findings, including appropriate charts and graphs.

21 Population

21.1 ▶ Importance of population

Consider making a list of every single item that you have consumed during the last three days. Assuming that you can remember every item, the list that you will end up with will be surprisingly long. But you will no doubt be well aware that there are people throughout the world who are suffering from malnutrition. In fact, two thirds of the world's population is in this position. The source of this problem can be found in our inability to grow enough food to feed an increasing world population. The shortage of resources required by the world population is not restricted to food alone; many other material shortages also exist such as housing, education, medical care, etc.

Obviously many of the existing shortages would be easier to resolve if there were fewer people in the world, yet some countries are actually trying to persuade their inhabitants to have more children to increase the size of their population. But serious consideration of the problem will lead you to realise that it is not just the size of population, but also the structure of it that is important. For this reason demographic (population) studies are important to economic planning. It must also be remembered that population not only provides the labour to produce goods and services, but it is also a source of demand for the goods and services which the labour produces. Population studies are also important because changes that occur require changes in planning strategies to ensure that resources are used efficiently. For example, a straightforward increase in population will require increased resources devoted to education, welfare services and medical care.

21.2 ▶ Factors influencing population size

Before 1801, when the first *official census* (official counting of the inhabitants of a country) was held, there was little information on the size of Britain's population although it has been estimated to have been about $5\frac{1}{2}$ million in 1688. In 1801, and periodically ever since, the government ordered the first official census of the UK.

The census does more than just count the total population. It breaks the data into a variety of categories, e.g. men, women, single, married, widowed, divorced, number of children, teenagers, working people, retired people, etc. The census counts people in relation to the types of houses they live in, the kind of job they do, how they travel to and from work, and their country of origin.

The data obtained from a census is used, particularly by the government, to decide what revenue it needs and how it should be used. For example, it is used

(2001 = projection)

12 m	22 m	38 m	50 m	56 m	57.1 m	58 m
1801	1851	1901	1951	1983	1988	2001

UK population growth (millions).

to work out how much is needed for pensions, health care, etc. The census also shows how the workforce is changing and moving to other areas. This information is used when planning building programmes, e.g. factories, housing, etc.

You can see from the diagram below that the population of the United Kingdom has steadily increased since 1801, with some levelling off in recent times.

There are three factors which influence the size of population – migration, births and deaths.

Migration

Migration refers to the movement of people from one country to another to live. More people may come into a country to live (immigration), and people may leave their home country to go and live abroad (emigration). Depending whether immigration exceeds emigration, or vice versa, the population increases or decreases.

Migration is influenced by economic conditions and official policies and controls. Poor economic conditions in one country and brighter prospects in another country encourage migration. But some countries may enforce controls which limit immigration or emigration, and this can influence population size.

Birth rate

The birth rate can be expressed as a percentage or as a figure representing the number of births per thousand of the population. From the diagram on page 360 it can be seen that the trend in the UK is one of a steadily decreasing birth rate since 1801. The birth rate is affected by a number of factors:

- *Standard of living* – where a standard of living is high, the birth rate tends to be low. When the standard of living is low, the birth rate tends to be high.
- *Attitudes, customs and beliefs* – religious beliefs (e.g. Catholicism) and attitudes to contraception influence the birth rate. A reduction in prejudice to women working,

359

UK birth rate from 1801.   *UK death rate from 1801.*

coupled with a desire for a better standard of living that can be achieved by both partners of a marriage working, affects the willingness of women to have children.

- *Women of child-bearing age* – assuming that the average number of children born to women remains unchanged, then the greater the proportion of women of child-bearing age, the higher will be the birth rate.
- *Government policies* – the birth rate is influenced by the level of welfare benefits, child benefit and rate of taxation, all of which are directly controlled by the government. The government also influences the provision of facilities which provide advice on contraception and family planning (e.g. through the education system), which also affects the birth rate as do laws and attitudes to abortion.

Death rate

The death rate is the number of deaths per thousand of population per year. It can also be expressed as a percentage figure. Obviously, if people begin to live longer this contributes to an increase in the size of the population. This is the case in the UK. It can be seen from the diagram above that there has been an almost continuous decline in the death rate since 1801, although the trend has evened out in recent times. The reasons for the fall in death rate are clearer than those influencing the fall in the birth rate.

- *Standard of living* – improved living standards such as better housing, clothing and diet contribute to better health and reduce mortality.
- *Medical knowledge* – advances in medical knowledge, new discoveries, drugs and inventions have all contributed to a significant reduction in the death rate.
- *Public health measures* – many basic services provided by local authorities have improved considerably and have contributed to a reduction in illness and disease. For example, improvements in services such as refuse collection, water purification and sewage disposal have contributed to a reduction in death from infectious disease.

Optimum population size

Overpopulation

This creates many problems, whether it occurs in a single country or worldwide. Poverty, food shortages and a low rate of investment are all features of overpopulation. It is a familiar feature of an agriculture-based society which experiences difficulty in accumulating sufficient capital necessary to industrialise the economy. The difficulty in accumulating capital for industrial development occurs because a large percentage of all available resources is needed to keep the population alive.

Declining population

This also creates problems. A falling population implies that the average age of the population is increasing. This reduces the mobility and the quality of the labour force. It also makes demands for higher welfare benefits and a higher taxation on the younger sections of the working population. There is a greater need for hospitals, old people's homes and related services. On the other hand, there could be a reduced need for schools and teachers.

If the population is declining, a smaller domestic market exists – there are fewer customers for the goods and services produced. This can reduce the opportunities for large-scale production and the economies of scale associated with it. It may also result in reduced enthusiasm and initiative in the workforce.

Optimum population

The optimum, or most beneficial, population is one which makes maximum effective use of the resources (land, labour and capital) available. Optimum population is that which gives the highest output per head of population.

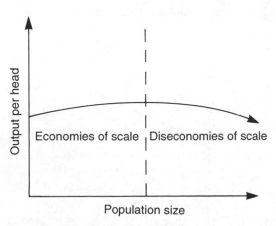

Optimum population.

- If the average output per head is rising as population increases, then the country is underpopulated.
- If the average output falls as population increases then the country is overpopulated.

21.4 Distribution of population

Age distribution

Age distribution refers to the numbers of the population in the different age groups. Age distribution is important because it is directly related to the proportion of producers to consumers. It is influenced by both past and present birth and death rates.

When looking at the age distribution of the population it is usual to classify the population into three groups.

1 Those below school leaving age.
2 Those of working age.
3 Those above retirement age.

Obviously, those of working age are required to support people within the other two categories.

Working population

All these people are at work or available for work. The size of the workforce will be influenced by:

- total population size
- school leaving age

- retirement age
- percentage of non-workers in the working age group
- people working who are beyond retirement age
- age distribution of population
- sex distribution of population.

In the UK we say that the population has 'aged' during the twentieth century. In other words, there has been a tendency for an increase in the proportion of those above retirement age; those leaving the workforce to retire are exceeding those entering employment. This trend has its origins in past and present birth and death rates, but it has also been influenced by an increasing number of young people entering full-time education and other 'non-employment' schemes beyond school leaving age, and a tendency for people to retire earlier than they used to.

Dependency ratio

The dependency ratio is the proportion of the working population to the non-working (dependent) population:

$$\frac{\text{Number of workers}}{\text{Number of dependents}} - \text{Dependency ratio}$$

Economic effects of an ageing population

1 *Changes in spending patterns* – as the population ages spending patterns change; there is an increased demand for goods related to the older population, and reduced demand for goods for the young.
2 *Increased dependence on working population* – as the proportion of non-working population increases there is an increase in the number of those dependent on the output of the current working population (increased dependency ratio).
3 *Less adaptive workforce* – there is a reduced mobility and adaptability of the labour force because an older population tend to be less energetic and enterprising than a younger population. Alternatively, we could say that there is a need for the younger proportion of the population to be more mobile, adaptive, energetic and enterprising.

Years of age	Further expectation of life		
NOW	MALE	FEMALE	
20	54.6	58.3	
25	49.9	53.6	
30	44.9	48.8	
35	40.1	44.0	
40	35.3	39.1	
45	30.6	34.3	
50	26.1	29.7	
55	21.9	25.3	

Expectation of life table.

Sex distribution

As long as the proportion of males to females is similar, sex distribution is of less significance to population than age distribution.

In the UK more males are born that females and men outnumber women of all age groups up to 44 years of age. But in the older age groups there are a greater number of women than men. Whilst this may at first sight seem a contradiction, the reason for the differences is quite simple; more women survive beyond the age of 45. Three factors explain this:

1 *Work pressure* – physical and mental pressure of work affects men more than women.
2 *Emigration* – more men leave the UK than women.
3 *Wars* – affect the male population more than the female population.

Geographical distribution

Geographical distribution refers to the distribution of the population in different regions at various dates. We can usually see a direct relationship between location or relocation of industry and geographical distribution of the population.

In the UK we have seen that as the location of industries has changed, so has the geographical distribution of the population. Prior to the Industrial Revolution, the population was located mainly in rural areas, and concentrated in areas where the farming land is good (particularly in the south-east). Following the Industrial Revolution there was a movement from the countryside into towns, and particularly into the northern parts of Britain where the major impact of the development of coal, steel, cotton and shipbuilding was taking effect. As these industries declined between the wars and after 1945, newer industries in light engineering located in the Midlands and the south attracted labour away from the north.

Occupational distribution

Occupational distribution statistics show the numbers of people employed in various occupations. Job distribution depends on a country's stage of development. Underdeveloped countries tend to have a large proportion (75 per cent) of their workforce employed in the agricultural sector, while developed countries have 10 per cent or less in this section of the economy.

By examining such statistics over a period of time we can see changes that have taken place. For example, prior to the Industrial Revolution Britain's workforce was largely involved in agriculture. The Industrial Revolution necessitated movement from agriculture into manufacturing and construction industries. This trend has continued and it has also contributed to increased employment in the tertiary sector. The table opposite shows the movement away from the primary industries such as farming, forestry, fishing and mining. However, the percentage of the total workforce employed in manufacturing has changed little.

	1841		1901		1981		1991	
	'000s	%	'000s	%	'000s	%	'000s	%
Agriculture, forestry, fishing	1 639	22.3	2 243	11.8	360	1.7	268	1.2
Mining, quarrying	225	3.2	944	5.0	337	1.6	154	0.7
Manufacturing	2 452	35.5	7 000	36.9	6 038	28.1	5 437	24.4
Construction	377	5.5	1 336	7.0	1 132	5.3	1 038	4.7
Transport/ communications	200	2.9	1 497	7.9	1 429	6.6	1 354	6.0
Others	2 014	30.6	5 954	31.4	12 229	56.7	14 021	63.0
Total	6 097	100.0	18 974	100.0	21.525	100.0	22 272	100.0

21.5 Mobility of labour

Mobility in this respect is the movement between occupations. The efficient working of any economy depends not only on the size and structure of the workforce but also how mobile it is, so that maximum use is made of it. Mobility of labour can be viewed in two ways.

1 *Geographic (lateral) mobility* – the ability to move from one area to another.
2 *Occupational (vertical) mobility* – the ability to change one's job, profession or industry.

Obstacles to mobility of labour

Look at the following list of factors that inhibit labour mobility. Which ones can you identify that can be clearly associated with geographic mobility and which are related only to occupational mobility?

- *Inertia* – the desire to remain in one place.
- *Family and friendship ties* have to be broken.
- *Education* of children may be disrupted.
- *Re-housing* involves costs and inconvenience.
- *Prejudice* – people may dislike particular jobs or areas.
- *Knowledge* of alternative jobs is not always readily available.
- *Wages* of alternative occupation may be unattractive.
- *Retraining* costs may be too high.
- *Skills* to do alternative employment may be lacking.
- *Trade unions* may resist occupation movement.

Make a note of it

1 What do you understand by the word demography?

2 Give four reasons why population studies are important.

3 What is a 'census'?

4 What has been happening to the size of the UK population since 1801?

5 Explain the meaning of the word 'migration' and show its relevance to population.

6 Define birth rate and list the factors which affects its growth or decline.

7 What trend can be seen in the UK birth rate over the last 150 years?

8 What factors influence the death rate and why is this figure important to population?

9 Why are overpopulation and declining population problems?

10 What do you understand by optimum population?

11 'The age distribution of the UK population has increased during the twentieth century.' Explain this statement.

12 What is the dependency ratio?

13 Explain the term 'sex distribution of population'.

14 Give a brief description of the geographical distribution of the UK population since the Industrial Revolution.

15 What does examination of statistics related to UK occupational distribution show us?

16 What is mobility of labour and what factors influence it?

Structured Questions

1 Consider the following diagram and answer the questions on page 367.

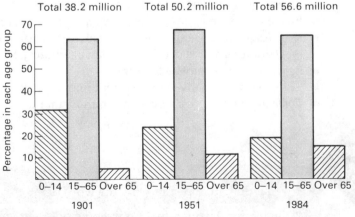

Changing age structure of UK population 1901–84

Source: *Annual Abstract of Statistics*, HMSO.

(a) What was the population of the UK in 1951? (1)
(b) What has happened to the percentage of the 0–14 year-olds in the population since 1901? (2)
(c) Calculate the number of 0–14 year-olds in the UK for 1984. (3)
(d) Why is the age distribution of the UK often shown using the categories that have been used in the data? (2)
(e) (i) What evidence is there in the data that the UK has an ageing population? (2)
(ii) What factors have contributed to the ageing of the UK population? (4)
(iii) What are the economic implications for a country of having an ageing population? (6)

2 The following table shows the changes in occupational distribution in Anytown, 1974–94.

Employment in Anytown, 1974–94

% of employment in:	1974	1984	1994
Primary sector	6	3	1
Secondary sector	70	40	30
Tertiary sector	20	52	58
Unemployed	4	5	11
Working population (000s)	500	520	540

(a) What do you understand by 'occupational distribution'? (1)
(b) Give two examples of jobs in each of the primary, secondary and tertiary sectors. (3)
(c) Summarise the main trends that can be observed in this data. (3)
(d) Complete the following table, showing all your calculations.

Anytown – actual numbers employed

No. of people employed	1994
Primary sector	?
Secondary sector	?
Tertiary sector	?

(3)

(e) Give four possible reasons for the changes in Anytown occupational distribution shown in the data. (4)
(f) Compare the data shown here with that contained in the table on page 365. What comparison can you make between the trend shown here for Anytown and the national data shown on page 365? (6)

3 (a) 'The census does more than count the population.' Explain this
statement. (2)

(b) Define the term 'optimum population'. (2)

(c) 'If the size of the population is too small the country may not be able
to fully use its productive potential.' Why is this statement true? (3)

(d) 'Beyond the optimum population size diseconomies occur.' Explain
this statement. (3)

(e) Give two examples of factors that influence the birth rate and two that
influence the death rate. (4)

(f) Refer to the data on page 365 showing changes in occupational
distribution of the UK population. Explain the reasons for at least three
of the changes contained in the data. (6)

Extended Answer Assignments

1 There has been a considerable increase in the number of people employed in
the tertiary sector in the UK. Use locally researched data to show whether this
is also the case in the area where you live. Write a report to summarise your
findings.

2 What effect has the national fall in the birth rate had in your local area?

3 To what extent is your local population economically mobile?

22 ► The role of governments

22.1 ►

The responsibilities of governments

In all countries the government plays a crucial role because it has such a wide-reaching effect on the community. The level of government involvement in the economy or the life of the country will be influenced by the type of economic system that the country has – free, planned or controlled, or mixed (*see* Chapter 1). The UK economy is largely a 'mixed' system, that is a mixture of the free and controlled economic systems. In other words, there is some government involvement in the economy and the life of the country. The extent of this involvement can be dependent upon political influences (refer also to Chapter 7).

The responsibilities of governments can be categorised into four major areas:

1 Promotion of law and order and defence

The government is the protector of the people. The general aim is to ensure that all persons in the community receive 'just treatment'. Law and order is important in society because it promotes economic stability. For example, tourists are not likely to want to visit a country where there is unrest and instability. Similarly, investors will be less likely to put their money into a country where law and order is not evident.

In order to meet this responsibility the government must promote appropriate legislation and provide police and courts of justice to administer law and order in the country. The government also has to make provision for defence (e.g. armed forces) against external dangers, and to provide diplomatic representation abroad.

2 Strategic planning

The government will develop plans for particular sectors of the economy. It may want to promote development in particular industries, or in specific locations. To support such a plan the government may provide grants, subsidies or 'soft' loans, advisory services and other agencies to industries or people it wants to influence.

As part of their strategic planning many governments provide public utilities, such as water and telephones, whereas some governments prefer these in private ownership. Many aspects of public transport are also provided or regulated by governments. Public ownership of enterprises such as these is examined in Chapter 4 and transport is covered in Chapter 13.

3 Provision of social services

The government will provide services which private enterprise would be unable or unwilling to supply at a price that all people could afford to pay, e.g. education, health, welfare, culture and sanitation. The provision of social services is examined in more detail later in this chapter.

4 Management of the economy

The government is charged with overall control of the economy. It will aim to achieve a high level of employment and to encourage economic growth through sound productivity. It will want to manage the National Debt, protect the country's balance-of-payments position and maintain its foreign reserves.

The Budget

In order to meet the foregoing responsibilities the government will need to raise the necessary revenue and exercise control over the economy. In Chapter 20 we have seen the part that taxation measures play, and in Chapter 15 we saw how governments can influence the financial markets. The Budget plays a key part in the government's strategies for managing the economy.

There are two main functions of the Budget:

1 *to regulate the economy* by influencing the demand for goods and services;
2 *to redistribute income and wealth* among the sections of the community.

The government makes public its Budget every year. The Budget summarises what services the government intends to provide for its citizens, how much money is needed, and how it intends to raise the necessary revenue. The Budget may also set out measures to be taken to stimulate or depress key areas of the economy and to encourage saving and investment.

The main source of government income is from taxation. Changes in taxation can affect businesses in a variety of ways. For example, if the government increased taxation on cars, people will probably buy fewer. This will lead to reduced sales and lower profits. This would, of course, result in increased unemployment, which in turn will mean that consumers have less money in order to buy cars, and so on.

22.2 Government assistance to entrepreneurs

It is in the interest of all governments to help businesses to achieve their full potential because in doing so businesses contribute to the ideal of full employment and add to national prosperity. Most governments will try to support businesses by providing the following :

- An environment that is conducive to economic growth. It will do this by setting rules for business operations, and providing utilities and other facilities which support business activities.
- Promotion and maintenance of competitive markets. Governments will prevent companies from abusing their power by taking action against monopolistic activities. This benefits businesses that are not in a monopolistic position, as well as safeguarding the consumer.

Trade promotion

The government provides various forms of assistance to encourage trade, particularly in respect of the exporting sector. The latter is recognised as of special importance in contributing to the balance of payments (*see* Chapter 11). The following are typical examples of government assistance in promoting trade overseas and at home:

- foreign market intelligence
- Export Credits Guarantee Department
- subsidies
- regional aid.

Foreign market intelligence

The government will provide information about foreign markets and trading opportunities. Fore example, it will advise on the market potential for an exporter's goods and provide details of regulations and other specific local requirements in the target market. The government will also assist in the process of advertising and marketing the country's products abroad, e.g. co-ordinating participation in overseas trade fairs.

Much of foreign market intelligence operations are carried out by governments through their embassies and diplomats abroad. These officials will also register protests on behalf of their country if free trade is unduly threatened by the import controls of foreign governments.

Export Credits Guarantee Department

This government department supports exporters by providing:

- insurance against non-payment of debts by foreign importers;
- grants or low-interest loans to assist exporters in meeting the initial expense of exporting (*see* Chapter 11).

Subsidies

When a government is faced with a persistent adverse balance of trade it might tackle the situation by imposing import duties (tariffs/taxes) which would discourage imports by making them relatively more expensive. This can have an adverse effect in causing overseas governments to impose taxes on our goods in retaliation.

An alternative strategy would be to give subsidies (grants) to home producers. This would have the effect of making UK goods cheaper and enable them to compete more effectively against cheap imports.

Regional aid

Regional aid refers to grants or loans or tax relief given to firms and local authorities to create jobs or to improve the infrastructure in areas where there is high unemployment and poor living conditions. The aid aims to attract firms into areas identified by the government for special treatment (*see also* Chapter 2).

22.3 Government intervention in business

Governments throughout the world intervene in business activities for a variety of reasons and to different degrees. Sometimes they might do so in order to support enterprises, in other circumstances governments might be motivated by a need to control or regulate them.

Consumer protection

Consumer protection refers to the range of measures that exist to help consumers to make wise purchases and to protect them from exploitation.

Governments accept some of the responsibility for consumer protection and demonstrate this in a variety of ways, including the following:

- by contributing to consumer education and advice;
- by establishing and enforcing appropriate legislation;
- by the control of quality and weights and measures;
- by the monitoring and control of prices;
- by the promotion of fair trading practices;
- by the supervision of credit facilities.

The National Consumer Council

The Council was set up by the government in 1975 to carry out research into consumer problems. It acts as a pressure group and has strong links with other consumer organisations. As such, the Council can give businesses advice to help direct their marketing strategies, and it can also put pressure on businesses when they are acting in a manner that is not in the interests of consumers.

Consumer protection is dealt with in more detail in Chapter 9.

Monopolies, mergers and restrictive practices

A *monopoly* is a situation where a firm holds such a large proportion (25 per cent or more) of the market that it could control the supply and price. A firm in a monopolistic position could exploit the consumer by restricting output and charging high prices.

Where a monopoly exists in the public sector the government has direct access to the means of protecting consumer interests. Where the monopoly exists in the private sector it is important that the government ensures that those with a large share of the market do not exploit their strong position in a manner that is not in the interest of consumers.

A *merger* refers to the joining together of two firms into a larger unit. This can be against public interests if it results in a monopolistic position which is exploited by the firm.

A *restrictive practice* is any activity by a firm aimed at reducing competition, e.g. by price fixing and forming groups of firms (*cartels*) to control output and other factors influencing conditions of sale.

There are two main elements which support the UK government's legal framework for preventing businesses from restricting competition or engaging in activities which are unfair to the consumer.

The Monopolies and Mergers Commission

The Commission can investigate to see if a firm or firms are operating against the public interest. It also investigates mergers and takeovers to ensure that firms with a large share of the market do not exploit their position against the interest of the public.

The Commission reports its findings to the Director General of Fair Trading. Action can be taken to remedy any trading situation found to be against the public interest, and recommendations are made to the government.

The Restrictive Practices Court

The Court investigates cases where firms are engaged in activities which have the effect of fixing prices in a manner that is against the public interest. For example, a group of firms might agree to fix their prices (*a price ring*) or a firm could decide that it will only supply certain retailers (e.g. those who do not cut prices).

Import controls

Sometimes governments may feel it necessary to place controls on goods being brought into the country in order to protect industries in the home market, or to secure a favourable balance-of-payments position (*see* Chapter 11). There are two basic methods of import controls – *quotas* and *tariffs*.

- *Quotas* – are a limit on the quantity of a product that is allowed to enter the country in a given period of time. Sometimes the government may implement an *embargo* which is a complete ban on the import of certain goods (or goods of a specific country).
- *Tariffs* – are a tax on imports which has the effect of raising the cost price of the import. The tax may be *specific* or *ad valorem* (for an explanation of these terms *see* Chapter 11).

Taxation

Taxation of income, goods and property can also be used to influence and to encourage industry and commerce. For example, increasing taxation on certain products can depress demand and discourage production, and vice versa. Taxation is dealt with in depth in Chapter 20.

Nationalisation

We have seen in Chapter 4 that sometimes the state will take over the ownership of certain industries. When a business is taken into public ownership in this way it is said to have been *nationalised*. Sometimes enterprises are in state ownership but have not been nationalised, in other words, they are enterprises that have been originally established by the government. State ownership of industries is a prominent feature of controlled economies, and to a lesser extent is found in mixed economies.

State control of industries in this way allows the government to ensure that certain goods and services are made available at an economic price, and it also makes it possible to plan for particular sectors of the economy. You should refer again to Chapter 4 for wider examination of state ownership of industries, and particularly the arguments for and against state ownership.

22.4 Social services

In modern society the responsibilities of government are now seen to include the provision of social services at a national and personal level such as social security, medical and health care, education and welfare facilities including sanitation, housing, roads and transportation.

It is generally recognised that a government has an obligation to provide its citizens with social services because without government intervention many in the community would be denied these basic material needs. In this respect the government takes a political decision to provide these services either free or at a cost subsidised by funds obtained from taxation.

Education

Education is an example of the high degree of specialisation in modern developed societies. In the UK, instead of every worker trying to provide their own needs, each specialises in doing one thing and pays others to provide everything else. This is the case with education. Parents do not have the expertise or the time to educate their children. So they pay for schools and teachers to do the educating whilst they carry on their own specialisms, which in turn help to supply schools and teachers with their needs.

The UK has a strong tradition of state-provided education. The government funds most education at the primary, secondary, tertiary and higher levels. A well-educated population is generally recognised as making an important contribution to commerce and industry. Better educated and healthier workers are more productive and less of a burden on the state than people who are not. Conversely, low educational standards generally lead to less output for the economy. Education not only helps to provide the knowledge and skills that enable workers to be useful to business, but it also helps to make the workforce more flexible and mobile. In this sense education contributes to human wealth.

Health

A healthy population is important to all countries and, therefore, promotion of healthy living and medical care is an important responsibility of government. This will include not only the provision of medical facilities such as hospitals, but also the broadcasting of information on health-related matters such as sensible diet, hygiene, contraception, etc.

Health care has become increasingly important in most developed societies. As income rises, people tend to demand more health care. For the whole UK economy, incomes have gone up fairly steadily since the 1950s and so has the demand for health care.

One of the reasons for the rising demand for health care services is due to the change in attitudes towards such care. We expect more and better health care in the UK today. In some ways this is a result of the government's efforts to raise public awareness of the need for healthy living, including dietary influences.

The UK is one of the few countries in the industrialised world to have a free health service. In effect the service is not truly free because it is funded by the National Insurance scheme (explained below). In most other countries health is looked after by private insurance schemes. In some countries every person is required to join a scheme, whereas in others it is voluntary.

National Insurance (NI)

National Insurance, which is a system contributing to health care, is operated by many countries as a social service. It should be noted that National Insurance is not only concerned with health care, although this is one of its main aims. In the UK National Insurance is compulsory for all working people and the benefits are available to all the population.

National Insurance is an example of the way that some governments ensure that medical and health care and other support services are available for all members of the community. National Insurance is a scheme which aims to raise money through premiums deducted from wages, with contributions (approximately two-

Some of the benefits from National Insurance.

375

thirds) from employers. The funds raised in this way are used to provide the benefits outlined in the diagram above.

National Insurance contributions are paid into the National Insurance Fund and are used only to pay for National Insurance benefits (e.g. retirement pensions, unemployment benefits) and a small part of the National Health Service. National Insurance contributions are paid by workers and their employers and are calculated as a percentage of wages.

Recreational facilities

Recreation also plays an important part in both the health, education and leisure of both citizens and tourists. The governments of most developed countries provide libraries, botanical gardens and recreational parks for the use of both local residents and visitors. Sport is also encouraged by the government, often with a Sports Minister as administrator. In addition, there are national galleries of art, museums and zoos, all considerably influenced by government.

The foregoing are just some of the many social services that countries provide for their citizens – it would be impossible to include all of them here. However, the importance of social services is demonstrated by the fact that most governments establish separate ministries or departments with responsibilities for the various areas of social services. For example, there may be a department of education, transport, health, etc.

Make a note of it

1 Describe the four main areas of responsibility of governments.

2 What is the purpose of the government budget?

3 Why is it in the interests of all governments to assist entrepreneurs?

4 How can a government assist the promotion of trade?

5 Why should a government be keen for a business involved in exporting to be successful? How could it help such a business?

6 How does the Export Credits Guarantee Department encourage foreign trade?

7 How could the use of subsidies help to solve a balance-of-trade deficit?

8 What is the purpose of regional grants?

9 Why do governments intervene in business activities?

10 How does the government demonstrate its responsibility for consumer protection?

11 In what way can the National Consumer Council help both the consumer and businesses?

12 Explain the meaning of the terms monopoly and merger.

13 What is the function of the Monopolies and Mergers Commission?

14 To what extent does the Restrictive Practices Court regulate business activities?

15 Why would a government impose controls on imports and what form might these controls take?

16 In what ways can the government's taxation policies affect businesses?

17 For what reason might a government want to own certain industries?

18 Why does a government have an obligation to provide its citizens with social services?

19 Why is education important to commerce and industry?

20 In what ways does the UK government try to promote a healthy population? How does it finance this?

21 How are funds raised through National Insurance used?

22 What sort of recreational facilities does the government provide? Which are particularly linked to local governments and which are not?

Structured Questions

1 Study the following information and answer the questions below.

Working hours

British trade unions have been trying for many years to reduce the working hours of employees, and governments have from time to time attempted to restrict the hours a business can operate. This has particularly been the case with regard to the times shops can open.

Unions and the government do not necessarily have the same objectives in mind, and in any case it seems that there are always workers who are willing to work unsociable hours.

(a) What do you consider as 'unsociable working hours'? (1)

(b) Give two examples of ways in which the government might try to restrict the hours a business can operate. (2)

(c) State two reasons why the government might want to influence the hours a business can operate. (2)

(d) State two differences in the reasons which unions may have to try to influence working hours from those of the government. (2)

(e) Give three economic or social reasons why some workers would be more willing than others to work unsociable hours. (3)

(f) Allowing all businesses to operate unrestricted hours can affect different groups of people in varied ways. Describe the ways in which it could affect each of the following:
   (i)   the employee
   (ii) the employer
   (iii) the government
   (iv) religious groups. (4)

(g) Write a report that argues against allowing businesses to operate unrestricted hours. (6)

2 Study the following information and answer the questions which follow.

The Budget

The Chancellor of the Exchequer presents the main Budget once a year, and occasionally mini-budgets in between. Sometimes a budget *surplus* is achieved and sometimes a *deficit*. The Chancellor may prefer a deficit at a time of high unemployment but a surplus to check inflation.

(a) What is 'The Budget'? (1)

(b) Explain the terms *surplus* and *deficit* used here. (2)

(c) State two examples of sources of government income as a result of measures contained in the Budget. (2)

(d) List three major elements of central government expenditure. (3)

(e) If there was high inflation because consumers were spending too much money, the government could create a budget surplus by increasing taxation and lowering its own spending. What could be the effect of this on business? (3)

(f) Describe four circumstances in which business organisations would want to influence government budgetary measures. (4)

(g) Give two examples of ways that individuals, and three examples where businesses, are affected by government fiscal policies. (5)

3 Study the information on page 379 and answer the questions which follow.

(a) Define the term 'monopoly'. (1)

(b) Why do monopolies occur? (2)

(c) Give three examples of how a monopoly can occur. (3)

Monopolies

In the UK economy there are many examples of industries that are dominated by a few very large firms. Even where there are a lot of firms the competition between them may not be particularly effective.

When the supply of a product is controlled by one or a group of firms acting together we say that a monopoly exists.

Monopolies can be granted by law. For example, if you invented something you would be given the right (by patents) to have complete control of the production and sale over a given period of time.

Sometimes the advantages of a monopoly outweigh its disadvantages and for this reason governments have sometimes not interfered, and may even encourage it. But the disadvantages of monopoly, particularly from the point of view of the consumer, have generally caused governments to exercise some control over it.

(d) Explain how a monopoly can bring advantages and disadvantages for the public. (4)

(e) In what ways might the government try to restrict mergers and monopolies? (4)

(f) What are the reasons for saying that monopolies should be the subject of state control? (6)

4 Consider the following information and answer the questions which follow.

Noland needs new life

Business activities in the country of Noland are slowing down. Many people are being laid off work and each week reveals substantial numbers of businesses going bankrupt. There are overpopulated areas where unemployment is abnormally high and there is insufficient industry. The government has an important part to play in reviving economic activity.

(a) State two reasons why business activities in a country might be 'slowing down'. (2)

(b) What could the government do to influence consumer behaviour, particularly in order to help increase economic activity? (2)

    (c) In what ways could a government relieve the pressure of industry and
          population in congested areas? (3)

    (d) Describe two social problems and two economic problems that could
          result from the situation described above if the government did not
          intervene. (4)

    (e) What strategies could the government use to increase employment in
          areas in which unemployment is abnormally high? (4)

    (f) Governments sometimes give tax relief and other incentives to small
          firms. Describe how such a policy could help to solve the situation
          described above. To what extent do you agree that the government is
          justified in interfering in business activities in this way? (5)

Extended Answer Assignments

1 To what extent do you agree or disagree with the view that the provision of
social services is too generous and, therefore, taxation is higher than
necessary? Provide examples to support your views.

2 Design a questionnaire which concisely states the social welfare services
provided by the state, and then present a series of questions aimed at
identifying the social services residents in your locality use most frequently.
Present your findings using tables and charts and present a summary.

3 'Cigarette smoking has a private cost to the individual and a social cost to the
economy.' Investigate this statement including data obtained by personal
survey to establish private costs and data from government departments to
identify social costs. Present your discussion of the statement in the form of a
report that aims to raise awareness of the real cost of smoking to the economy.

4 What evidence can you find to support the view that there is a difference in
living standards between the South East and the rest of the UK? What influence
can the government have on this?

5 Make a collection of newspaper articles from your local press related to
matters of local concern, and related to business activities. Divide your articles
into issues that you feel could be solved by local government and those that
are central government responsibility. Write a summary report, in two parts, to
say how you feel the issues should be tackled:
(a) by local government;
(b) by central government.

Index